The New York Times

SIMPLY SUNDAY CROSSWORDS
From the Pages of *The New York Times*

Edited by Will Shortz

ST. MARTIN'S GRIFFIN ❧ NEW YORK

10 9 8 7 6 5 4 3

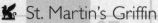

1 VAMPIRE'S DELIGHT

ACROSS

1 One of the Brady Bunch
7 "___ Darlin'" (Neal Hefti song)
10 Some W.W. II service personnel
14 Public relations effort
18 Consecrate
19 River or reservoir in Hesse
21 Saudi Arabia neighbor
22 Corn ___
23 Showed no emotion
25 "Dracula" miss
26 Epithet for Adenauer
27 Daughter of Teddy Roosevelt
28 Natterjacks
29 Like chicken fingers
31 Hanukkah item
33 Singer Garrett
35 Where the Clintons met
36 ___ de coeur
37 Sculpture material
38 Pakistani river
40 Sister of Helios
42 Fortress parapets
47 Related through the mother
50 90-Down's land
51 Crocus and gladiolus
52 Whit
54 Broadway belter
57 Wrongs
58 Valse, e.g.
59 Southern capital
61 "The Hundred Secret Senses" author
62 Movie theater
63 Pro ___
65 Riot

67 Mexican President, 1946–52
69 Allowance
72 Painter Childe ___
74 Some undercover operations
76 Make
77 List ender
79 Verdi's "___ tu"
80 Leave
82 Tallinn natives
84 Disturb
85 Word with buddy or binary
86 Kind of prize
87 Spa feature
88 Con game
91 Daughter of Juan Carlos
94 Prince Philip's surname
96 Sense of taste
99 Hat designer Lilly
101 Water channel: Abbr.
102 Partook of
103 Like outer space
106 Stage telephone, e.g.
107 Coppice
112 Attempt
115 North of Virginia
117 Task
118 Rick Blaine's love
119 A Turner
120 1992 Michael Keaton film
122 Barbary beasts
123 One of Chekhov's "Three Sisters"
124 Like Rioja wine
125 Execrate
126 Beverage from une vache
127 Vegas night sight
128 Boxer's title Abbr.
129 Deals with

DOWN

1 Word heard in fine stores
2 Id-womanish
3 "Le Penseur" sculptor
4 Mexican holiday ___ de Mayo
5 Lulls
6 Up
7 Big star at night
8 Don Quixotes
9 Rembrandt's birthplace
10 Aussie marsupial
11 "Jaws" setting
12 Former capital of Crete
13 Tangles
14 Bicker
15 Keeps up the beat?
16 "ER" extras
17 More strapped
20 Live
24 Demosthenes, e.g.
30 Charge
32 Point of no return?
34 Amusing
39 Polynesian tongue
41 Fencers' movements
42 Castro predecessor
43 Bar events
44 Old World finches
45 MS. vetters
46 Pitches
48 X rating?
49 Messes up
53 Forward pass, in football
55 Some ice cream orders
56 Acoustic
58 Airheads
59 Secured, with "down"
60 Let go tactfully
62 Critic Vincent
64 Lender's letters

66 Iwo Jima flag raiser
68 Toxic atmosphere
70 Made a yoke
71 Part of a "Star Wars" name
73 Where to see "The Last Supper"
75 Venue
78 Spacecraft part
81 Cartoonist's transparency
83 Here or there
84 African capital
87 More rigid
88 Dimensional
89 Tree with white flower clusters
90 Comrade Kosygin
92 Pile
93 Tumblers, e.g.
95 Utmost
97 Wilson Dam org.
98 "For Your Eyes Only" singer, 1981
100 Fictional mastermind
104 Fence feature
105 Albeniz's "___ in D"
108 Amusement park attraction
109 Park land?
110 Artist Max
111 Dips one's toe in
113 90 degrees
114 Wayne film "Back to ___"
116 A party to
121 Summer hours in D.C.

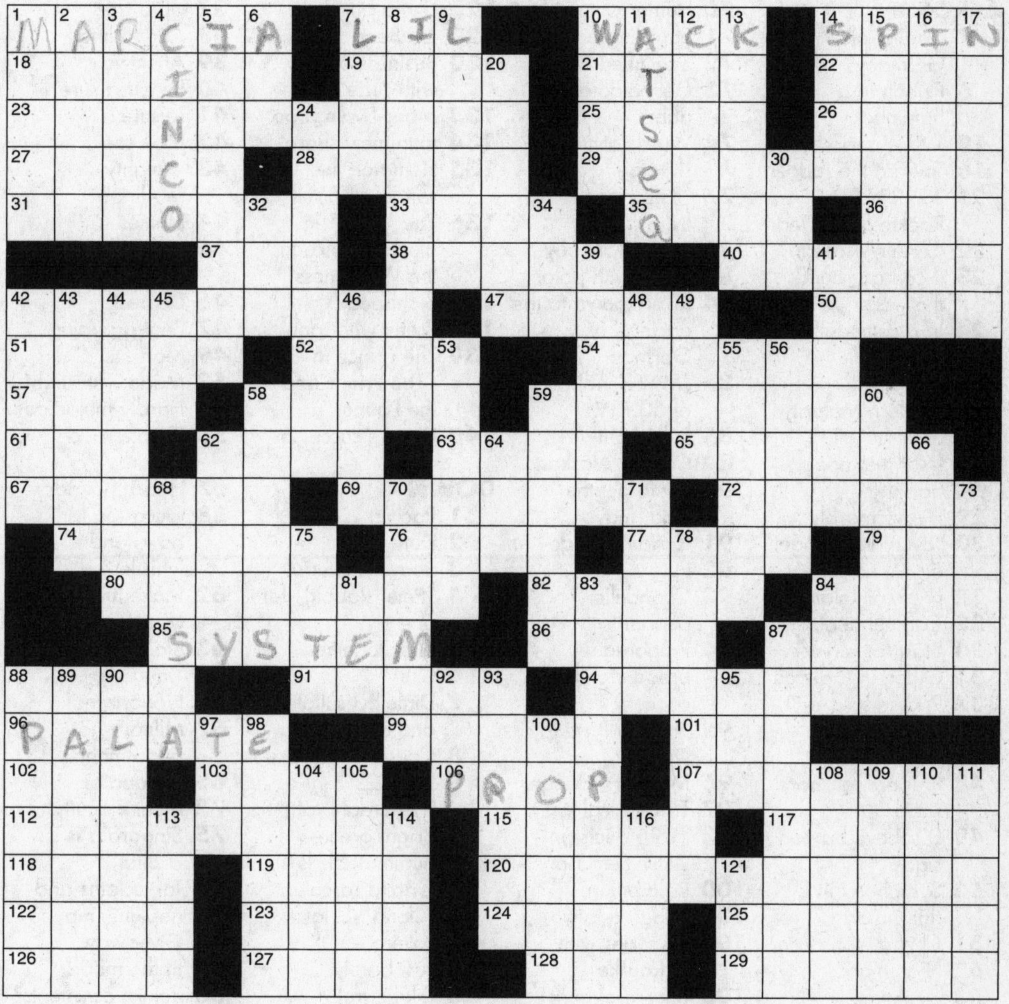

by Nancy Nicholson Joline

2 POKER SET

ACROSS

1 Capital of Germany?
6 Person in a hammock
12 TV's Maverick
16 Toward the rudder
21 1993 N.B.A. Rookie of the Year
22 Certain Alaskan
23 It can go round the world
24 In a distinguished way
25 Move
27 Modern Maturity grp.
28 [Not that one again!]
29 Heavy marble
30 Joyce and Synge, e.g.
32 Fresh air, slangily
33 Cabinet dept.
34 Start for girl
35 Other, in Oaxaca
37 Price discount factors
42 Avoid guile
48 Prepare for more shots
49 Disobeyed a zoo sign?
50 Symphony in E flat major
51 Chef d'état, once
52 High mark
53 Stroke
56 Dashboard letters
57 Street fight?
59 Academy freshman
60 On one's toes
61 Jimmies
64 Unhappy one
65 Sound of laughter
66 Part of Q.E.D.
67 They are round and pound
68 Emulates Delilah
69 French 101 verb
70 Humerus neighbor
71 Soup ingredient
72 Sanctified
73 Genealogical abbr.
74 Words at a shootout
77 "It's ___ cry from . . ."
81 Boardwalk buy
83 Prefix with polar
84 River known to the ancients as Obringa
85 "My Friend" of 50's TV
86 Pulled out
89 Certain Alaskan
90 Try to get the lead, maybe
91 Certain Dodge
92 Put
93 Chandelier pendant
94 Prepared with bread crumbs, in cookery
95 "Happy Birthday" writers
96 Mariners' danger
97 Theological Inst.
98 1896 decision ___ v. Ferguson
100 Prohibition
101 Keogh relative
102 TV series with Sgt. O'Rourke
105 Source of cork
106 Scientific discovery of 1868
107 1939 film with a Best Actor performance
111 Like some stockings
113 Hardly humble
114 ___-mémoire
115 Farthest: Abbr.
116 Agree
119 Pirates' domain
123 Works
128 Like a bunch
129 ___ Bear
130 Business book, with "The"
133 Mark Twain prop
134 Extremely sharp
135 Home on the range
136 The "voice" in Bloch's "Voice in the Wilderness"
137 S-shaped
138 Prefix with -gon
139 The prince in "The Prince and the Pauper"
140 Grant's successor

DOWN

1 Pacifier
2 Duty
3 Beaver material
4 "Peter Rabbit," for one
5 Stick together
6 Quit
7 Dimethyl sulfate and others
8 Cousin of calypso
9 Kon-___ (Heyerdahl raft)
10 Bright green hummingbirds
11 Garcia Lorca's "Dona ___ la soltera"
12 Just barely
13 Globe-trot
14 Fictional Jane
15 Bang-up
16 Sweater material
17 Russian wolfhound
18 Peek follower
19 Spanish custard
20 Sharon's co-star in 80's TV
26 Checks on clothing
31 Red-eye cause
36 Song syllable
37 Up a tree
38 Abounding
39 Attentive
40 Be extra sure
41 Leisure
42 Look-see
43 Weighty reading?
44 Nurses
45 ___ Hall (Robert Southey's home)
46 Dearest
47 Seat groupings
49 Man ___
53 Made watertight
54 Hardly melodious
55 Private road feature
57 Hooch hounds
58 Occasion for bows and whistles?
62 Make further corrections
63 Black
64 Tiny
66 Not original
67 Military hat adornments
68 Banana oil
72 Mental acuity
75 Singaraja is its capital
76 Tablecloths and napkins, maybe
78 Giveaway
79 In the mood
80 Return payments?
82 Horace volume
86 Young fellow
87 The gold of the conquistadors
88 Important West Indies crop
89 Kind of plate
93 It can curl your hair
94 Stew ingredients
95 It's on the agenda
97 Tablet
99 Like dachshunds

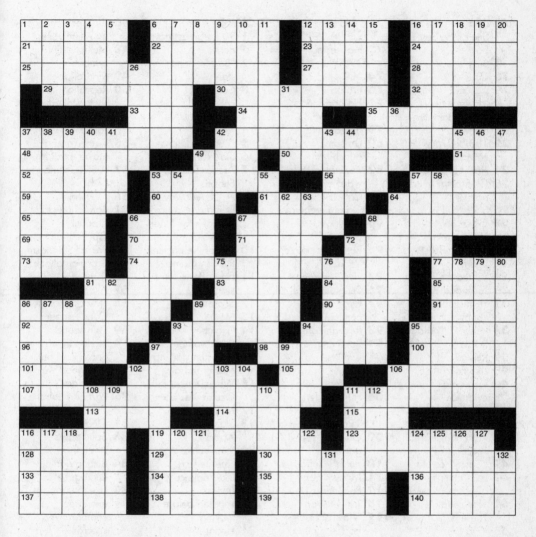

by Manny Nosowsky

ACROSS

1 Site of the Sun Bowl
7 Busy
13 Couch
19 ___ acid (preservative)
20 Biblical tempter
21 Honors
22 1837 literary collection
24 Hairy-chested
25 Gloaming, to poets
26 Shift
27 Expert at ledger-demain?
28 "Paradise Lost" figure
29 Visited the future
36 Tad's dad
37 Yevtushenko's "Babi ___"
38 Reply to "Who's there?"
39 Repute
40 Like Falstaff
43 Turn state's evidence
45 Continue without the words
46 Rush-hour traffic speed
47 "Cosby" co-star
49 ___ in the right direction
51 She loved Theseus
53 Kind
54 Silent signals
56 Bridge or wrestling feat
59 Bran source
60 Tinker with, in a way
62 Reprimands
66 Covering
70 Winsor McCay's "Little" one
71 Game-winning cry
72 Auto's comfort quality
73 Pioneering 1982 film
74 100
76 Pronto
77 Fine-grained wood
79 Out of here
80 Do some punching
82 Beginning Latin word
83 Caboose
87 Grimm creature
90 Noted X-1 pilot
92 Romantic painter Vedder
93 "Up" positions
96 Religious ideal
97 Greenpeace concern
98 Recognition
99 Bowwow
101 Zeniths, e.g.
103 ___-mo
104 Hit song lyric of 1929 and 1968
109 Green garnishes
110 Sugary suffix
111 Many moons
112 Part of i.p.s.
115 Trinket: Var.
117 Show once hosted by Bud Collyer
121 Gentleman thief Lupin
122 Torments
123 Barbara Bush's maiden name
124 Van Dyke Emmy-winning role
125 Prepared for a blow
126 Excoriate

DOWN

1 90 (degrees) from norte
2 "Bad Influence" star
3 Computer command
4 Epitome of simplicity
5 "Buttery" legume
6 Staff range
7 Alaska Senator Stevens
8 N.Y.C. subway
9 Difference in days between the lunar and solar year
10 Site of the ancient Pythian Games
11 Find after a long search
12 Scores: Abbr.
13 Maul
14 "Dombey and Son" woman
15 War film starring Martin Balsam
16 Where singer Billy Ocean was born
17 Migratory fish
18 Storm heading: Abbr.
20 With subterfuge
23 Cuprite, e.g.
28 Like some college honors
30 Leaping before looking
31 Headset, to hams
32 "Phooey!"
33 The Buckeyes
34 Cut down
35 First name in mysteries
40 Point in the right direction
41 More obvious
42 Sealskin wearer
44 Convincing evidence
46 Org. once headed by Allen Dulles
48 Multiplication symbol
49 Kind of price
50 Repetition for rhetorical effect
52 Anti-Communist soldier
55 Dinner and a movie, perhaps
57 A.B.A. members: Abbr.
58 ___-tung
61 Bandanna-clad product "spokesman"
63 Prefix with plasm
64 Scorpion attack
65 Transude
67 Aspect
68 "My Cup Runneth Over" singer
69 Gun sound
74 Its slogan was once "Find out how good we really are"
75 Part of a count
78 French shield
81 Clear-eyed
83 Southpaw's strength
84 Betting game ending
85 Like a warm-up exercise, comparatively speaking
86 Heritage
88 Words to live by
89 Shake a leg
91 Straddling
94 Classic Japanese theater
95 Miser
99 Shorty
100 "The African Queen" director
102 Rotisserie league concern

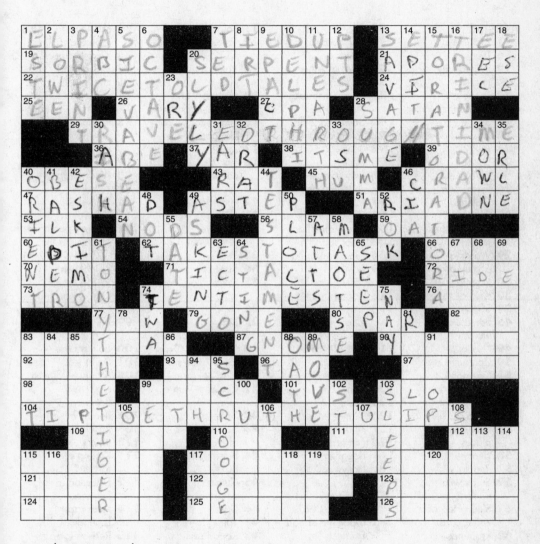

by Ray Hamel

4   THANKSGIVING SHOPPING LIST

ACROSS

1 Perfume
6 Tie
12 Individually, in a way
20 Truman biographer Miller
21 Sub feature
22 Ups and downs
23 TURKEY
25 SWEET POTATOES
26 Town near Oakland
27 Closeout
28 Home in the woods
29 Words of acquiescence
30 Rose fancier
33 Kind of chair
38 SQUASH
45 Some Dadaist works
49 "Voila!"
50 Conduct
51 Composer Khachaturian
52 Funny ones
54 "That __ lie!"
55 Gathering places
56 Henry __
57 Regulars
59 Suffix with Rock
61 Skill tested with Zener cards
62 Resounds
63 BRUSSELS SPROUTS
66 The Way
68 Lobster part
69 Pen noise
70 Big name in sportswear
75 Kind of jet
76 STUFFING
79 Stings
83 One who looks at books
85 "Flash Gordon" originator __ Raymond
86 Rival of Athens
87 Separated
88 Equips with better materiel
90 Soundstage cry
92 Theater drop
93 Scope
94 Soul
95 What wine shouldn't be
97 Earth tones
98 GRAVY
102 Stage direction
103 Hoof sound
104 Kind of ground
109 Ball Ha'i, in "South Pacific"
113 Iranian money
116 "My Left Foot" Oscar-winner Fricker
117 CHESTNUTS
121 APPLE PIE
123 Band attraction
124 San __
125 Harden
126 Dinner ender
127 Atlas features
128 Father-and-daughter Hollywood duo

DOWN

1 Perth __, N.J.
2 Opposite of eau
3 Dumas's Les __ Mousquetaires
4 King and others
5 More rubicund
6 Civil War Inits.
7 They may be caught at the shore
8 Italian sports car, informally
9 Bordered by a ridge
10 Protozoan
11 Pointer
12 "Sweet Swan of __!": Jonson
13 Valenciennes, e.g.
14 Eastern V.I.P.'s
15 Business combine
16 Uris hero __ Ben Canaan
17 __ Tin Tin
18 Hot spot, in lunch counter lingo
19 Tee predecessor
24 Attended
31 "Where's Daddy?" playwright
32 Elicits
34 Sisal or yucca
35 "West Side Story" song
36 Send
37 Rigs
39 X, to Xenophon
40 "One Flew Over the Cuckoo's Nest" author
41 Goddess with a lyre
42 Some pens
43 Screenwriter, often
44 Bandleader Baxter
45 Curacao neighbor
46 Up
47 Young fowl
48 Rocket section
53 Hamlet's "__ and arrows"
55 Greek brandies
58 Mideast capital
60 March need
62 Sea anemones, e.g.
64 Dawning
65 Salute
67 Beggar's quest
71 Do a legislator's job
72 Missionary Junipero __
73 Kind of sleeve
74 Red-coated cheeses
76 Airstrip
77 Style of furnishing
78 Part of a metropolitan region
79 Satisfy
80 Actor Redgrave
81 About
82 Gettysburg general
84 Hosiery purchase
88 "A Yank in the __" (1941 movie)
89 Knightwear
91 W.B.A. result
95 Office machines
96 "__ dabba doo!"
99 Baltimore's __ Park
100 Saxon's foe
101 Deflected
105 Marie Antoinette, e.g.
106 Bring on
107 Beautify
108 Spare locales
110 It's a put-on
111 Kipling's "__ we forget!"
112 Direction in Durango
114 Auto racer Luyendyk
115 Reason for a brushoff?
117 Gametes
118 Cambodia's __ Nol
119 Seventh-century date
120 N.T. book
121 Bon __
122 Nasdaq listings: Abbr.

by Nancy Nicholson Joline

5 THE LADY CHANGES HER NAME

ACROSS

1 "It" in the old slogan "Gotta have it"
6 Stinky
11 Crescent's tip
15 Scepters' go-withs
19 Liquid part of fat
20 Poem's farewell
21 "God ha' mercy on such ___"
22 Pullover
23 "The Goodbye Girl" star suffers audibly
25 Look from Groucho
26 Foreign statesman whose real first name was Aubrey
27 Annex
28 Beggar's cry
29 Philippine lady ricochets
32 Aproned advertising animal
34 Destinations
35 Kickback
36 Reproductive cell
38 Parsonage
40 Sup
41 Tequila source
42 Foldaway
43 Novelist-critic dances
49 Form of a thank-you
50 Theater acronym
52 Bottom line
53 "To a Steam Roller" poet
54 1942 Oscar winner reacts to a bad pun
58 Troubadour
61 Locker room supply
62 Set upon
63 Twosome
65 Member of the order Isoptera
67 "The Munsters" actress sang
70 Popular Polynesian port
73 E.T.O. battle town
74 Shining
78 Big name in Hawaii
79 Shows curiosity
81 Two-time Tony winner did a no-no
84 Its symbol is a crescent and star
86 Mausoleum opening?
88 Steak order
89 Old dagger
90 "Casino" co-star does firming exercises
94 Shaver
95 Pantheon figures
96 Manner, as of writing
97 Headwork
99 Noted Egyptian temple site
100 One of the Clintons
103 Memo order
104 Port of Crete
105 1964 Oscar winner roams
107 Part of B.A.
108 Canadian politician Bob
111 Like most cupcakes
112 Super's apartment number, maybe
113 Newswoman stops
116 Rooster locale
117 Coin in Kerman
118 Kett and James
119 Six-time U.S. Open tennis champ
120 Pizazz
121 Moolah
122 Several Peters
123 She was a lady in a 1932 tune

DOWN

1 Fleshy fruit
2 Airline since 1948
3 Ambassador takes a husband
4 Sonny's sibling
5 Slapdash
6 Wife abroad
7 Genesis name
8 Tellico Dam overseer: Abbr.
9 Sea between Italy and Greece
10 Send away
11 Salesman's duties
12 Like some books
13 Administer an oath to
14 Rate
15 "Lulu," e.g.
16 Perfect slave
17 Mame's onus
18 King's desires
24 What George couldn't tell
30 Cousins of cassowaries: Var.
31 Perpendicular to the keel
33 They protect banks
36 Police target
37 Hub of old Athens
38 One-track
39 Win
40 New York Senator
42 Parking places
44 Pinch hitter
45 Reply to the Little Red Hen
46 Annapolis mascot
47 Shield border
48 Not long to wait
51 Pennies, perhaps
55 50's TV's "The Martha ___ Show"
56 ___ hoot
57 Nazarenes and others
59 Forwarded
60 Hardly the creme de la creme
64 Of the cheekbone
66 Year in Ivan the Terrible's reign
68 Marine organisms
69 Jimmy's successor
70 Swanky
71 ___ breve
72 Liqueur flavor
75 Nail down
76 Columnist reacted angrily
77 "If a body ___ body . . ."
78 Bad-mouth
80 End of Madama Butterfly's name
82 Sturdy wagon
83 Escritoire
85 Flick
87 1980 Carly Simon hit
91 Make business connections
92 Shakespeare's Fairy Queen
93 Hollywood hopeful
95 Wailer
98 Tournament news
99 Lady of a stuttering song
100 Almost princely
101 Jean Renoir film heroine
102 Ream
103 Allan-___ (Sherwood Forest figure)
104 Salad ingredient
105 Baloney

by Maura Jacobson

106 Patricia of
"A Face in the
Crowd"
107 Controversial
apple spray
109 Longfellow's
bell town
110 Isabella d'___
(famed beauty)

114 Times Sq.,
e.g., on the IRT
115 Film "Contessa"

ACROSS

1 "The Cape Cod Lighter" writer
6 Speak abusively to
11 Swear words
15 Hunt assemblage
19 Like a shoe
20 Add ___ of salt
21 Cicatrix
22 Classic New Yorker cartoonist
23 The God, literally
24 Undeliverable piece of mail
25 Toaster, e.g.
27 Crystal-lined stone
28 Ample shoe width
29 Precious one
31 Progeny
32 With 39- and 54-Across, the beginning of the story
36 Javits Center designer
37 Dark grayish green
38 Dolt
39 See 32-Across
50 Takes too much, briefly
51 Chinese truth
52 Lloyd Webber musical role
53 Code word for "K"
54 See 32-Across
63 Take care of
64 Start for bees or breeze
65 Noted Expos name
66 Put away
67 Dental mold
70 S.A.T. subj.
72 Flash
74 Insult, slangily
77 Bangkok teacher, on Broadway
78 Anonymous one
80 Literature Nobelist Pirandello
83 With 94- and 106-Across, the end of the story
90 Panache
91 "I told you so!"
92 Harris of "thirty-something"
93 Fluffy scarf
94 See 83-Across
103 Newton of the N.F.L.
104 "O Henry, ___ thine eyes!": Shak.
105 Put ___ show
106 See 83-Across
117 Tidal flood
118 Island near Quemoy
119 Louis who said "L'état c'est moi"
120 North of Virginia
121 Heating conduit
123 Early pamphleteer
125 Rope with a loop
126 Say "z" imperfectly
127 Ready for service
128 Church V.I.P.
129 Flower with a showy head
130 Pot builder?
131 1985 Cher film
132 Baby Moses was hidden among them
133 Author Hite

DOWN

1 Midwest tribe
2 Used an awl
3 Grant
4 Make suitable again
5 Holds fast
6 Best-selling 1993 pop album
7 "Bye"
8 Simonized
9 "Do ___ say . . ."
10 Mark Twain novel whose plot is encapsulated in this puzzle
11 Hollywood statue
12 Barbados cherry
13 Count, as votes
14 It ended in 1806: Abbr.
15 Problematic construction site
16 Clear
17 Boredom
18 Shopper, often
26 Silvers sarge
30 Like some humor
33 Radio code sound
34 ___ piece (consistent)
35 Doce meses, en España
39 Dangerous group
40 Popular ice cream brand
41 Suffix meaning "to become"
42 Stock page heading
43 W. C. co-star
44 Foldable items
45 "It's O.K. with me"
46 Old studio
47 Carnival girl, in the movies
48 Actor McCowen
49 Shot
55 Males
56 ___ of roses
57 Very much
58 Part of a bray
59 Card
60 Whole
61 W.W. I soldier
62 Increase
68 Wind dir.
69 Mai ___
71 Sentimentality
73 Stockbroker's offering
74 A couple of bucks?
75 Not occupied
76 Valuables
79 Lucci's elusive prize
81 Mongolian desert
82 Smooth
84 Literary olio
85 Calendar abbr.
86 Overhead figures?
87 Flandre flavoring
88 Pavement caution
89 ID of a sort
95 Like some court proceedings
96 Scotch refusal
97 Marathoner's need
98 Shoots over
99 ___ canto
100 Persuade by trickery
101 Some sweaters
102 Somewhat high
106 Electronics pioneer Nikola
107 Toss one's ___ the ring
108 Get rid of
109 Kool-Aid flavor
110 Hearty dinner entree
111 Zinc ___
112 Penalized
113 Diamond middleman?
114 Winged
115 Potassium compound
116 "The Wreck of the Mary ___"
122 Spitz-type dog
124 Bath beverage

by David J. Kahn

ACROSS

1 Title sister of a 1970 film
5 50's pitcher Maglie
8 Shelley, for one
13 Bobybuilder's intake
18 Hydrangea, e.g.
19 A Khan
20 Further shorten, as a board
21 1982 Tony nominee Milo
22 One-one and two-two
24 Women's shoe style
26 Bridger
27 Ends of lines
29 Classical earth goddess
30 Kind of cracker
32 Hamilton's prov.
33 Glow
34 Those who work
38 Given life, perhaps
43 See 7-Down
46 Contemporary author-illustrator Jon
47 Unvarnished
48 Roar of a crowd
49 Love personified
50 React angrily
51 Illinois city
52 "De ___ Poetica" (ancient treatise)
53 Arles article
54 Orchestra member
56 Caruso was one
57 Feature of James Monroe's estate
59 Palindrome girl
60 Lourdes is one
61 Coif
63 Trauma sites, for short
64 Suntanning areas
66 Ran for one's wife?
68 November honorees
70 Armada component
73 Teases
74 Quieting down
78 Tee follower
79 Western Hemisphere abbr.
80 ___ team (assault unit)
81 Extreme amount
82 Bug shots?
83 Scale notes
84 List in a hurry?
85 Ancient Brit
86 All, in stage directions
87 Difference
89 Sound mind, in a phrase
91 Partner for Clark
92 Crosspiece
93 Potato choice
97 Kind of panel
100 Sandwich filler
105 Parade figure
106 Indy 500 gear
108 Beyond control
110 Words with eye or fore
111 Certain repairman
112 Cockpit reading: Abbr.
113 Furious
114 ___ a time
115 Song much played on the radio
116 Shaft
117 To ___ (exactly)

DOWN

1 Bake, as eggs
2 Betel palm
3 Honking time
4 Its slogan was once "Wide world of entertainment"
5 Delhi gown
6 Long time
7 With 43-Across, a 1940's movie cowboy
8 Bean and others
9 Stop
10 Writer Dinesen
11 ___ doute (certainly): Fr.
12 Prefix with light
13 Stuck
14 Dump
15 Pearl player, in a 1996 sitcom
16 Shade of red
17 Red tag locale
18 Alone
23 "For the life ___ . . ."
25 Confined
28 Monopoly equipment
31 Barbary beast
33 Off ___ (occasionally)
35 Extended
36 "___ in Calico" (1946 song)
37 Saint Philip ___ (Renaissance figure)
38 Fashionable shop
39 Bag
40 Holiday bird
41 "Rocket Man" John
42 Tractor man John
43 Kind of land
44 Brothers' name of 40's–50's music
45 Monthly synagogue observance
47 Lyricist Sammy et al
50 "Pretty stupid, huh?" declarer
52 Old Houston hockey team
54 Lake Indians
55 Raspy
56 Addams Family member
58 VCR
60 Public relations gambit
62 Small eggs
63 One of filmdom's Coen brothers
65 Certain discriminators
66 Daughter of Mnemosyne
67 Restrict
69 "Women Who Run With the Wolves" author
71 French suffix
72 Split ___
74 Toast start
75 They're a pain
76 Looked over
77 Rijksmuseum artist
80 From Odense
82 Standing-room-only show
84 Do needlework
86 ___ hunch
88 Biblical miracle worker
89 Hardly a naif
90 Bullets
92 Extort from
94 Nautical order
95 Bud Grace comic strip
96 Connecticut Senator
97 Prefix with morph

by A. J. Santora

98 1982 Disney film
99 More than a peeve
100 In addition
101 Old Dodge
102 Frost
103 Kind of skirt
104 Dist. ___
107 Greek letter
109 Marlins locale: Abbr.

8 BUMPER TO BUMPER

ACROSS
1 Hosp. areas
4 Orbital extreme
9 Fed
13 Mea ___
18 "I reckon not"
19 ___ Affair (Civil War imbroglio)
20 Michener title
22 1995 N.B.A. scoring leader
23 Business firm, in France: Abbr.
24 Page 2, usually
25 Ratify
26 Software buyers
27 Wing it
29 Relief pitchers
31 Hardy grass
33 Measuring system
35 Popular sporting fish
37 Gen. Pershing's command: Abbr.
38 Spread the word?
39 Tarlatan skirt
40 Masks
45 Georgia, once: Abbr.
46 Day, to Dayan
48 Campaign pro
49 Sample
50 Divvy up
51 "Behold," to Boethius
52 Harper's Weekly cartoonist
54 Singer Harris
56 The tiniest bit
59 Slugger's stat
62 Opposite of paleo-
63 Def Jam records genre
64 Traffic jam
72 Traffic jam
73 Traffic jam
74 Fleur-de-___
75 Author Stanislaw
76 Young socialite
77 "The Flowering Peach" playwright
78 He wore a top hat in "Top Hat"
82 First word of "Send in the Clowns"
84 Overdue
86 Earthshaking event
87 White House inits.
89 Sports governing body: Abbr.
91 Author of "The Island of the Day Before"
92 Vacation spot
95 Even more distressing
97 Optimist, of sorts
99 Neptune moon
101 The dovekie is one
102 Film heptad
105 Plan out
106 TV dinner name
110 "Semiramide" composer
112 Gossip
113 Day of la semaine
114 Like some traffic barriers
116 Battlefield V.I.P.
118 Sticky stuff
119 Club publication
120 Paris cultural center
121 Be behind
122 Poetic preposition
123 Troll's cousin
124 Flagstone, e.g.
125 Davis of "Get On the Bus"
126 Wino's woe

DOWN
1 Prepares to spend the night
2 Al Davis's men
3 Harbor
4 Traffic jam
5 Post's opposite
6 Lord's lackey
7 Put one's foot down
8 Save for a rainy day
9 Traffic jam
10 Jason's wife, in myth
11 Nerve fibers
12 Tot's time-out
13 Traffic jam
14 With risk
15 Groucho expression
16 Auditioner's aim
17 Plus
21 Sault ___ Marie
28 "Cybill" character
30 Popular brand of stationery
32 ___ Jacinto Day (April 21)
34 Kiss flavor: Abbr.
36 Poli ___
41 Ready to be turned on
42 Best effort
43 Elton's john
44 Good name for a cabin attendant
47 Diving ducks
49 Had a tantrum
51 Fragrant resin
53 Large chain
55 City on the Ocmulgee River
56 Parts of days, in the classifieds
57 Flag
58 Saroyan hero
60 ___ fond farewell to
61 It can cause a shock
65 Asphyxiation cause
66 Diminutive endings
67 Heckled
68 ___ Island
69 Hitchcock title
70 "___ a man who wasn't there"
71 Sheepskin alternatives, for short
78 Matter of fact introduction?
79 One in it for the long term?: Abbr.
80 Prescription abbr.
81 Construction of 1898–1902
83 Balzac's birthplace
85 Is decisive
88 Mayo, e.g.
90 Words before fame or after lay
92 Pinched pennies
93 Toaster snack
94 Scorpio's brightest star
96 Howard Hughes studio
98 Record holders
100 Incense
103 Synthetic fiber
104 Shearer of "Peeping Tom"
106 Kind of alert
107 Alert
108 Ship to Colchis
109 Bilko, for one: Abbr.
111 Castor's killer
115 Photo ___
117 Grandson, maybe

by Randolph Ross

ACROSS

1 Madrid's Paseo del __
6 Swagger
13 Modern dance giant
19 Reading on the Richter scale
20 Declaimed, as "A Visit From St. Nicholas"
21 Barrio resident
22 Start of a verse
25 Outdid
26 Introduction to conservatism
27 Not the lowest prices
28 Social reformer Dorothea
29 Word with guard or chard
31 Take steps
32 Order to the "Ship of State"
36 Like Atalanta
37 Its point is to make holes
38 Swarthy
42 Yearn
43 Zoom
44 Matty or Moises
45 Chief Theban deity
46 Part 2 of the verse
52 Writer Santha Rama __
53 Plains Indian
54 Slickers
55 Word from a fencer
56 Seat of an empire?
58 1980 Oscar winner
60 Theodor __ (Dr. Seuss)
61 Name that means "heavenly"
63 Wild asses
65 "Passages" writer Gail
68 Most like the Magi
70 Joining forces
74 Thomas of TV
75 Tolkien tree-men
76 It has a Minor part
77 PBS benefactor
78 Part 3 of the verse
84 Cobbler's form
85 Rival of Scipio
86 Hecuba's home
87 Mariposa lily
88 W.W. II landing craft
89 Printers' widths
90 Letter opener?
92 Famous Christian
94 Bee: Prefix
95 On the sordid side
96 From __ Z
97 Rubble
100 Socks, e.g.
101 D'Oyly Carte offering
106 End of the verse
110 New Jersey's state tree
111 Engine fluid
112 She played Anastasia in "Anastasia"
113 Begets
114 Popular Mousekeeper
115 Chart holder

DOWN

1 Shore (up)
2 Zebras
3 Last of a Latin trio
4 Fish also called mahimahi
5 Source
6 Thin nail
7 Padre, for short
8 It's not returnable
9 Barbarino on "Welcome Back, Kotter"
10 Certify
11 Deejay's disks
12 Harem room
13 Group in robes
14 "Nick of Time" Grammy winner
15 Girl lead-in
16 Sound setup
17 Indigo source
18 Epigram
19 Nashville sch.
23 Put the whammy on
24 Make use of
29 Pole, for example
30 "The stockings __ hung . . ."
32 Gerald's predecessor
33 Shoot for
34 Ideas, opinions, etc.
35 Sign of summer
36 Liver, in Le Havre
37 Subject of an 1867 sale
38 67-Down, for one
39 Cherubs
40 1950 Max Ophuls film "La __"
41 Prepare to propose
43 Pit
44 Sign of stress?
47 By hook or by crook
48 Po land
49 Muldaur's "__ Woman"
50 They have edible shells
51 Women advisers
57 Cousins of margays
58 Strong ale
59 Genoese creation
60 Bottled spirits?
62 Dieter's bane
64 Not reserved
65 Slight
66 Laugh track sounds
67 Artist Max
69 N.Y.C. zone
71 Enlargement, maybe
72 Mont Blanc covering
73 Burt Reynolds flick
76 Energy source
79 They produce chips off the old block
80 Leave no trace
81 News squib
82 Carhop's burden
83 O.T. book
90 "'Tis the __ to be jolly"
91 Be a snitch
92 Glenda Jackson biopic
93 Name in 1993 headlines
94 Indo-European
95 Offshoot
96 Galoot
97 Like still waters, maybe
98 "Das Rheingold" earth goddess
99 Knitted item
101 Bone: Prefix
102 Work units
103 King Hiram's home
104 Drudgery
105 What's more
106 "__ Winterbourne"
107 Elvis's label
108 Welcome giver
109 Sugar lover

by Frances Hansen

A HOST OF SINS

ACROSS

1 Attack severely
7 Sweet, dark wine
14 Saw-billed duck
18 Dutch city on the Rhine
19 Bacchanalian activity
20 Silly
21 Venomous snake
23 Girl, informally
24 "M*A*S*H" regular
25 Noted Riverdale High student
26 Insanity and others
28 Ballerina Spessivtseva
29 Philbrick's "___ Three Lives"
30 Some wts.
32 Silver coins of ancient Greece
33 Pot-au-___ (meat and vegetable dish)
34 ___ were
35 Bossy remark?
36 Spanish arm
37 Rat Pack member
44 Make, as bread
45 Captain of the Half Moon
46 Quarterback's cry
47 Sugar source
49 Victim in a 1932 mystery, with "the"
51 It comes from a fountain
54 Perfect
55 Division of a long poem
56 List shortener
57 Swamp
60 Separates
63 Writers Meyer and Ira
64 One who wails
65 Other: Fr.
66 "The Dark at the Top of the Stairs" writer
67 Planetarium
68 Comic punctuation from a drummer
70 Prepares, in a way
72 Chivvy
73 Help the cause
74 Pitch
75 "Arabian Nights" hero
84 First name in hoteliers
85 Charles, e.g.
86 Offend olfactorily
87 Suffix with portrait
88 Schubert piece
89 Schmear
90 Million-selling
91 Jack-o'-lantern feature
92 Bargain hunter's joy
94 Axis divisions
96 Tropical tree of the soapberry family
97 Commence
98 Popular cocktail
102 Hold off
103 Blows to smithereens
104 Rouge roulette bet
105 Some beans
106 Solvent compounds
107 Like most gates

DOWN

1 Shortens
2 Worm for bait
3 One of the Leeward Islands
4 Head of Thermopylae?
5 One of L.B.J.'s beagles
6 Mystery author Lathen
7 Chopper
8 "This is ___ !" (police cry)
9 1948 Hitchcock thriller
10 South of Mexico
11 "___ live and breathe!"
12 Cheryl and Diane of Hollywood
13 Nautical direction
14 17th-century rationalist
15 Hypothetical animal
16 Abbreviations for weekend days
17 Reasons
19 Year St. Augustine was born
20 They undergo mitosis
22 Prayer
27 Ones voting yes
30 Vociferous
31 ___ nova
34 Plot to plant
35 "The Ten Commandments" location
36 Michael Jackson's first #1 hit
38 Where Triton is
39 ___-El (Superman's real name)
40 Doodad
41 United Nations vote
42 Opinions
43 "Relax!"
47 Feldspar, e.g.
48 Uniqueness
49 Horned Frogs' sch.
50 Solo in space
51 Come together
52 Arapaho foe
53 Trattoria offering
54 Vietnamese river or delta
58 Celtic Poseidon
59 Small swimmers
61 Man of courage, to Kipling
62 Hollywood workplace
68 Emerson of tennis
69 Chief Vedic god
70 Wine shipment
71 Biographer Winslow
73 Kind of fingerprint
74 Branch railroad, e.g.
76 Intelligently planned progresses
77 Flipper
78 Suitable for service
79 Blast furnace apparatuses
80 Chariot-driving Greek god
81 Ready to ambush
82 The East, en España
83 Broke a rule of play
88 Migratory songbird
89 Al ___
90 Just touch
91 Pioneer in medicine
92 Macarena and others
93 Jacob's first wife
94 Opposed, in Dogpatch
95 Clockmaker Thomas
99 ___ angelica (organ stop)
100 Singer Sumac
101 Overseas title

by Bryant White

WATER, WATER EVERYWHERE

ACROSS

1 Blah
6 Airplane engines
13 Remind again and again of an error
20 Stopped lying
21 Get hot under the collar
22 Very hot under the collar
23 Buck Rogers's female companion
24 It opens with a 75-bar bassoon solo
26 Poor surfer
27 Ref. set
28 Zodiac symbol
29 Like Abner
30 "1,001 Arabian Nights" hero
31 Quills
34 Roman way
35 Fr. religieuse
36 Charged
39 Parade decorations
41 Monumental
42 Esophagus
44 Completes a graveside ceremony
45 Country singer Black
46 Droopy-eared one
48 Follow, as advice
49 Social activities
50 Noted Dixieland clarinetist
52 Unequaled
54 The sun, the moon and the stars
55 Implant
56 Notorious London prison
58 Like some stocks, for short
61 Initials on a rocket

62 Rum cocktail
65 Circles and such
66 Fiesta, e.g.
67 Mystery writer Josephine
68 Italian province or its capital
70 Disney deer
71 Caesar's well
72 Sitcom originally titled "These Friends of Mine"
73 Bouquets
77 Scotland yards?
80 Corps unit
81 Basins
82 Neural transmitters
83 "Happy Days" role
85 Papal capes
86 Engine stats
87 It gives players a cushion
89 Bird calls
92 Meteorological datum
93 Tennis player Ramirez
94 ___ del Fuego
96 Bailey's bailiwick
97 "Walking on Thin Ice" singer
98 Those playing the role of Boris Godunov
100 Athos, to Porthos
101 Writer Rogers St. Johns
103 Like a samaritan's help
107 Tangle
108 Implement
109 Staffing
110 Goddess of peace
111 Crook
112 Understanding
113 Cause for an insurance claim

DOWN

1 Derisive laugh
2 Jim Palmer, notably
3 Preventing an attack, in a way
4 Cadets' inits.
5 Drink for Beowulf
6 Camera setting
7 Not the prayerful sort
8 "You ___ worry . . ."
9 Clash
10 Major record co.
11 Sounds of reproof
12 Display item
13 Ransackers
14 Indy 500 family
15 Some Protestants: Abbr.
16 Sale item abbr.
17 Pilot's nightmare
18 Firing up
19 Overlooks
25 Gene Autry pic
31 His feast day is April 11
32 The unmarried woman in "An Unmarried Woman"
33 Submitted
37 Ditties
38 Arabic letter
40 Makes amends
41 Writer Wiesel
43 Hard to describe
45 Holiday decorations
46 State oratorically
47 Intrinsically
48 Fighting
49 Show senility
51 Idle
52 Capital of Guam
53 One of the Canaries
57 The place
58 1960 Sinatra movie

59 Roberts of "Charlie's Angels"
60 Salad green
62 Fr. girls
63 Bothers
64 Actually
69 Behind the times
71 It gets into a pickle
72 Seabirds
74 Small African antelope
75 Noted workshop chief
76 Ship, in poetry
77 English writers Derek and Christopher
78 Advocate
79 "The Electric Kool-Aid Acid Test" author
80 1974 Chicago hit
83 Furniture protector
84 Roulette player's opponent
85 Unrest
87 Steed's movement
88 Position oneself to hear better
90 Pageant element
91 Low tracts
95 Chip feature
98 Engage in logrolling
99 Cartoonist Drake
101 Dry
102 Defy
104 Mauna ___
105 Bank figure: Abbr.
106 "___ moment"

by Wayne R. Williams

I WANTED TO BE A . . .

ACROSS

1 "___ It Be Magic" (Manilow song)
6 Country place for Yeltsin
11 16-Down, for one
16 Recipe amt.
20 Prefix with -pathy
21 Contemporary author Canin
22 Kind of cross
23 They get what's left
25 More aloof
26 Car in a Beach Boys song
27 Irregular
28 Longhorn rival
29 . . . faith healer, but I . . .
33 Cadiz Mrs.
34 "The heck with you!"
35 Large group
36 Cherish
37 Trig figure: Abbr.
38 Grenoble's river
40 It's good in Paris
42 Benchmarks: Abbr.
43 Exchange
48 Convertiplane, e.g.
49 Shipping hazard
50 . . . publisher of e. e. cummings's works, but I . . .
55 Country singer Tillis
58 Each
59 "Shrovetide Revelers" artist
60 Coeur d'___, Idaho
61 Crockett's last stand
63 Past its prime
64 "Mister ___" (1957 Tony Curtis film)
65 Go through
66 Visit
67 Singer Janis
68 Cha, cha, cha, e.g.
69 Neologism
70 . . . masseur, but I . . .
78 Works into a passion
79 Cowboy gear
80 Smithfield product
81 Combs
82 Collapses
83 Product of Sweden
85 Former chairman of CBS
90 Say "fo'c'sle," e.g.
91 San ___, Calif.
92 Eastern title
93 Violinmaker Amati
94 Address book info: Abbr.
95 . . . mime, but I . . .
99 Wasn't straight
100 Many paintings
101 Releases, in a way
102 Runner Zatopek
106 Cover
107 Word on all U.S. coins
109 Misc. ending
110 Corelli composition
112 Office
113 Dinsmore the prig
115 Cousin of "ugh!"
118 . . . sumo wrestler, but I . . .
124 Free
125 Disinclined
126 Tropical palm
127 Triangular peninsula
128 Minneapolis suburb
129 Big name in the metals industry
130 Do
131 Baylor of basketball fame
132 Overcharge
133 Limitlessly
134 Hell, with "the"
135 It's a wrap

DOWN

1 Prepares to strike, maybe
2 March honor
3 Punic War city
4 National emblem of Wales
5 Quiz whiz Charles Van ___
6 Oust
7 One of Pete Rose's records
8 Does gym-class exercises
9 Like Hannah's heart, in song
10 Connective tissue of prose
11 Warm-up act
12 Made without milk or meat
13 Thermosetting resin
14 Farrier's tool
15 On the safe side?
16 Massenet work
17 Sires
18 Official impression
19 Set an asking figure
24 Has the earmarks of
30 Figure
31 Daggers, in printing
32 Dancer Jeanmaire
38 Autostrada's place
39 Bribes
40 Word with date or trust
41 Slime
43 Moore starter
44 Intent
45 Polo grounds?
46 Field of honor fight
47 Suffix with differ
48 Badge of battle
49 Work on a whaling ship
51 River of Avignon
52 Retina layers
53 Israeli opener
54 "Mack the Knife" singer
55 Tree also called a custard apple
56 Bygone computer
57 It may be advanced
62 Extended
64 Tops off
65 Galley notations
66 Popular PC shooting game
67 Mid-month, in old Rome
68 Go downhill, in a way
69 Complain
70 Furnace button
71 Truce word
72 Swelter
73 Unit of data transmission
74 Casmerodius albus, commonly
75 Spieled
76 Carpetlike
77 Slip
82 Like Hitler's "diaries"
83 Got wind of, old-style
84 Feels punk
85 Small songbirds
86 It stands for something
87 François Boucher's "Nude Lying on a ___"
88 Fast pace
89 Have the ___ for
91 Year in St. Leo IX's papacy

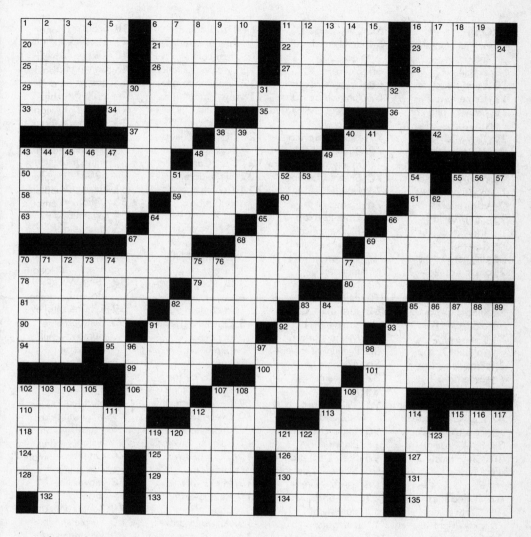

by Mel Rosen

13 CLINTON PUNDITRY

ACROSS

1 Mogul capital of India
5 Pundit
10 Dead duck
15 Torme forte
19 Dinner's often on him
20 "Les Miz" setting
21 1836 battle site
22 Like some traffic
23 Movie about a boy's presidential aspirations?
25 ___ Drusilla (mother of Tiberius)
26 Trigger puller?
27 Home of the Minotaur
28 Tango maneuver
29 Places for races
30 95-Down finisher
31 Cause of inflation?
32 Presidential biography by Noel Coward?
36 Italian wine region
37 ___ Hall (historic Princeton site)
39 Bank deposit
40 Great time
41 "That is to say . . ."
42 Stuffed shirt
44 "Dirty Hands" playwright
46 China setting
47 Spruce
50 Gulf
52 Christie's "___ M?"
53 Country guitar player, e.g.
56 At bat stat
57 What the First lady's critics did over a bottle of bathtub gin?
61 Indianapolis's ___ Dome
62 Cliff hanger?
64 Rembrandt van ___
65 Skittish
66 Dreamscape artist
67 One of the Horae
68 Current choice
70 Exclusive
71 Pickle flavoring
72 Basketball maneuver
73 Shelved for now
75 Hollow
76 Pizazz
77 Gained a lap
78 Mathematical rules governing a vice president's macarena?
81 Hard-rock connection
82 Turn into something big
84 Memo starter
85 Prominent tower
86 Agonize
87 Rec center
88 At the scene
91 1984 Peace Nobelist
93 Children's author Eleanor
95 New Deal proj.
96 Narrowly defeats
98 S.A.T. score
102 60's draft deferment category
103 Vice president's wife at the Starlight Diner?
106 Belfast grp.
107 Baseball Hall-of-Famer Waite ___
108 Basil's "Captain Blood" co-star
109 Catch on
110 Pert
112 Flood avoider
113 Timex rival
114 Head and tail of the victorious First cat?
116 Avalon, for one
117 Chihuahua bites
118 Bye word
119 Atlantic City attraction
120 "Clueless" lead role
121 "___ Canyon"
122 Skein game?
123 Contemporary of Garbo

DOWN

1 Depth charge
2 Extolment, in hymns
3 Cowboys
4 Be a partner in crime
5 Obsolete geog. abbr.
6 Like unkept yards
7 Stands by for
8 "Aida" setting
9 Returns home?
10 Lively dance in duple time
11 "Sleuth" co-star
12 Old 48-Down kingdom
13 Iago's wife
14 Rake over the coals
15 Arrive in droves
16 Star of a sitcom in which the First daughter learns syntax?
17 Whitney Houston's record label
18 Get, as a radio broadcast
24 Prohibit
33 One of Nintendo's Mario Brothers
34 African antelope
35 Detroit brew
38 Scout
41 Essex exclamation
43 Kitchen fixture
45 Comings and goings
46 With a twist?
47 Gallivant
48 Basque, e.g.
49 Where the president went without collecting $200?
51 Hitchcock classic
53 Defiant words
54 Overshadow
55 Umbrella alternative
57 Balmoral Castle river
58 "Star Wars" moon
59 Off one's trolley
60 Humbert Humbert's obsession
63 Publicity
66 Burns and Allen, e.g.
69 Staff leaders
71 Inc. listings
73 "The Three Sisters" sister
74 On the clothesline
78 Moves like a comet
79 Band command
80 Purple shade
83 Into the wind
86 It's a wrap
88 Not neat
89 60-Down's creator
90 Show piece?
92 Clipped
93 Italian or Mexican, e.g.
94 Rushing sound
95 Terrorist tactic
97 Coin of the realm

by Bob Klahn

ACROSS

1 Alternative to orchestra
5 Indispensables
10 Puts in stitches
14 1965 jazz album
18 Where Innsbruck is
19 Bubbling
20 One of the Baldwin brothers
21 Thwart
22 City NNE of Tampa
23 Jefferson's portrayer in a 1995 film
24 Java neighbor
25 Kind of collar
26 Mangles
27 Dickens novel transmuted
30 Bargain
32 Hale
33 ___ Fein
34 Effort
35 Boxing titlist with 57 KO's
37 60's Secretary of the Interior
41 More to the point
45 U.S. ship transmuted
48 Prefix with gram
49 Music hall
51 Opening word?
52 Believer, informally
53 City on the Rhein
54 Eagerly expectant
56 Bandar ___ Begawan (Brunei's capital)
57 Addition column
58 "L.A. Law" lawyer
59 Native of the Land of the Thunder Dragon
62 Write painstakingly
64 1955 play transmuted
70 Schoolmarm's hairdos
71 Spread ingredient
72 Ottoman authority
75 Bettors bet on them
78 "___ la guerre"
81 Billionth: Prefix
82 Drink on the drink
83 Fab competitor
84 Atheist Madalyn et al.
86 Rock's opposite, often
89 Fiend
90 50's TV catch phrase transmuted
93 Deer playmate, in song
95 Consummate
96 Idyllic spots
97 Twosome
98 C minor and others
101 "Xanadu" rock group
102 Water-skier's need
107 Cary Grant movie transmuted
111 German poet Heinrich
112 Astronomer's sighting
113 Lounge
114 Story subtitled "The Yeshiva Boy"
115 Tuckered out
116 Another time
117 Stylish gent, in Britain
118 Knobby
119 Like non-oyster months?
120 Ivy League team
121 Want ad listings: Abbr.
122 "Holy cow!"
123 Storied Phoenician port

DOWN

1 Ecote
2 Clint's "co-star" Clyde, for one
3 Cable channel transmuted
4 Adaptable
5 Decreed
6 W.W. II menace
7 Crack
8 Small, reddish monkey
9 Santa's load
10 Throws a monkey wrench into
11 Airline name drawn from Hosea
12 Joins
13 Some Asimov books
14 Eastern pooh-bah
15 Lounge
16 Produced fiction
17 ___ maison (indoors): Fr.
18 No longer mint
28 Prepares for action
29 Not free
31 Passionate about
35 Masquerade mask
36 Rose bouquet
38 Deuce follower
39 ___-majesté
40 Amphibious vehicles, for short
41 Dutch tourist attraction
42 What's all the screaming about?
43 Holdover
44 Rope used to hang banditos
46 Town in many an oater
47 One of the Karamozov brothers
50 Jazz players are found here
55 Scaler's spike
57 "Well, well, well!"
59 Furnace measure, for short
60 El jefe
61 Open
63 Maj.'s superior
65 Sit-ups strengthen them
66 Cooper of "My Fair Lady"
67 Wine: Prefix
68 Irish lullaby syllables
69 1996 Coen brothers film
73 Trail mix
74 "The Night of the Hunter" screenwriter
75 Soft drink brand
76 Lifeless
77 Singer Marvin
79 Incidental
80 Considerations pro and con
82 Blues singer transmuted
84 Eyeballed
85 Jim-dandy
87 Exists as an activating force
88 Case for an ophthalmologist
91 Chicago suburb
92 Pain reliever
94 "Lady Lindy"
99 Resort east of Sevastopol
100 Prier
102 Non-bear bear
103 Rowing team

by Suzie Elliott

104 Dorothy, for the Tin Man
105 Cordial flavoring
106 Addition column
107 Vanished
108 Where Hansel was headed
109 A penny short of a dime
110 Actor ___ Carroll
112 Drop off for a bit

15 COLLEGE CATALOGUE

ACROSS

1 Spanish poet Federico Garcia ___
6 Jacuzzi user
12 Look everywhere in
17 Indisposed
19 Make it big
20 Popular porters
22 Welty's "One Writer's Beginnings," e.g.
23 Stretched one's neck
24 Mexican state or a product that originated there
25 Whole-grain food
27 Specialist in a duck blind
29 "___ Where My Money Goes" (early 1900's song)
30 Chuck alternative
32 The thing is?
33 G.P. grp.
34 Highest honor
35 Colorful clumps of grass
40 Trimming tool
42 Platitudes
44 Army leader?
45 Province in Italy's Northern League
46 Blue Eagle initials
47 Adult
48 Locate
49 Conviction
52 Kingdom of Minos
53 Lies limply
56 Drink for Drac
57 Nurse
58 Street of mystery
60 Go cold turkey
62 Columbia athlete
63 Fill the hold
64 Flying jib, e.g.
65 Pull strings?
66 Get fresh with
67 More than miffed
69 Toiling
70 Christmas ___
71 Advanced course
73 Whiz
75 "___ a Moon Out Tonight" (1961 hit)
76 "___ Three Lives"
77 Missouri, e.g.
78 East end
79 Jelly ingredient
82 Secretary, at times
83 Crime statistics
87 Western airline name
88 Emma Lazarus
90 Muscle-building unit
92 Put up
93 To be, to Benita
94 Word in a promise
95 Hot issue?
96 Area near the crown
102 One who teases a nobleman
105 Squeaking
106 "Stalag 17" star
108 Inherent character
109 They're dispensed in litres
110 Ancient
111 School of painting
112 Marsh plant
113 Break
114 Cobbler's stock

DOWN

1 Kind of particle
2 "Saw the air too much with your hand," in Shakespeare's words
3 Like Uranus vis-à-vis Jupiter
4 A cock does it
5 Speller's phrase
6 God of wine
7 Unpaid debt
8 Sing-a-long syllable
9 Posterior
10 In any way
11 The scarlet letter
12 Bygone kings
13 Philippine island
14 City WNW of Mascara
15 Overshadow
16 Flower clusters
18 Not be perfect
20 Changes back
21 Guy Lombardo hit of 1937 or Jimmy Dorsey hit of 1957
26 Silo occupant
28 Franklin's flier
31 Grabbed
35 Hung out to dry
36 Bomber initials
37 Bring (out)
38 Single
39 Cod piece?
40 "___ Peach" (Allman Brothers album)
41 Got lucky at poker
43 General Grant's horseshoer
45 Like the flu
47 Hail
48 Alley challenge
49 Beer holders: Abbr.
50 Walt Disney's middle name
51 Unbound
52 Chest material
53 Done in
54 Like some excursions
55 Go furtively
57 Unit of capacitance
59 Distillation product
61 Chuck
63 Closet contents
68 "South Pacific" hero
69 Fends off
70 Make confetti
72 Trojan princess of a Mozart opera
74 Maintain
75 Alas., once
77 Costa, anatomically
79 Get ready to leave
80 Renowned Manhattan eatery
81 Suggest
82 Concern
83 Overflows
84 Captain, e.g.
85 Slander
86 A fistful
88 Home of England's Opera North
89 Off-peak calls?
91 ( ), informally
93 Marker
95 Loose-limbed
97 Prepare for action
98 Toil wearily
99 "___ Lap" (1983 film)
100 Balcony section
101 Engr.'s specialty
103 Bambi's aunt
104 Devil-may-care
107 Bambi's aunt

by Richard Silvestri

THAT'S AMORE

ACROSS

1 Lake name of two Olympics
7 "Pardon me, Marcello"
12 Bay
19 The dawn
20 Seesaw
21 Nervous system stimulant
23 Amore from Judy Garland, 1948
25 Amore from Jan Garber and His Orchestra, 1926
26 Jonathan's father, in the Bible
27 Sour
28 Romance, e.g.
29 "Too-Ra-Loo-Ra-Loo-___"
30 When dinner may be served
32 Amore from Dean Martin, 1955
35 Reply courtesy, briefly
36 ___ embarrassment (be mortified)
37 Where black is white, for short?
38 Muse for Milton
39 All alternative
40 It turns out Its
41 Footnote abbr.
43 Griffith and Gibb
44 Rundown
45 It may be picked up in bars
46 Ruth's "Laugh-In" foil
47 "Bye!"
48 Star of 50's TV's "Private Secretary"
51 Amore from Andy Williams, 1965
54 "I do," e.g.
57 Express
58 Like an oxeye window
59 Example of Peke speak?
60 Metro entrance
62 Above, in Berlin
63 Subway passages
65 "Good ___!"
67 Lick ___ promise
68 Music for a baseball team?
70 Ore delivery, maybe
71 Vacation spot
72 Striking likeness
74 "The Spanish Tragedy" dramatist
75 Amore from Anita Baker, 1986
78 Actress called "The Jersey Lily"
79 Kentucky Derby times
80 W. Hemisphere land
81 Strike down
82 Aim
85 Certain South Asian
87 Initials in a 1991 financial scandal
88 Org. at Constitution Hall
91 Investigator's sources
92 Purplish
93 Verb for you
94 Relative of an onion
96 About
97 Amore from the Archies, 1969
99 Rapper ___ Shakur
100 Grunts
101 Simoleons
102 "The Age of Reason" writer
104 Cold Adriatic wind
105 Amore from the Beatles, 1968
107 Amore from the Diamonds, 1957
110 Parent's armful
111 Singer Waters
112 For one
113 The sun and moon
114 Sillies
115 Meals in a hall

DOWN

1 Thrusting fencing maneuver
2 Kook
3 Provokes
4 "Gangsta's Paradise" singer
5 Provoke
6 During office hours
7 Needed smelling salts
8 Encrustation
9 Part of the soft palate
10 Pastor's sch.
11 Major C.P.A. employer
12 Strokes for Solti
13 It's inclined to provide shelter
14 Dark area
15 Ravel's "Ma mère ___" ("Mother Goose")
16 Franklin's 1936 foe
17 Like a beauty queen
18 Contained
22 Where to catch a moray
24 View
28 Gloomy
31 Scully and Mulder's obsession
33 Telepathic
34 Court demand
35 "Away!"
39 Common online activities
42 Military wear
43 Precincts
44 ___ Winston Churchill
45 It's just south of Des Plaines
46 Coming
47 ___ noir
48 Spirit
49 Cry of delight
50 That's the way it goes
52 "Bury Me in a Free Land" poet
53 Presque Isle locale
54 French score
55 On in years
56 Pooped
58 Relative of the English horn
61 Code letter after Sierra
64 Uintah Reservation Indians
65 Auctioneer's aid
66 Coin worth about 19 cents
69 Autocrats
71 Sunday reading
73 Charge
76 Fourth of July?
77 Truman's Missouri birthplace
78 Swiss tourist center
79 Lapel item, sometimes
82 Land
83 Kind of tour
84 Garden root
85 Fierce woman
86 Wings
87 Words read with feeling?

by Dean Niles

88 Some antennas
89 Cupidity
90 Fixes, as furniture
92 1937 DuPont invention
93 Marbles
95 Classic cause of a fall
97 ___ Tuesday
98 ___ creek
101 1977 Cy Young winner from the Yankees
103 Dutch treat
106 Letter from St. Paul: Abbr.
107 Standing prerequisite
108 Suffix with Samson
109 Do a Little bit

ACROSS

1 Suffix with land or city
6 Hanged
14 Unhitched?
20 Clio contender
21 Attack
22 Like socks in a drawer
23 Noted guitarist
26 Some learning
27 Kernel
28 The Thames borders it
29 Word of reproach
30 Tiny type size
32 Numbskull
34 Bandleader Paul
38 Roman mine
39 Atom
40 Chiang ___-shek
43 Marcus and George
44 Four-time Indy winner
50 Noted youth grp.
51 ___ Mujeres, Mexico
52 Furtive sort
53 They don't want to fight
55 Should
57 Attached at the base, botanically
63 Druggie
64 Early empire builder
65 Recipe amt.
67 Italian city where Giotto painted
69 "Surprised by Joy" autobiographer
74 Metric weights
75 It may be high in the afternoon
76 Count
77 Introductory material
78 Loss by decay
81 Wasn't sociable
83 Strike location
84 General announcement?
86 Stagger
88 Not the best service
89 "My Little Chickadee" star
96 Medieval weapon
97 Laugh syllable
98 Artillery shell component
99 A substantial amount of Louisiana
100 Goes around
102 Tricked
103 Rolls
107 Vitamin C source
108 Refuse
112 No longer stuck on
114 Understanding words
115 Three-time N.F.L. M.V.P.
121 Understanding
122 Computer offering
123 Not be fast
124 They're out in a game
125 Prepares for a rough ride
126 Cardinal points?

DOWN

1 Buffalo wing?
2 Modern information medium
3 Tiny amount
4 Where gelato was invented
5 Like a member of the U.S.N.
6 Sober-minded
7 Comaneci achievements
8 Kind of comb
9 City area
10 "Frasier" character
11 Lions' prey
12 Indians with a sun dance
13 It may be struck
14 Eponymous Belgian town
15 Actor Holm
16 An end to peace
17 1994 A.L. home run king
18 Soft
19 Garden tools
24 Homes with domes
25 Cold war threat
31 Elvis Costello's "My ___ True"
33 Grave marker
35 Silver treat
36 First name in 1936 politics
37 Early 80's sitcom
39 "Othello" courtesan
40 Name in 1993 news
41 Bill the Cat pronouncement, in the funnies
42 Alibi ___ (liars, of a sort)
44 Shanghai
45 G.I. entertainment
46 Greek cafe
47 Shrovetide dish
48 Legal grounds for action
49 Poetic preposition
54 Gray and Moran
56 Argot
58 Getting around well
59 "My gal"
60 The best
61 Kind of estimate
62 Got a flat boot?
64 "___ deal!"
66 Some government appropriations
68 The plus column
70 Pin down
71 Kind of oil
72 Ogle
73 "The Courtship of Miles Standish" character
79 Travel (about)
80 Drop acid?
82 Preceded
83 Travels back and forth
85 Abbr. in a help wanted ad
87 Application
89 Lynette ___, first female Harlem Globetrotter
90 Took in, maybe
91 Actor Stephen
92 Congratulations, of a sort
93 Palindromic English river
94 Chants
95 Authorize
96 Beseech
101 ___-Anne-des-Plaines, Quebec
102 Lake Volta's country
103 Ho-hum TV fare
104 Adlai's '56 running mate
105 Like some apartments
106 Most likely winners
109 Butts
110 Rat-___
111 Pokey
113 Start of a classic Latin quote
116 Broodmare
117 Had fare
118 Med. specialty
119 Tiny terror
120 ___ Saud (former Mideast leader)

by Matt Gaffney

SOUND EFFECTS

ACROSS

1 Erect
6 "Casablanca" role
10 Legend, e.g.
15 Winston Churchill's "___ Country"
19 ___ vincit amor
20 Distress
21 Signals are used to switch them
22 Leader of philosophical skepticism
23 What a tipsy actor does?
26 Priests' vestments
27 Sets for med. dramas
28 "Video Companion" author
29 Pool
30 Reine's spouse
32 Year in Claudius's reign
33 Wallace of "E.T."
34 Like 20-Across, often
35 It may drip
36 Brought about
38 What a sweet tooth demands?
41 Words with hole or two
42 Commercial thoroughfare
45 "Gunsmoke" bartender
46 Mme., in Madrid
47 Nuts
48 "On Broadway" co-writer Cynthia
49 Social climber's goal
52 Loose overcoat
55 Like the Archbishop of York
57 Code word
59 Plenty
60 Yup's alternative
61 Aisle?
65 Some are holy
68 Access
70 Work done on the premises?
71 Broadway hit subtitled "A Musical Arabian Night"
72 Italian auto maker Bugatti
73 Had one's foot in the door?
76 Prefix with sphere
77 "thirty-something" actor
78 Social addition
79 Disney World transport
81 Wingdings
83 "Love Affair" star, 1994
86 Der ___ (Adenauer)
87 Striker's cry
89 "The Crying Game" star
91 Student datum
92 Fools
93 200 milligrams
95 San Diego Zoo attraction?
100 Conquered quickly
102 Fleet fleet?
103 Deep blue
104 Nobelist Hammarskjold
107 Maria, for one
108 List ender
109 Constrain
110 Rush
111 Low note
112 Biting
114 Goings-on at the church fair?
118 "___ la Douce"
119 Had dinner delivered
120 Like one side of a ship
121 Laertes and Ophelia
122 They, in Trieste
123 Nashville ___ (60's pop group)
124 Trade center
125 Año nuevo time

DOWN

1 Enticed, with "in"
2 Dean Martin topic
3 Taken
4 ___ Roger de Coverley (country dance)
5 Abated
6 Flip
7 Emulated Groucho Marx
8 Miro compatriot
9 Holly Hunter in "The Piano"
10 Recess
11 Plains family
12 Cycle starter
13 Payback
14 Luxury car ___ Martin
15 "Gotcha!"
16 Offerings at a downscale eatery?
17 Encompassing
18 Lives
24 They go to waist
25 Spurts of activity
31 Uganda's Amin
35 "___ was a cunning hunter": Genesis
37 Relaxes
38 Nursery rhyme girl
39 L.I. zone
40 Veridicality
42 Classic Gershwin song
43 Landlord's need
44 Government fashion decree?
49 Summer needs
50 Mai ___
51 Or's go-with
53 Stirring up
54 City WSW of Milano
56 European airline
57 Place for a throne
58 Problem for a suited-up diver?
62 "___, 'tis true I have gone here and there": Shak.
63 Preoccupied
64 Tour organizer, for short
66 Enumerate
67 Wraps
69 Sports car feature
73 Having learned a lesson
74 Japan's largest lake
75 Waiting period, seemingly
80 Tabula ___
82 Curtail
83 Persiflage
84 Easter features
85 ___-Freudian
87 F.D.R.'s Fala, e.g.
88 Blini accompaniments
90 Forbear
92 "The House of the Spirits" author
94 Sei halved
96 Kurds and Turks
97 Ice-T or Eazy-E
98 Sulking
99 Word for the diet-conscious

by Nancy Nicholson Joline

101 In a box,
    in a way
104 "Death, Be Not
    Proud" poet
105 Choler
106 Artist's
    plaster
110 Large hall
113 ___ kwon do

115 Small section
    of a dictionary
116 Country ___
117 Golfer Woosnam

ACROSS

1 Follow
8 Cases
15 Unmemorized words
20 Begin, e.g.
21 Less stirred
22 Winslow Homer's home
23 Be ecstatic
26 King of the 18th dynasty
27 Parodied, with "up"
28 Poetic contraction
29 Even though
30 Tiny bit
33 Go to bat for
35 Sault __ Marie
36 Okla. football rival
37 "Women and Love" author
40 Neighbor of Minn.
41 Garish
42 Paris-to-Marseilles dir.
43 Song from the Beatles' "Sgt. Pepper" album
48 Rocker Joan
49 Principle of philosophy
50 Old Alka-Seltzer mascot
51 Finder's cry
53 Slippery __
54 Land of the Chosen people
55 "Diary of a Genius" author
57 Bring upon oneself
61 Stout relative
62 With 86-Down, partner of buts
63 Brunch beverage
65 __ incognita
66 Musical measures
68 Some gold diggers
72 Watch word
73 Not chronic
75 Approached
76 Nice view
78 Fraternity letter
79 Pool contents?
80 "It's __ . . . World"
81 Bow in the theater
83 Reunion group
84 B flat's equivalent
87 1985 N.L. Cy Young Award winner
88 Ally of the U.S.
89 Raised
92 Slots
96 King's title: Abbr.
97 Melville foretopman
98 Singer Janis
99 Rockefeller Center muralist
100 Chemical suffix
101 Hosp. areas
102 Sandinista foe
105 Cruise in style
109 Reception helper
111 Performs, for King James
112 Downwind
115 Dauphin's father
116 1970 Chicago hit
121 Waste maker
122 Partly coincide
123 Show up
124 Vocalist John
125 Hounds
126 American and Swiss

DOWN

1 Strains, in a way
2 Exhaust
3 Where Sir Arthur Evans excavated
4 Hall-of-Famer Hubbard
5 Slimmer swimmer
6 Some Ivy Leaguers
7 Water barrier
8 It's quarried in Vermont
9 Continuous sound
10 Celebrated
11 Galore
12 Like some floors
13 Presumptive person?
14 Full house indicator
15 Sashayed
16 Brush carelessly
17 Poet's prerogative
18 Most pitch-black
19 Optimal option
24 Objective
25 First published work by 39-Down
31 Antonio's role in "Evita"
32 Aguirre portrayer
34 Very alluring
35 Whisky drink
38 Alert
39 The Sage of Concord
41 Charpentier opera or its heroine
43 "Ben-Hur" author
44 Round trip of sorts
45 Spot
46 Humphrey's "High Sierra" co-star
47 Malefactor
48 Jamie Lee's mom
49 It's often in hot water
52 Supplies
55 Treated to supper
56 Surrounded by
58 Fair play
59 Ragamuffins
60 Yard chore
63 "__ Breckinridge"
64 Easily maneuverable military forces
67 Place
69 Raised
70 City with a Latin quarter
71 Composed
74 Drain trap shape, at times
77 Petered out
81 Provincetown catch
82 Tennis shot
85 Like some wages
86 See 62-Across
87 Chap
89 Get some air
90 Urban modernization
91 Chomolungma's more familiar name
93 "Do the Right Thing" extras
94 Way down?
95 Spanish diminutive suffix
97 Hammered
102 Recesses
103 Coarse files
104 Former ring king
106 Riding accessories
107 Representative location
108 Rollers?
110 Division word
111 Midler's "__ Las Vegas"
113 Big cheese
114 Use acid
117 A gift in O. Henry's "The Gift of the Magi"
118 Squeal
119 Good __ boy
120 Old-style interjection

This is a crossword puzzle grid with some cells filled in by hand.

1 S	2 U	3 C	4 C	5 E	6 E	7 D	■	8	9	10	11	12	13	14	■	15	16	17	18	19
20 I	s	r	a	e	l	i		21							■	22				
23 F	e	e	l	l	i	k	24 e	a	m	i	l	l	i	o	25 n	b	u	c	k	s
26 I		■		27			■	28				■		29						
30 S		■	31	32		■	33		34			■	35				■	36		
■			37		38	39	■	40			■	41				■	42			
■	43	44					45	46			47			■	48					
49			■	50					■	51			■	52						
53			■	54				■	55	56			■	57		58	59	60		
61			■	62		■	63			■	64		■	65						
66		67	■	68		69	70					71	■	72						
73			74	■	75				■	76		77	■	78						
79				■	80		■	81	82				■	83						
■		84		85	86		■	87					■	88						
89	90	91		92		93	94						95			■				
96		■	97		■	98			■	99				■						
100		■	101		■	102			103	104	■	105		106	107	108				
109		110		■	111		■	112		113	114		115							
116				117			118					119	120							
121		■	122					■	123											
124				■	125				■	126										

by Harvey Estes

ACROSS

1 Sponge
6 Iconoclastic comedian
10 South Africa's first P.M.
15 Sap
20 Think a lot of
21 Ensemble part
22 Commandment subjects
23 Pineapple island
24 Sailor's cry
26 Forty?
28 Continue to the end
29 Stuffing seasoning
31 Clear
32 1936 Loretta Young title role
33 Itches
34 Second person in the Bible
36 Approaching
38 First name in society
39 Take the wrong way?
40 1932 skiing gold medalist Utterstrom
41 Agamemnon's sister-in-law
43 Dog on "Frasier"
46 Heiress, maybe
48 Subject of monthly reading
49 Indy racer Guthrie
52 Monitor
53 Flushing stadium
54 Onetime SAC chief and family
55 Downyflake rival
56 Put on a show
58 Virus type
60 Part of the Winnebago nation
61 Less ruddy
62 Dreary
65 New York nosh
67 Trembling
69 Hydrocarbon suffixes
70 Class division
73 Sandhurst send-offs
75 Earned a citation?
76 Barber of renown
77 Lure of New Orleans
79 Churchill Downs drink
81 "We Do Our Part" org.
84 Parsley's pungent relative
86 Where Mocha is
88 Hardly enthusiastic
89 Largest land carnivore
90 Concerns
93 Pluck
95 Dessert wine
97 Part of "the works"
98 Women's casual slacks
100 G.I.'s suppliers
102 Truth, to Trotsky
103 Senator succeeded by Cleland
104 Liturgy
105 8-Down sound
108 Beauts
109 Sound of reproach
110 Deposit
112 Guard of myth
114 Kind of footing
115 Plug
116 Blue-green
117 Not yet scheduled
119 Head for the ranch?
121 "___ Playing Our Song" (1979 song)
123 Calyx components
124 Pizarro's capital
128 Home of the Riksdag
129 Stalemate
130 Joss
132 Odysseus, e.g.
134 Antique sale listing
137 Lure of New Orleans
139 Reference marks
140 A la King?
141 Individual share
142 Two-time U.S. Open winner
143 First name in cosmetics
144 Stumped
145 Dallas Cowboy's emblem
146 Assignation

DOWN

1 Like some skits
2 Allan-___
3 Single-named 60's singer
4 Zane and Lady Jane
5 A Saarinen
6 Reassure
7 Former org. of the Pacers and the Spurs
8 Guffaw
9 Mother of 41-Across
10 "Phooey!"
11 It circles Uranus
12 Morrison and others
13 Lunch counter request
14 Start of a Faulkner title
15 TV family name
16 "Dallas" co-star
17 Kind of suit
18 Heavenly gift
19 Site of a famous campanile
22 Boxcars
25 Western copper center
27 Feverish
30 Place to put a tiger?
35 ___ Bridge, St. Louis
37 La Méditerranée, e.g.
39 Parts of pedigrees
42 And the following: Lat.
43 Fine fur
44 Mickey
45 Spoils, with "on"
47 "What's with ___?"
48 CH$_4$
49 Heebie-jeebies
50 The Rome of Hungary
51 Loyalist
52 Westernizer of Russia
54 Became unglued
55 Leaf gatherer
57 Make squiggles
59 Tunnel traveler
61 Founder of New York's Public Theater
63 Claustrophobe's nightmare, for short
64 Tense
66 Cartesian conclusion
68 Gone
71 Monk, maybe
72 Branched
74 Motor oil additives
77 Prized game fish
78 Reason for an R rating
80 Addams portrayer, in film
82 Produced no more
83 Some are restricted
85 It's a scorcher
87 Frostiness
89 Vegetarian's staple
90 Practice
91 ___ probandi

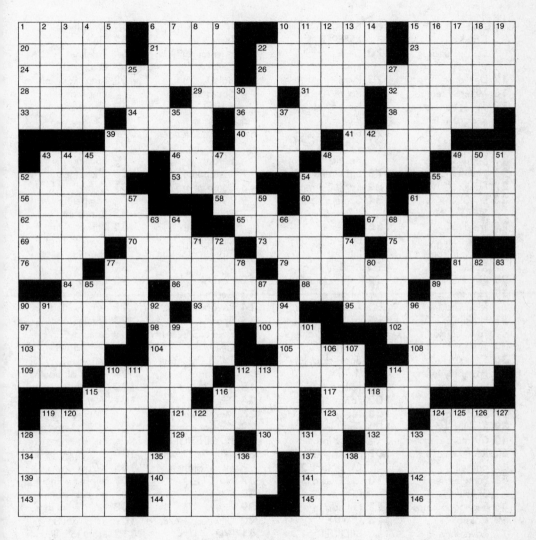

by June Boggs

92 Beat it
94 Gave off, as vapor
96 Steelhead, e.g.
99 Fruit pastry
101 Slump
106 Philodendron, e.g.
107 Held on the stage
110 Early arrival
111 Blackmore heroine

112 "Blue River"
    actress, 1995
113 Collectible, maybe
114 Sauce made with
    pine nuts
115 Hawk
116 Crow's home
118 Dell necessity
119 Lab specimens

120 Principle
122 Like good
    computer screens,
    informally
124 Great Western
    Forum player
125 With aloof disdain
126 Prides of lions
127 Existential woe

128 Last item
131 Wood sorrels
133 Graft recipient
135 Bing Crosby's
    record label
136 Org. founded in
    1970
138 Interim rulers

ACROSS

1 Cruelty
7 Conspicuous success
12 Deliver
16 Metered rental
19 1979 Vanessa Redgrave title role
20 "You ___ Beautiful"
21 Naturalness
22 Santa ___ winds
23 PLASTIC SURGEON
25 Trisyllabic cadences
27 Landon from Kansas
28 GARDENER
30 Play to ___ (deadlock)
31 Hamlin's "L.A. Law" co-star
32 A pop
33 "Yikes!"
34 Fraternity letters
35 Lively ones
36 Storm type
38 ___ Friday
39 Reddish brown
40 Curator's deg.
42 Really enjoys oneself
45 Female friend of Franco
46 Feel-good times
49 Cassio's adversary
50 Injured, in a way
51 Eye problem
52 Herb used in cooking
55 Order
57 Valueless item
58 Neighbor of Turk.
60 Take-home
61 Slave of Amneris
63 St. Louis pro
65 Old English letter

66 BASKETBALL REFEREE
70 Quite some time
71 Even
72 Royal Ascot time
73 House vote
74 Blue
75 Economic stat.
76 Org. involved in Bosnia
78 Small endocrine
82 Early German
84 Some schools, informally
86 Perceive
87 Baby oil brand
89 Interest
90 Kind of error
92 Crisis points?: Abbr.
93 Actress North
94 Tricked
95 Lime and others
98 Zestful
99 Short dog, for short
100 Joined
102 Force: Lat.
103 Ax
106 Old Norse collection
107 MARRIAGE COUNSELOR
110 ___ Piedras, P.R.
111 Enhearten
113 CATTLE BREEDER
115 Bird with a white tail
116 Expos V.I.P.
117 Copier, for short
118 Anna Pavlova, e.g.
119 37-Down, in Oberhausen
120 Squeal
121 Fatty ___
122 Longed

DOWN

1 Leaves for a restaurant?
2 Quick
3 Bats
4 Sheraton's parent
5 Boutique
6 "The ___ redden in the sun": Bryant
7 Take home
8 Bomb aftermaths
9 1969 Paul Revere & the Raiders hit
10 Drenched
11 Rip, but not Van Winkle
12 Harbor sight
13 Certain hose
14 Bavarian river
15 Sparkle
16 FISHING BOAT CAPTAIN
17 1493 Columbus landing site
18 Most abject
24 Ribald
26 More primitive
29 Kind of computer
35 TOY DESIGNER
36 With 96-Down, movie pioneer
37 N.F.C. ___
38 Dotty
39 Pasty
40 City near Hartford
41 BAIL BONDSMAN
43 Exposer
44 JUDGE
46 Judy Blume best seller
47 CHIROPRACTOR
48 Words with were or know
50 Joins
53 Amazon, e.g.
54 It fits in a lock
56 Florida game fish

59 Stepping places
62 Finis
64 Pipelines
67 Bro. or sist.
68 King, Pope or Emperor
69 Fleischer's Olive ___
77 March ender, maybe
79 Burning
80 Shortage
81 Comet competitor
83 Brings into play
85 Part of a bray
88 "Twelfth Night" countess
89 Overhangs
90 Become emotional
91 Arm-twisted
93 Family room feature
96 See 36-Down
97 Leftovers?
99 Word of mouth
100 ___ nerve
101 Wynonna's mother
103 1993 Aerosmith hit
104 Seating request
105 Wrote down
107 Slipper without a back
108 West Point inits.
109 Ring results
112 Right to influence
114 Cambodia's ___ Nol

by David J. Kahn

22 POP CULTURE

ACROSS

1 Haughty refusal
6 Sternward
11 Surveyor's chart
15 Where scissors are made?
18 St. Theresa's birthplace
19 Edit, possibly
21 "An American in Paris" actress
23 ___ Orchestra (popular 30's band)
24 The Beatles' "I'm ___"
25 Case
26 Slangy refusal
27 Pop setting for a Mussorgsky work?
29 Spiral ___
32 Products of gamma rays
33 Thatching palm
34 Horus's father
35 Kind of fence
38 Comes down pretty hard
40 Pop Anthony Burgess novel?
43 Prefix with drama
44 Louis I, to Charlemagne
45 College building
46 "___ beam up" ("Star Trek" order)
48 Big dogs, for short
52 Glides
57 Pop title role in a 1993 film?
62 Epithet of Athena
63 Pitchers, in a way
64 Trifling
65 Disagreeable sorts, in slang
66 Actress Russo
67 Pop dance team, informally?
71 Hero sandwich
73 Joule fragments
74 Containing the 58th element
75 Alaska's first governor
77 Dig
78 30's crooner Columbo
82 Pop western of 1960?
91 Garden section: Var.
92 Catacomb recess
93 Weed with purplish flowers: Var.
94 Old alms box
95 ___ de pont (bridgehead)
96 Phoenician, e.g.
97 Pop 50's–60's TV star?
105 A season: Abbr.
106 Medieval kingdom in western Europe
107 Morgan le Fay's brother
108 Sheepherders of the Southwest
110 Commences, as an adventure
111 Gaines rival
112 ___ Rogers St. Johns
113 Scale notes
114 Aid for Santa
115 "Oh boy!"
116 ___-tresses (orchid)

DOWN

1 Collar
2 Dissolve
3 Where charges may show up
4 Pop Peace Nobelist?
5 "Norma ___"
6 Kind of summit
7 Hungarian revolutionary Kun
8 M.P.'s prize
9 Fearless one
10 Vibrating effect
11 1957 Nabokov novel
12 Scourge of serge
13 Amphora handle
14 "Jour de Fete" star
15 Kin of "Sacre bleu!"
16 Swallows
17 Shallow bay on England's east coast
20 Swedish money
22 "Cleopatra" extra
28 Jimmy Carter alma mater: Abbr.
29 Linguist Chomsky
30 Tavern need: Abbr.
31 Solicit
35 Obsession, e.g.
36 Soph. and others
37 Cricket wicket
38 Mideast inn
39 Math amts.
41 1984–88 Olympic figure-skating gold medalist
42 "No kidding!"
47 Cyst
48 Truman's birthplace
49 Burlesque activity
50 Part of morning calisthenics
51 Holdup
53 Pop product at a barbershop?
54 "It was ___ joke!"
55 Protest in no uncertain terms
56 Ed.'s request
57 1978 Irving character
58 Graphic beginning
59 Alphabet quartet
60 Tormented
61 Draws
65 Language authority Mario
67 Unclear
68 Fastballer known as "The Express"
69 Bills
70 Waves at, perhaps
72 One of a storied threesome
76 Goose egg
77 Lion's prey
79 Open, in a way
80 How a siren walks
81 He sank with the Scharnhorst
82 Park item
83 Insulin, e.g.
84 Ones providing arms
85 Thin, overseas
86 Picture, commercially
87 Cold pack?
88 Dance
89 Hero robot of the comics
90 Certain intersection
98 Rank below marquis
99 ___ prius (trial court)
100 Grandson of Adam
101 Tiny payment
102 Mississippi feeder
103 Bergman in "Casablanca"
104 Without ___ of hope
108 Old-time Yankee great Chase
109 Eur. airline

by Bryant White

23 PARADOX

ACROSS

1 One may be checkered
5 Night light
9 April honoree
13 Fairy tale figures
17 Baseball's Tommie
18 Devour
20 ___ Fjord
21 Part of a monk's title
22 Beginning of a thought by the 72-Across 102-Across 80-Across
26 Bedtime genie
27 Stamp of approval?: Abbr.
28 Patsies
29 Sushi supplies
30 Scrooge's look
31 Quilters' klatch
32 "Dr. Zhivago" name
34 Type choices
35 Mocking
40 End of the thought
44 ___-de-sac
45 Seat of Garfield County, Okla.
46 Olympics jump
47 Not theirs
48 Canon competitor
49 P.M. hours, to a bard
50 80-Across's field
54 Practices girth control
55 With grace
58 ___-class (airplane section)
59 Two Tudors
60 Regatta
61 Catch of the day, maybe
62 Somewhat, to Salieri
63 Part of a rainbow

66 Palestrina piece
67 Ale, e.g.
71 Tearjerkers, sometimes
72 Like 80-Across
74 Lacto-___-vegetarian
75 Beer variety
76 Lady Macbeth, for one
77 Crazy quilt
78 Corp. V.I.P.'s
79 "Peer Gynt" character
80 See 22-Across
85 E-mail
87 Bar, at the bar
88 Taxi door info
89 Personals, e.g.
90 Isle on which Apollo was born
91 Protection for some I.R.A.'s
93 Item on a list
97 Each
98 Vexes
102 What 80-Across became in 1996
106 Start of a Dickens title
107 River to the Fulda
108 Certain string ensemble
109 "Eugene Onegin" mezzo-soprano
110 Famous tiger
111 Root beer brand
112 Eliot character
113 Old news agency

DOWN

1 Dog's "dogs"
2 Mideast title
3 Spotted
4 Bid
5 Only U.N. member whose flag is not rectangular
6 Clears
7 Ear: Prefix

8 Mother Teresa, for one
9 Most enamored (of)
10 Pianist Levant
11 1982 country hit "Same ___ Me"
12 Gobs
13 Peddled
14 ___ vera
15 "Dumb & Dumber" actress
16 Caesar and others
19 Jump (on)
21 Trickery
23 "That is . . ."
24 "___ directed"
25 Chutzpah
30 Not go directly
32 Eye makeup
33 Dress style
34 Godliness
35 Oporto's river
36 Young Fontaine role
37 With increased reserve
38 Cuckoo
39 Bar request
40 Trickle
41 Black, yellow and white
42 Jean-Claude Duvalier, e.g.
43 Big bar order
48 Second-fiddle
51 Prefix with linear
52 Plottage
53 Liking
54 Art style, familiarly
56 Rubbish
57 Yard sale staples
59 Associate
61 Roman sandal
62 Jewish holiday
63 Faith in Turkey
64 Static
65 Historical info
66 Gangster's gals
67 Nodule

68 Verb for thou
69 Call to mind
70 Santa ___, Calif.
72 Sit for a photo
73 Nincompoops
76 Erects, as a contraption
78 Loon
80 Duck walk
81 Sorry sorts
82 "It must have been ___ news day"
83 Visit
84 Bit of NASA equipment
86 With a level head
90 In a fog
91 Overexposed to the sun
92 T.S. Eliot book-essay
93 Premed class: Abbr.
94 Computer programming phrase
95 Israel's Abba
96 He once had stable work on TV
99 Wife in "Come Back, Little Sheba"
100 Brain scans, for short
101 Timetable listings: Abbr.
103 Rhoda's TV mom
104 Head, in slang
105 Liverpool-to-Newcastle dir.

by Elizabeth C. Gorski

ACROSS

1 Brawl
7 Presence
15 Brothers' titles
19 Place
20 Cleared out, in a way
21 Matter
22 Reckless arrival?
24 ___ Arenas, port in 93-Down
25 Tropical cuckoo
26 ___-Cat
27 University V.I.P.
28 Former Met conductor Bruno
29 Prefix with fuel
30 Smallville, U.S.A., family, in the comics
33 Jettison
36 Mother ___
37 Punkie
39 Figure at a roast
41 Word before Rodham, perhaps
42 "___ no idea!"
43 Become, with "to"
45 Actress Peeples et al
46 "Hardy Boys" character
47 Naldi of the "Ziegfeld Follies"
48 Extols
49 Real estate ad abbr.
50 Zero hour for Will Kane, in a film
51 Convened anew
52 Computer magazine
53 Biblical heirs, with "the"
54 "No food or drink" site, perhaps
56 "I knew it!"
57 Storyteller
58 Grating
59 Exchange figures
62 Philippine Island
64 Early 20th-century French art style
66 Diamond status
68 Alley sounds
69 Warren Moon, once
70 A lot of time
72 Norwegian coin
73 Made a lot of noise
75 "A Hard Road to Glory" athlete-author
76 Baker
77 Loquacious
80 Anatomical passage
81 Rumple
82 Colgate rival
83 Hall ___
84 Bulbous flower, for short
85 Blue of baseball
86 Plans, as a course
87 Muslim's House of God
88 Boost, with "up"
89 Acting baseball commissioner Bud
90 Maintained
91 Jack London's "Martin ___"
92 Hoists
94 Glacial ice formation
96 ___ rigueur (literally)
99 Agent 99 portrayer
101 Jobs, figuratively
103 Be a pain
104 Reach capacity, slangily, with "out"
105 "In other words . . ."
106 Decisive spa service?
111 Spica's constellation
112 Consign
113 Groundhog, notably
114 Slacken
115 D'Oyly Carte production
116 Puts in

DOWN

1 Causes of some scratches
2 Cox of "St. Elsewhere"
3 Temporary talent scarcity?
4 Saturn, for one
5 Their motto is "North to the future"
6 "Keystone Kops" producer
7 Alphabetic sequence
8 Sailing pronoun
9 Inst.
10 Name of 11 ancient Egyptian rulers
11 Transfix
12 Actor Vincent of "Alive"
13 Writer Wolitzer
14 "Fables in Slang" author
15 Questionable ancestry?
16 1961 Bobby Vee hit
17 Come before
18 Eyed
21 One doing a balancing job
23 Trick
28 Stimulate
31 Romantic bit of film making?
32 Brat's look
34 Atheist's e-mail, maybe?
35 She played Thelma in "Thelma & Louise"
38 Marcel Duchamp subject
40 Sky-___ (TV news aid)
43 Austrian composer Berg
44 Tumult
46 Some apartments
49 "___ dear . . ."
50 Polite refusal
51 They exist from hand-to-mouth
53 Beethoven's "___ Solemnis"
54 No longer dirt
55 River at Avignon
57 Humble
58 Schoolbag item
60 Vacuum malfunction result?
61 Least equivocal
63 Prehistoric medical supply?
65 Was shown
67 Revival gear
71 Words of understanding
74 American record holder Steve Scott, e.g.
75 Quattros and others
76 Kind of testimony
77 Get some coffee, perhaps
78 Don's world
79 Identifying equipment
81 .001 inch
82 Arrives, officially

by Rich Norris

84 Baltimore suburb ___ Burnie
85 Trace
86 It may involve finger-pointing
89 Ancient Greek coin
93 Where the Bio-Bio flows
95 Margin
97 Bar selection
98 Managers, sometimes
100 Experimental rock pioneer
102 Jazz style
106 ___-Magnon
107 Part of a workout
108 Court figure: Abbr.
109 Rural sight
110 Lt. hopeful

ACROSS

1 Workplace overseer, for short
5 Placido domicile
9 Diamond, e.g.
13 Beatles hit of 1965
17 Popular newspaper column
19 Alma mater visitor
20 ___ vincit amor
22 Water color
23 JUST LISTED!
26 Hardly Herculean
27 Have a yen (for)
28 Jennifer of "Flashdance"
29 Winkers and blinkers
31 Instrument for a merengue
34 Award for Eric Bogosian
35 Inclined
36 Address
37 OPEN FLOOR PLAN!
42 Miniature sci-fi vehicles
43 French possessive
45 Sea dog
46 Milo of "Barbarella"
47 Comic Philips
48 MANY UPGRADES!
54 Two in a million?
55 Unfortunate price to pay
57 Mideast pooh-bah
58 Blue book filler
59 "___ Tu" (1974 hit)
60 Two caliphs
61 Start to byte
62 Milanese monsieur
64 Stadium stats
65 NICE MOLDING!
69 Flat parts
70 They pay for quarters
72 Pervading tone
73 Bondman
74 120-pound Australians
75 Actors McKellen and Holm
78 Art Deco designer
79 Lincoln's first Vice President
82 Chinese dynasty
83 COLONIAL CHARM!
86 That: Sp.
87 Terminator
89 Suffix with cash
90 ___-Cat
91 Hold up
92 FULL BASEMENT!
98 Rower, e.g.
100 Some earrings
101 Dagwood's sweetheart before Blondie
102 Sweetheart
103 Shot glass?
106 The "tacho" in tachometer
107 Short story-writer
108 Secular
109 PARKLIKE SETTING!
115 Actor Alan
116 Collar
117 Bath cooler
118 Saint Catherine's birthplace
119 It's out on a lime
120 Skates in water
121 Part of B.P.O.E.
122 Not own

DOWN

1 Mo. when oysters "R" in season
2 Cinema admonition
3 Laugh syllable
4 Fireplace receptacles
5 Clicker
6 Cold porter
7 Water-light phenomenon
8 Protozoan
9 Makes out in a lawsuit
10 Reformer Jessie
11 Genetic carrier, for short
12 Bread for tacos
13 Unfortunate
14 Latin counterpart of "iso-"
15 Bergman's "Casablanca" surname
16 Yields
18 Words of agreement
21 Shakespearean title start
24 Reveals, as a secret
25 Web user's woe
30 Matriculate
31 Sad sort
32 Subject for a wine connoisseur
33 GAS INCLUDED!
35 Glass cookware brand
38 Renowned "regretter"
39 INDOOR POOL!
40 Some fishermen
41 Out
44 Drum major's hat
48 Banging
49 Not orig.
50 Pop musician Lofgren
51 Dog show worker
52 Like the Sahara
53 Brit. record label
56 Diets
59 Huge, old-style
63 Gather gradually
64 Oft-grated cheese
65 Hurdle for an atty.-to-be
66 ___ song
67 Campus military org.
68 "Awake and Sing!" playwright
70 Make new A-line lines
71 ___ Tin Tin
73 Oater action
76 Innocents
77 Ragout
80 First-generation Japanese
81 The Hunchback's "our"
83 Oldest known city in Belgium
84 Tramps
85 Hooks up or lays down, e.g.
88 Upright
91 Holy Roman Emperor, 840–55
93 Hindu ascetics
94 Kitchen drawer item
95 Waste allowance of old
96 Crop up
97 Kind of symmetry
99 Writers Henry and Philip
103 Put-down
104 ___ Bowl
105 Use a shuttle
106 Skier Chaffee
110 Domingo, for one
111 Hunky-dory
112 Pipe joint
113 It's accommodating
114 Put an end to something?

by Cathy Millhauser

BAR NONE

ACROSS

1 Appears
6 Tackle
9 Certain apartment
13 Fly out of a jungle
19 Implied
20 Like a bairn
21 "Are you __ out?"
22 Terrigenous rocks
23 Ballet dancer's cookout?
26 Sublet
27 Polaris, in Paris
28 Bottle contents, perhaps
30 Lao-__
31 Not dorsal
34 Applications
35 Feather's partner
36 Rations
39 Litter's littlest
40 Most like sphagnum
43 Hit man
44 Biblical no-no
45 Special-interest grps.
48 "The Day the Earth Stood Still" star Michael
49 Timeline division
50 X years before Hastings
51 Wash. Sq. campus
52 Quiescent
53 Showman's good buys?
56 Certain skirts
58 Finds an easy chair
61 Where basketball and volleyball were first played
62 "Yer darn __!"
64 Position
65 Envelope abbr.

68 Sir Charles's pet fish?
71 V-neck garment
72 Unruly hair
74 The "A" of A&M Records
75 Its pitch is high
77 Orange __
78 Provokes
79 Silent screen star's drink makers?
84 Oxford's skyline
86 Mother of Zephyrus
88 "B.C." cartoonist
89 Stadium sound
90 Glycerol-based solvent
91 Congenial song ending
92 Apr. addressee
93 Single out for praise
94 Beat against
96 Wood stack
98 Spiked staffs
99 Camera type, for short
100 Big name in games
101 Kind of shopping
103 Exclamation of surprise
104 Scrapes
107 Codeine, for one
111 Tell
113 French sculptor's weather-front detectors?
116 It's a fault's fault
117 High water alternative
118 Average fellow?
119 Day to remember
120 "__ Fables"
121 Drifting
122 Ogle
123 Acclivity

DOWN

1 Palpebral swelling
2 How the Amazon flows
3 Effect in the recording studio
4 Cheevy of Edwin Arlington Robinson verse
5 Old rural sights
6 Tangoing number
7 Prepare to drag
8 Rubber stamp
9 Played fast and loose with the facts
10 As soon as
11 Boners
12 Braid, to Brigitte
13 Simpson attorney?
14 Nickname for a big dog
15 Canal site
16 Quotation compiler's singer?
17 Feeling
18 Benzocaine, for one
24 This guy's a doll
25 "How Can We Be Lovers" singer
29 Favorite game of President Clinton
32 Nugatory
33 Tiff
36 Manner
37 Beige hue
38 Pair with a plow
41 Bumbling
42 Bound
44 Pants
46 Noted acting family's nobleman?
47 Fandango accompaniment
50 Thalberg's studio
52 Hokkaido native
54 Phonetic contractions
55 Pens and needles

57 Pronouncements
59 Desktop pub. items
60 Match maker?
63 Fish hawk
64 Warmongers rattle them
65 Cleo's undoing
66 Useful article
67 Hungarian composer's boat songs?
69 Chow
70 Senile ones
73 The "K" of RKO
76 Neighbor of Minn.
78 Transmitter
80 Queen's county
81 Language maven Partridge
82 Interest level
83 "__ a Woman" (Beatles tune)
85 Scottish playwright's haircutters?
87 Silver category
90 Like the gang, in song
91 Stores
93 Lawmaking locale
95 Hercule's creator
97 Behind the line of scrimmage
98 Power bikes
99 Rather, informally
102 Tabby's mate
104 On
105 Maiden loved by Hercules
106 Pueblo pot
108 Dynamic introduction
109 Junket
110 To be, to Brutus
112 "Yo te __"
114 Tofu base
115 Have markers out

by Charles M. Deber

ACROSS

1 Campus cafeteria arrangement
9 Soft drink brand
15 Spot, biblically
20 "The Witching Hour" author
21 Dorsal part of the midbrain
22 Merchant Nordstrom
23 Flip through a magazine?
25 "The Canterbury Tales" pilgrim
26 Returnee's "hello!"
27 Dickens boy
28 Mars's opposite
29 Bogies
30 Appearances
31 Powerful Washington lobby
34 "If ___ broke . . ."
35 Near, in Niedersachsen
36 Get a 3 on a 3, e.g.
37 Blackens
39 From the source
40 From the capital of Eritrea
43 Gets mentioned by a magazine?
45 Unvarnished
46 Says a myth that's amiss?
47 Prefix with god
48 Three-time Masters winner
51 Manx or Persian
52 Present
57 One magazine's view?
61 Neighbor of Mauritania
62 When repeated, comment to an apologizer
63 Stiller's comedy partner
64 Left-lane type
67 Movie segment
68 Like an oversized magazine?
70 City of Brittany
72 A.T.M. need
73 Guards
74 Coordinate in the game battleships
76 Back way
79 Spill, as blood
80 Force behind a magazine?
85 Herons' haunts
89 "Deal!"
90 X's on a map
91 U.S.S.R. successor
92 "Die Meistersinger" soprano
93 Bellyached
94 20 Questions category
96 Prominent U.S. mayor
98 Held off
99 Old car with a 389 engine
101 Shining example?
102 Fades (out)
103 Adler of Sherlock Holmes stories
104 Gracing a magazine's cover?
108 Around
109 "___ serious?"
110 Southeast Asian tongue
111 More fitting
112 Saddam Hussein, e.g.
113 They're useful in making contacts

DOWN

1 Cousin of the xylophone
2 Them
3 Orange County city
4 Inveigled
5 Big balls
6 "You come here often?" e.g.
7 Whiz
8 Counselor at Troy
9 Stands
10 "And I love ___"
11 Show biz group
12 Dazes
13 Sandwich filler
14 Green card, Informally
15 Certain neurotransmitter
16 Finely done
17 Some professors
18 Common alarm clock setting
19 Bridge support
24 Piece of disinformation
31 Larrup
32 Ninja's motion
33 As the crow cries
34 "___ not back in an hour . . ."
36 Foe of the Sioux
38 Red Sea nation
41 Amounts to carry
42 Files
43 Jazz group member
44 51-Across, for one
46 Switzerland's ___ Leman
48 Poultry plant worker
49 Florida Congressman ___ Hastings
50 Operation locations, for short
51 Get tough
53 Brunch fare
54 Point of depression
55 G, F and C
56 St. Patrick's locale
57 Recent fighter
58 According to
59 Make it
60 Disgruntledness
64 Any car, affectionately
65 Goddess mentioned in "The Raven"
66 Computer key
68 "Peanuts" boy
69 "Lord's Prayer" pronoun
71 Like some sports contracts
72 Vim
75 One First Lady's maiden name
76 Piedmont wine city
77 Collateral, maybe
78 Gets the short end of the stick
80 Where Montego Bay is
81 Braggart's vacation?
82 1955 Wimbledon and U.S. Open champ
83 Sinners do it
84 Fine porcelain
85 Fraction of an inch
86 Curtis and others
87 News locale of 5/28/53
88 Assents
91 "That's Impossible!"
95 Bank worry

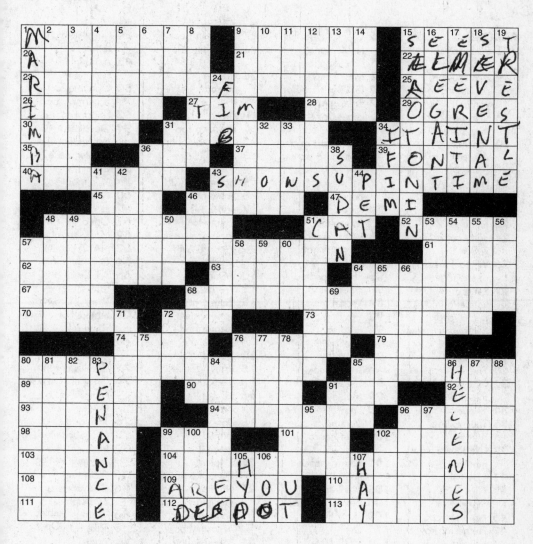

by Matt Gaffney

96 Resign,
as an office
97 When lunch
may end
99 Sheepskin
holder
100 Rubber roller
102 Brazilian
national hero

105 Under: Prefix
106 Overly
107 Silver filling? CAP

LOCATION IS EVERYTHING

ACROSS

1 Pod used in cooking
9 Fish usually caught in the winter
13 Was upset and then some
20 "Enemies, A Love Story" actress
21 De __ hotel
22 Prismatic, as a stone
23 Stubborn
24 Early comic writer
26 Without means of support?
27 With 30-Across, where to find a snowcap
28 Symphonic poem inventor
29 Big snowfall
30 See 27-Across
32 One way to get things down
34 Like Jack
36 They roll on a Rolls
38 Old White House moniker
41 Flake off
43 Nice 'n Easy maker
46 Northern capital
47 Friend for Rover or Fido
48 Mad as a hornet
49 Lose forward momentum
51 Jack Mercer supplied his voice
53 Kind of personality
55 With 63-Across, pretty good
58 "__ coffee?"
59 African ranger
63 See 55-Across
65 "__ It Kinda Fun" (1945 song)
66 PBS supplier
68 Most blue?
70 Gil Blas's creator
72 Emergency room cases, for short
73 "__ joy keep you" (start of a Sandburg poem)
75 See 81-Across
77 Arrive, but just barely
79 Kick up __ (complain)
81 With 75-Across, unmentionables
82 Jack
85 Sharp-toothed creatures
87 Vegan morsels
93 Way up a hill
94 Prior to, poetically
95 Warm, so to speak
98 Livestock feed
99 Medley
100 French surname start
101 "I've heard enough!"
103 Some speech sounds
105 Lt.'s inferior
106 See 116-Across
109 Lecherlike
111 Drops
116 With 106-Across, phrase said with a sneer
117 Bonelike
120 Revolutionary turned politico
122 Thrust forward
123 Noble
124 Düsseldorf donkey
125 Exhaust
126 Is of value, colloquially
127 Name in book publishing since 1943
128 Having no spark left

DOWN

1 Hardly a fop
2 Colo. neighbor
3 See 67-Down
4 Saint in Brazil
5 Had to do with
6 Some bands
7 British Isles
8 Tampa-to-Jacksonville dir.
9 Wounds with words
10 Wounds
11 Words to live by
12 Democrat's opponent?
13 Astaire and Rogers, e.g.
14 O.K.'d: Abbr.
15 Willy Wonka creator
16 Jai __
17 Platy propellers
18 Don Juan's mother
19 Feeler
25 Onetime Olympics host
27 North of Virginia
30 Book after Amos: Abbr.
31 Pound sound
32 Call to attention
33 Hello, of sorts
35 Year in Edward the Confessor's reign
37 Fire damage
38 See 39-Down
39 With 38-Down, almost positive
40 Puts forth
42 Judge to be
44 King Harald's father
45 Actionable statements
50 Opening for a dermatologist
52 Linguist Mario
54 Classified information?
56 Mantel piece
57 Cousin of "Omigod!"
60 Parenthesis, essentially
61 Oner
62 Many years
63 NATO capital
64 Oriole's origin
66 Allegedly at fault
67 With 3-Down, features of some ads
69 F.C.C. concerns: Abbr.
71 Comics cry
74 Gray of "Gray's Manual of Botany"
76 Jocular suffix
78 "__ each life . . ."
80 In __ (harmonious)
83 Puffed up
84 God offended by Daphnis
86 Clothes line
88 Take the grand prize
89 "The Bell Jar" writer
90 Uncomplicated
91 __ Khan
92 Gets rid of, as stock
96 "Who'll volunteer?"
97 It's added to the bill
102 Colored
104 Parlor piece

by Manny Nosowsky

107 Some Canadian fliers
108 Actor Conrad of old films
110 "If I __ betting man . . ."
111 Halls of music
112 Skirt style
113 __ uproar
114 Knight fight
115 Clockmaker Thomas
117 French department or river
118 Out of action
119 Proof of ownership
121 Shepherd's setting
122 Walker, briefly

INFESTED!

ACROSS

1 Device
7 Crescent features
12 1986 P.G.A. Championship winner
19 Tell el ___, Nile excavation site
20 Richards of "Jurassic Park"
22 Fair
23 1980 Oscar winner
25 Makes available
26 Faint
27 Alvarado of "Little Women," 1994
29 Primatologists' subjects
30 More like Mrs. Rumpole of books and TV
33 Some are deciduous
34 London park name
36 Scarlett's mother
37 Three-time Pulitzer-winning playwright
41 Tiny one of fiction
44 Candy counter name
45 " ___ go bragh"
46 Mark of uncertainty
48 Tombstone letters
49 Like a streaker
51 ___ Na Na of rock
54 St. Francis ___ (French prelate)
55 Prevarication
59 View from Chamonix
61 Indian prince
62 Perkin's killer role
63 ___ Detoo, "Star Wars" android

65 They blow with the wind
66 Boggy land
67 Form of ID
70 Tolkien forest giant
71 Insults
73 Where Diana Vreeland reigned
74 Milne creature
76 Like some stories
77 Special-care job at the cleaner's
79 Reads the riot act to
84 Accommodates
86 Dallas-to-San Antonio dir.
88 Contest in "Ivanhoe"
89 Bachelor's last words
90 One in an incubator
91 Uffizi attraction
93 Storage area
95 Fairy tale creature
96 Sailor's top
101 Bit of earthenware
102 Tax ___
104 Waterfall
105 Museum guides
107 1960 #1 hit "___ Angel"
109 First name on "Saturday Night Live"
110 Deficiency
111 Mother-of-pearl source
114 It might make a report for a construction crew
120 Duped
121 More crushed
122 "South Pacific" nurse
123 Pedal parts
124 Yucky
125 Requiring a tie

DOWN

1 Hood's rod
2 Aramis, to Athos
3 Weir
4 Brings in
5 What vines do
6 1,600-foot-deep lake in the Western U.S.
7 "All the Way" lyricist Sammy
8 Neighbor of Arg.
9 Word to a boxer, maybe
10 Paisleys, e.g.
11 Rumbled, in a way
12 Hope-Crosby film destination
13 Prefix with duct or form
14 Gunn of "Treasure Island"
15 Escalator feature
16 Sulked
17 Flu feature
18 Cowboy affirmatives
21 Santa ___, California track
24 Time past
28 Whaler's org.
30 "The game ain't over till it's over" speaker
31 Kind of acid
32 Was quiescent
33 Red ___ (sushi order)
34 "___ Johnny!"
35 Senate sounds
38 Mocking
39 St. Paul's architect
40 Eliot hero
42 Personification of my peace, in myth
43 Painted Desert features
47 New York's ___ Lakes
49 Lunch counter order

50 Passing remarks?
52 Mad one of fiction
53 Santo Domingo–born All-Star
56 First U.S. college to admit women
57 Strikes out
58 Hindus' holy river
60 They may be felt on the head
64 Writer Santha Rama ___
65 Dramatist Lope de ___
66 Like Watergate-era Washington
68 Balder and Odin
69 Knicks great Monroe
71 Problem for a lawn mower
72 Classify
75 Sondheim's "___ While I'm Around"
77 Like some stoves
78 Worn
80 Cry of Caesar
81 Arrive at, as a solution
82 It's the law
83 Drawer oddments?
85 Word with park or plan
87 Big circus name
92 Bunk
93 Whistle-blower
94 Valley crosser
97 British mil. decoration
98 Feet containers
99 Maker of the Grand Canyon, in myth
100 Touch up
103 Shoreline feature
106 Upright
107 M. Hulot's creator

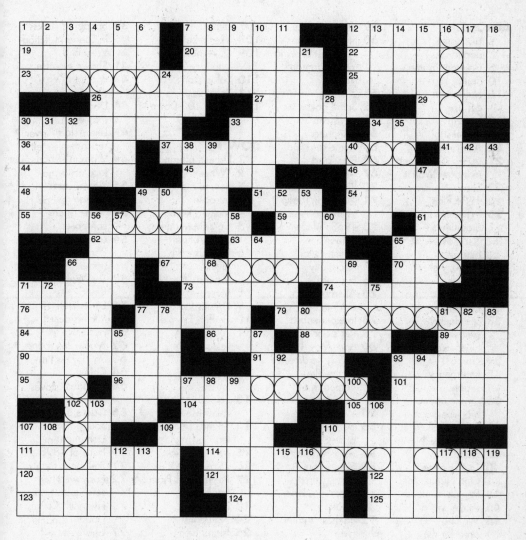

by Nancy Nicholson Joline

30

IN HONOR OF 80-ACROSS

ACROSS

1 Like some appliances
5 Cremona name
10 Spite
16 Halloween get-up
19 Inveigh (against)
20 Actor Alain
21 50's–70's Dodgers manager Walt
22 Slip
23 1936 film
26 Where Maracana Stadium is
27 "La Navarraise" heroine
28 Wheezy chest sounds
29 Girl with a crook
31 Daiquiri flavor
33 ___ clock (self-winding timepiece)
34 Fiasco
35 Emergency supply
36 Of the upper hipbone
37 Started eating
38 City on the North Platte
40 "It Happened One Night" star
42 Printemps month
45 Prayer word
46 Waiting area for the Robert E. Lee
48 One of a Latin trio
49 Ursula Andress's birthplace
50 Get better, so to speak
52 "Meet John Doe" star
56 P.C. Wren's Beau
57 Rank below abbess

59 Kind of space
60 Name in Keats's "On First Looking Into Chapman's Homer"
61 3-2, e.g.
62 Some poker payments
63 Faineance
64 Home for Heidi
66 Plow part
67 Abel, for one
70 Put an edge on
71 "You Can't Take it With You" star
73 1958 Pulitzer author
74 British royal, informally
75 Former Eur. airline
76 Alternative to Corinthian
78 Inexperienced
79 Ref's decision
80 Born May 18, 1897, he directed all the films named in this puzzle
84 Wheedle
86 60's series set in post–Civil War
88 Appropriate
89 Spread out
90 St. ___, first American links locale
92 Pakistan's chief river
93 Odalisques serve them
95 Contradicts
96 Respected one
97 Barbecue offering
98 One of Princess Yasmin's names
99 1946 film
105 Private eye
106 Tennis doubles player

107 Utters
108 Like some votes
109 St. Agnes's ___ (January 20)
110 Salad start
111 Ballet ___
112 Like a 103-Down, maybe

DOWN

1 Usher's offering
2 "Wheels"
3 Served the purpose
4 Make a killing
5 Contribute during preparation
6 Famous party giver
7 Marine ___
8 Moreover
9 Physics topic
10 Griffith TV role
11 Fugard's "A Lesson From ___"
12 W.W. II transports: Abbr.
13 Four-time Japanese P.M.
14 Sounds from the lea
15 Make heroic
16 1951 film
17 Posthumous Plath book
18 Fumble
24 Nail polish
25 Island next to Leyte
30 You can stand this!
31 Oregonian
32 1944 film
33 Part of a tennis court
34 Except
35 Rascal
36 Their work goes down the tubes
37 Hall-of-___

39 Shopping street in London's West End
41 Shows surprise
43 Puccini's "Vissi d'___"
44 Don Juan's mother
47 Like Asia's reaches
49 Woman's wide lace collar
51 Pianist-actor Wilson
53 "Over There" composer
54 Louise de la Ramee's pen name
55 The Water Rat's friend
56 Sticky stuff
58 Reconsidered
60 Father
62 Typewriter sound
63 Snub, in a way
64 Chin
65 It means "Out of my way!"
66 Game of chance
67 Young hog
68 Dominions
69 Hero of 1898
71 Steinbeck family
72 Early weather satellite
75 Plymouth Colony leader
77 Character actor J. ___ Naish
80 Emancipation
81 Western backdrops
82 Caller on Miss Mullens, in Longfellow
83 Sack
85 Guy in the street
87 TV actress Meyers
90 Moderate
91 Beersheba's locale

by Frances Hansen

92 Grant Wood, notably
93 Knife handles
94 Wrong
96 Title for Kiri Te Kanawa
97 Rap duo __ Kross
100 Bernadette, e.g.: Abbr.
101 Six-foot runner?
102 George's brother
103 Certain letter
104 Nevada county seat

ACROSS

1 Where heads are put together
6 Skater Harding and others
12 "__ behold!"
17 Tulle's schools
19 Popeye's son
21 Founding editor of the O.E.D.
22 How jewelers get absolution?
24 Per
25 "Le Comte Ory" composer
26 Cut forage
27 Super Bowl XXIX winner, informally
28 Midwestern jewelry article?
33 Cut forests
36 Ends
37 Mechanical method
38 Character actress Tessie
41 Oscar-winning "Love Story" composer
42 More than big
44 Tamperer hamperer
48 Patron of jewelers?
52 Exudation
54 Fills the cracks
55 "Snow White" dwarf
57 Notorious Bugs
58 Subjects of planning
61 Actress of "Fame" fame
62 Pippi Longstocking creator Lindgren
63 Green
65 Where crazy jewels end up?
68 Powers that be
69 Section of a pas de deux
72 Diamond great
73 "Hansel and Gretel" role
76 Stale
77 Mustachioed detective
79 Run
82 Bend
84 Jewelry disaster?
87 Surprise cries
88 "Picnic" playwright's kin
90 __ Canals
91 Second-oldest country in the Western Hemisphere
92 Adenauer, a k a Der __
93 Position
96 Family man
97 Part of a jeweler's education, with "the"?
103 Sal and others
104 Kind of diagram
105 Comeback
110 Banderillero's target
111 Jeweler's ultimatum?
115 Late-night name
116 "The Mighty Ducks" star
117 Bring to a boil?
118 Angora, merino, etc.
119 "Springtime-fresh" smokes
120 Wind-up toys?

DOWN

1 Fourfront?
2 Dos cubed
3 Wing tips' tips
4 Country rocker Joe et al.
5 Triage team member
6 Literary inits.
7 Mine __
8 Sparks on the screen
9 Aches
10 Breathing problem
11 Assail
12 Predatory
13 Rocket gasket
14 Spinning
15 Button material
16 Photography supplies
18 __ depth finder
20 Shoot for, with "to"
21 Possible source of mermaid legends
23 Long
29 Math class, for short
30 Writer Dinesen
31 Diamond and others
32 Jersey girl?
33 "Chicago Hope" setting: Abbr.
34 Biblical barterer
35 Platinum item of jewelry?
39 Tolkien tree creatures
40 Plugging away
42 Wide expanse
43 Acting family of TV and film
44 Smudge
45 Help at the jeweler's?
46 Over
47 Imparts
49 Peachy-keen
50 O.T. book
51 Driving hazard
53 German river
56 Perry Como's "__ Loves Mambo"
59 Gateway Architect, to friends
60 Floodgate
62 Song words before gal or shadow
63 Mariner's need
64 Fictional Italian town
66 Others: Sp.
67 Acad.
70 Hair applications
71 Ugandan with abandon
74 A lot
75 Turkish title
77 Prefix with dactyl
78 Preference
80 Grammy-winning Ford
81 Tennyson heroine
83 Swedish soprano Birgit
85 Land subjugated by 106-Down
86 "The Last Days of Pompeii" heroine
89 Washer setting
92 Honors
93 100 agorot
94 Writer famous for locked-room mysteries
95 Roman title
97 "The Hobbit" hero Baggins
98 Opening
99 Do maintenance work on
100 Rubbish
101 Anatomical roofs
102 Grit
103 Word in Morris code?
106 Ahab's father
107 Showed disdain
108 Shoe-touting bulldog
109 Tours seasons
112 Figurative brink
113 Pro __
114 Bar measures: Abbr.

by Cathy Millhauser

FORMAL FUNNIES

ACROSS

1 Stew
7 Like tea
13 These might play into the wrong hands
21 Two-time Wimbledon winner Gibson
22 It goes "pssst!"
24 Positively planning
25 Funnies romantic
27 ___ of habit
28 Penn name
29 Shade of purple
30 State of agitation
32 Award for Samuel Beckett
33 Features on some stationery
34 Peak of eastern Greece
36 Former service site
38 Funnies flapper
43 Shadowy places
48 Exceeded
49 Like some vbs.
50 Capital of Togo
51 H.S. subject
52 Baseball's Duren and Sandberg
53 Talk of the town?
56 The Mustangs: Abbr.
57 Mountain transport
58 Word repeated in "Elegy in a Country Churchyard"
59 Funnies flier
62 In ___ (beset by difficulties)
63 Little one
64 Spoilers
65 Singer Billy Ray
66 W.W. II Japanese aircraft
67 "Far out!"
69 New York Met tenor Alfredo
70 Flavors
71 Another funnies flier
78 Tired of everything
81 "All ___" (1967 Temptations hit)
82 University officials
86 Emulate Romeo and Juliet
87 Like some computer encoding systems
88 They give you fits
92 Rock-and-Roll Hall of Fame architect
93 Took steps
94 Funnies victim
96 Strike out
97 Mucho
98 Balmoral, e.g.
99 Untrustworthy types
100 Like some keys
101 Midsummer ___ (June 23)
102 Tree protuberance
104 Part of a drying-out period, maybe
105 Loud voice from the "Iliad"
107 1960's Maoists
110 Funnies fighter
113 ___ Lingus
114 Professor's prize
116 Ombrometers measure them
117 Carbon compound
120 Check, in a way
122 More or less, informally
123 "Things"
127 Vista
129 Big-eyed funnies character
133 Like a Carreras concert
134 Holes in the head
135 Coveted
136 In peace
137 Feeds a crowd
138 Actress Katharine et al.

DOWN

1 Aphorisms
2 Nobelist Wiesel
3 Pillar of heaven, to Pindar
4 Like a dime
5 Nickname in magazine publishing
6 Ring site
7 Spoiled bunch
8 Work on a tough stain, e.g.
9 10th-century explorer
10 Got the gold
11 Northern Amer.
12 Cream serving
13 Big-eared funnies character
14 Memo starter
15 Chest protector
16 Raiding grp.
17 Lay to rest
18 "Three men in ___"
19 Actress Petty
20 Old-time dagger
23 Grazing sites
26 "The ___ Sanction" (1970's thriller)
31 Cookbook amt.
33 Johns
34 Dunderheads
35 Doughnutlike
37 French soul
38 Typos
39 Knock down
40 Natural
41 Writer Akins and others
42 Dirty fighter
44 Proper words
45 Like some Christians
46 Science fiction magazine since 1930
47 Way out
53 Corral
54 Penn., e.g.
55 Anatomical prefix
56 Chocolate ___
57 Start of a how-to title
59 Ring sport
60 Even
61 Swimming great Diana
62 People of the Sun
64 Based (in)
68 Pilfers
69 Pasted but good
72 Funnies gumshoe
73 Available
74 Become tiresome
75 Places for drawings?
76 Brag
77 "Show Boat" composer
78 Medicine man
79 Breakfast place
80 Like Seurat paintings
83 Inviting, as inspection
84 Do a double take
85 Club name since 1892
87 Come to mind
88 Cause of jungle fever
89 Lower
90 Ruffle
91 "___ Amigos" (1973 western)
95 "Star Wars" planet
96 Classic Ferrari
100 Where Alice worked
102 Letter before ar
103 Tell tales

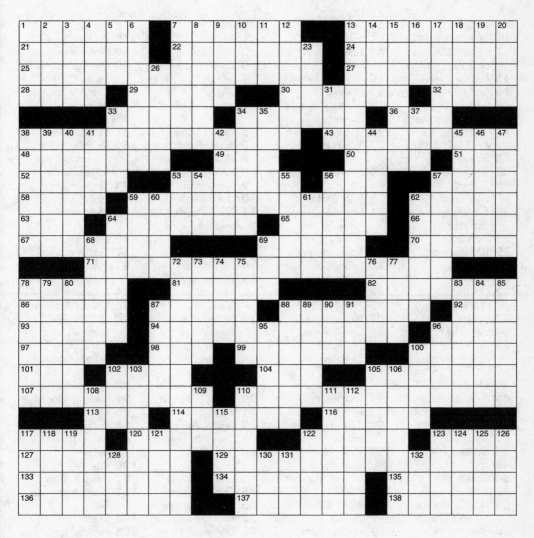

by Randolph Ross

33 ET TOO

ACROSS

1 Take for a spin?
7 Lincoln's Secretary of State
13 Pop follower
16 Curly conker
19 For him and her
20 Information like 15-Down
21 Aerialist's get up
23 Shoot-out?
25 Ran against
26 Journal conclusion
27 Everglades deposit
28 Bolts down
29 Without words
30 Mr. Hyde, for one
32 Cousin of a bandore
33 Drained
34 Stood by
36 Some of the best Impressionist art?
40 DH stat
43 Scots tongue
44 Riding for a fall
46 Construction piece
47 Go over
48 Jerk
50 Canute's foe
52 Mining waste
53 Year St. Eugene became Pope
54 Second-rate missile?
57 Harangue
58 Teacher's deg.
61 Exmoor exclamation
62 Surrey, e.g.
63 "Stand By Me" director
64 Scholarly
66 Formal accessories
67 Pelts
68 Dieter's temptation
69 Lose one's balance?
70 With the intent
71 Monogram of Macavity's creator
72 Swedish imports
73 When to go shopping?
75 "When You __ Love" (1912 tune)
76 Olympus Mons's locale
77 "Phooey!"
78 Spot maker
83 Sounds of disapproval
84 Personal quirks
85 "Phooey!"
87 Naturalness
88 Comic Philips
89 Trip fare?
93 Cretaceous
95 Middle of a TV trio
97 Touched the tarmac
98 1944 Preminger movie
99 Positions of authority
102 Obote's deposer
103 Post
104 1959 Kingston Trio hit
107 Photography aids
108 Tennis player's bad end?
111 Cheese dish
112 C_4H_8, e.g.
113 Tickled pink
114 Affirmative on board
115 Connections
116 Heavy
117 It's good for what ails you

DOWN

1 Rustic
2 Responsibility
3 Catch of the day, perhaps
4 Digital communication?: Abbr.
5 Crow's home
6 Spreads out
7 Galley mark
8 Vocalized pauses
9 Get smart
10 Use a joystick
11 This person's revolting
12 Fancy fellows?
13 Gobs
14 Do the walls over
15 Officer Dibble's nemesis, in cartoons
16 Setting of a sci-fi slave story?
17 Pitcher Hershiser
18 Where debris gets caught
22 Peg away
24 Down
31 Bit of gossip
32 Senate Agriculture Committee head
34 Basketball Hall-of-Famer Unseld
35 Cycloid section
36 Pacer's burden
37 Four-minute men
38 Die down
39 Old bay, maybe
41 Fishermen, at times
42 Opposite
45 Simple organism
47 Money substitute
49 Two cents worth
51 Promotes
52 Slipped in sleet
53 Not coastal
55 People on line
56 Big piece
57 Sunfish
58 Put on a pedestal
59 Good form
60 "Backdraft" by the Bolshoi?
65 Shankar and others
66 Spread out
67 Exact moment
69 Directly
70 Cremona collectible
74 Fortuneteller's tool
76 Short time?
79 Honey
80 Sled dog
81 Set, as a price
82 Marshal at Waterloo
84 Receptive
86 Checkout device
89 "I, Claudius" star
90 Hot dish
91 Thunderhead's mother, in film
92 Sounded swinish
94 Giant get-together
96 Pluckable
98 Pastoral setting
99 Other, in the barrio
100 Row
101 Mach 1 fliers
102 Uzbekistan's __ Sea
103 British gun
105 Headed for overtime
106 Capp of the comics
109 Pilot's heading
110 1971 McCartney album

by Richard Silvestri

OF COURSE!

ACROSS

1 Must
6 Dispute
10 Strip name
14 Thrash
19 Make suit, as a suit
20 Noted Sao Paulo-born athlete
21 Pastoral pipe
22 "God __ refuge . . .": Psalm 46
23 Wingding
24 Jive men
25 Golf pro?
27 Play 18 holes of miniature golf?
30 Place for a lace
31 It's a matter of pride
32 Mr. __ (old mystery game)
33 Rodents, jocularly
35 Weekend golfer's club?
41 Golf course?
45 Pizzeria __ (fast food chain)
46 Sunken treasure locale
47 Bouquet __
48 French biography
49 Prepare garlic, perhaps
52 Victimizes
54 Stamps
56 Go quietly
57 Dino, to Fred and Wilma
58 Canaanite's deity
60 Bird holder
61 __ del Corso, Rome
63 1770 patriot Attucks
66 The stuff of folk tales
67 Divots, for instance?
72 "__ gut" (German praise)
74 Nonets
75 __ Gabriel
76 Where the action is
78 Recognizes
79 Overseas relative
82 Word before and after "of the"
86 Fails to
88 Preppy, e.g.
91 Robert Devereux's earldom
92 Woodworker's tool
93 Lacking fresh air
95 Approaching
97 Kind of scores
98 Golfer's coverup?
100 Nostalgic for golf?
103 "Slithy" creatures
104 Fine, informally
105 Staff
106 "King Solomon's Mines" plot line
109 Like some bad golf shots?
116 L.P.G.A. player?
120 Haphazard collection
121 Spotted animal
122 Corn
123 Hollow
124 Ivy League team
125 Daughter of William the Conqueror
126 "Er . . . um . . ."
127 Less than solid
128 Laze in the tub
129 Introvert

DOWN

1 Instrument held between the knees
2 Baseball brothers' name
3 Copy of a photo, briefly
4 Like a Car and Driver car
5 Spanish essayist __ y Gasset
6 Abbreviation for a pound
7 Oviform : egg :: pyriform : __
8 Quarter of a quartet, maybe
9 Check the boundaries again
10 Teacher, frequently
11 Federal agcy., 1946–75
12 Lexicographer's conclusion
13 Pother
14 Many a Beijing commuter
15 Out
16 Music category
17 Couch potato's passion
18 At one time, at one time
26 __ pain
28 Rogers and Clark
29 Basic __
33 Wharton degree
34 Swimmer's stopper
35 Arithmetic homework
36 Condo
37 Have __ of (not allow)
38 "Ed Wood" star, 1994
39 Not easy to find
40 "Oh, right!"
42 The Land of the Blessed
43 Exactitude
44 New Hampshire college town
47 Grind
50 Popular tourist attractions
51 "Essays of __"
53 Parting words
55 Ancient money
59 Act like
62 Last word of Shelley's "Adonais"
63 Take it easy
64 Mail abbr.
65 Graduating class: Abbr.
67 Old joke
68 Waiting
69 Storm dir.
70 Whiteheads, e.g.
71 Rest
72 Time's 1977 Man of the Year
73 Slowly destroy
77 Rather and Jennings, e.g.
79 Sri Lankan exports
80 Cross inscription
81 Memo starter
83 Org.
84 Furniture wood
85 Office phone nos.
87 Mrs. Walton of "The Waltons"
89 Wedding
90 Work areas
94 Blvds.
96 Brute
99 Verse
100 By and large
101 Diet
102 Enthusiastic yes
106 Ventura County's __ Valley
107 Composer Khachaturian
108 Pate base

by Karen Hodge

ACROSS

1 Sleeping spots
7 Rats
12 Mark of official approval
18 White-knuckled
20 Pointless
21 Breathing aid
22 1944 film
25 See 45-Down
26 With 60-Down, bid
27 Blasted a hole in
28 Boots
29 "The Road Runner" background sights
33 "__ mud in your eye!"
35 Pitcher Fernandez
37 Fan letdown
38 "The First Wives' Club" members
40 Latin clarification
42 Make an outstanding design?
45 1965 film
51 Skirt
52 English churchyard features
53 Dealer in piece goods
54 Literally, "goddess"
55 They're toasted at luncheons
56 Shooting match
58 Domingo y lunes
62 Word of encouragement
63 City of northern Finland
64 Certain drop
65 Singer Jackson
67 1986 or 1994 film
72 Habituates
73 "James and the Giant Peach" author
74 Dole's Senate successor
75 Intl. air hub
76 Big name in video games
77 Golden __ (seniors)
79 Ball throwers
80 It played the Platters' platters
81 Hoglike animals
84 Auto with models 900 and 9000
85 Locale of ancient Ur
86 1951 film
91 Unfair shake
92 Relaxation in 63-Across
93 Exciting experience, in slang
94 En-graved letters?
95 "That feels good!"
97 Was in knots
100 Recesses
103 If A = B and B = C, then A = C, e.g.
106 "Serpico" author Peter
108 Glass-__ Currency Act, 1913
110 Impolite reply
112 1948 film
118 Helmsman
119 Like some walks
120 Successful person
121 Bootlicker
122 Theroux's "The Happy __ of Oceania"
123 Bay, county or city of Ireland

DOWN

1 Super Bowl XIV participants
2 Late bedtime
3 Daisy variety
4 Request to a guest
5 Kenyan independence leader __ Mboya
6 Look for damages
7 Former Chief Justice Harlan __ Stone
8 Breaks
9 More than nod
10 Contentious political assembly
11 Antivenins
12 British F.B.I.
13 First name in folk
14 Third Chinese dynasty
15 Two-time president of Texas
16 Snob
17 Actress Harper and others
19 Computer game __ City
21 Isao __ of the P.G.A.
23 Slangy turndown
24 Coming up
30 Crayola color
31 Canceled
32 Questionnaire datum
34 Author LeShan
36 "Edward Scissorhands" star
39 Strait of Messina menace
41 Iron: Prefix
43 "The Simpsons" bartender
44 With 111-Down, vulture or hawk
45 With 25-Across, voiced an opinion
46 Satanic moniker
47 Southern swarmer
48 Lull
49 Sympathetic sounds
50 A Turner
55 Pays the price for
56 Namesakes of a son of Adam
57 Swiss theologian Barth
59 Site of a famous flag-raising
60 See 26-Across
61 Real-life sailor on whom Crusoe was based
63 Words of praise
64 Paul I, e.g.
65 Pot contents
66 18, 19 and 20 of a series
68 Henry Clay, for one
69 West-central Texas city
70 Double fold
71 Challenger of the dragon Smaug
77 Boost
78 "The Pelican Brief" author
79 Case workers, for short
80 Arches
82 90's film autobiography subtitled "My Story"
83 Bear of literature
84 Fish that sings when mating
85 Bit
86 Embodiment of impractical chivalry
87 They make calls from home
88 Some TV's
89 The Tar Heels: Abbr.

by Matt Gaffney

90 Mouths
91 Loud and rude
96 1944 Bing Crosby hit
98 Cuddly film creatures of 1983
99 Opium __
101 Jostle
102 Historic rival of Florence
104 City near Provo
105 Vidal's "__ Breckinridge"
107 Prefix with –vert
109 Riot-stopping grps.
111 See 44-Down
113 Mid.
114 Wheaton of "Stand By Me"
115 Seasonal drink
116 Actress Thurman
117 Country singer McDaniel

ACROSS

1 Unrehearsed
8 Clear, in a way
13 Two-time U.S. Open champ
18 Showing again
20 Starting again
21 Jump for joy
22 MAC
24 Action star Jean-Claude Van ___
25 Tear down, in England
26 Taro root
27 Mom's specialty
28 Palette color
29 ___ Na Na
31 HARD DRIVE
35 White-tailed bird
36 Site of the Outback Bowl
38 One
39 One-___
41 Baseball's Moises
42 Theater group, for short
43 Lugubrious
46 Asian open sedan chair
49 Wipe the floor with
50 With 87-Down, early commercialists
51 "Happy" first name
53 Place for a cashier, maybe
54 Author Auletta
55 Coups de grace
56 BACKUP
58 Test killer
59 Vermeer contemporary
61 It means "place without water" In Mongolian
62 Wide shoe specification
63 Interviewed
64 CHIP
68 Some cuts
71 Anthem contraction
72 TV Maverick
73 Words on a quarter
76 Fire ___
77 MOUSE
79 Technique
80 A.C.C. team
82 Volcano near Catania
83 Warner on horseback
84 Press into service
85 "Are you ___ out?"
86 Discuss
88 Roman or Greek, e.g.
89 Not a picky specification
90 A year in the life of Attila
91 Tic-Tac rival
93 "The Last Supper," e.g.
96 "Somewhere in Time" actor
97 Har-___ (tennis surface)
99 WEB SITE
103 Legal point
104 Took on
106 Le Figaro article
107 Contender
108 Author Dinesen
110 Limber
111 NETWORK
116 Recruit's response
117 Luncheonette
118 Radiator features
119 Certain Art Deco works
120 Show off
121 Traveled by double-ripper

DOWN

1 Ball
2 Not agin
3 BIT
4 ___ run of bad luck
5 Bristle, botanically
6 Second-generation Japanese
7 Pol. designation for Gov. Jeanne Shaheen
8 Mark
9 Envelope abbr.
10 "The Young Man From Atlanta" playwright
11 Tracks
12 Nabber's cry
13 Noted ice cream maker
14 Conclusion of a term
15 HACKER
16 Bugs's foil
17 Grave
19 Not as accomplished
20 Shakespearean verb with thou
23 Soaking
29 Cheerless
30 Lunar phenomena
32 People of influence
33 Auto with Teletouch transmission
34 Eight is enough for this
37 Fix
40 Surrounded (by)
44 Executor, sometimes
45 Word in some magazine titles
47 ___ arch
48 Square
50 Church receptacle
51 FLOPPY DISK
52 "Mermaids" actress
55 Florida vacation spot, with "the"
56 Blackmailer, e.g.
57 1860's White House name
60 Get ready to fly
61 Shin armor
63 Scads
65 Bind, so to speak
66 Direct ending
67 Menace
68 Film director Nicolas
69 Doing
70 DIGITAL MONITOR
74 PRODIGY
75 Unfold
77 Soup for a cold
78 40's–50's TV drama sponsor
79 "Do ___ like"
81 Early spring sign
84 Opens
85 Word with bag or cap
87 See 50-Across
89 Best seller "Angela's ___"
92 Speaks impertinently to
94 Fall back
95 Uplift
96 Kind of price
97 Macduff was one
98 Hardship
100 Bad luck, old-style
101 "Cool!"
102 Kind of hemp
105 Mario of the N.B.A.
109 Not much
112 Suffix with bow
113 Up, as a vote
114 Tpke.
115 Either of two books of the Apocrypha: Abbr.

by David J. Kahn

PHRACTURED FONETICS

ACROSS

1 It comes in a scoop
5 Small club, say
9 Underlying
14 Essential parts
19 Butcher's cut
20 Luxembourg town where George Patton is buried
21 Daughter of William the Conqueror
22 On ___ (reveling)
23 First name in mystery
24 Grand
25 Tree knots
26 ___ Domingo
27 Seat setting
28 1997 Stanley Cup finals player
31 Unexplained skill
32 Harried
33 Scraps
34 "Little House on the Prairie" co-star Karen
35 Counts, e.g.
37 20's–50's papal name
38 Transfer and messenger materials
39 Yoga practitioner
40 Film maker Gus Van ___
41 What to call a lady
42 Letter trio
45 F-4's
48 Former Toronto pitching ace
50 Noted name in civil rights
51 Dark times, briefly
52 Good cheer
53 Where Europe was divided
54 Sales worker
55 Country name, 1937–49
57 With 17-Down, a temporary urban home
58 Characters in "Julius Caesar" and "The Merchant of Venice"
60 Stadium sounds
62 Close one
66 Spa: Abbr.
67 Like a prize-winning witch's costume
69 Rightful
70 Financial page inits.
72 ___ kwon do
73 Reams
74 Zip
75 Former Eur. carrier
77 Like very few games
79 Aldrin's craft
80 Strength
83 Lao-___
84 Sugar ___
85 Somewhat
86 Kick
87 Handful, maybe
88 It may be laid on thick
89 Scythe handle
90 Ogle
94 Word with pepper or paper
95 Covering
96 Intl. group since 1948
99 Voltaire, e.g.
102 Color of some hummingbird throats
103 Noted Civil War biography
104 Big name now out
105 Start of a cheer
106 Site of a 70's revolution
107 "___ my case"
108 Violate a treaty, perhaps
109 Land of literature
110 One of the Ringling Brothers
111 They run in the blood
112 Pick up
113 Depilatory brand
114 Throw off

DOWN

1 ___ France
2 Charles and others
3 They have suns and red, white and blue fields
4 Small roll
5 Title site in a Sondheim musical
6 Tippy canoe area
7 Microphone inventor Berliner
8 Place to play b-ball
9 Charter Baseball Hall-of-Famer
10 "___ only"
11 They're bound to work
12 "___ Have to Do Is Dream"
13 Pasta dishes
14 Turkish pooh-bahs
15 W.W. II Axis members: Abbr.
16 Prizes for Tommy Tune
17 See 57-Across
18 Outlet
29 Accomplishments
30 A pusher may push it
32 Give more medicine
36 ___ 'acte
37 Annoyance
38 Recherche
39 Try
40 Basic Halloween costume
41 Breakfast offering
42 Divisions politiques
43 King called "le Bel"
44 Be rewarded at work
45 Ring around the end of a post
46 1996 biography "Citizen ___"
47 Spelling on TV
48 Med. nation
49 Hounds
56 Conditions
57 Any vessel
58 Coll. course
59 Ahas
61 Edge
63 Horace, for one
64 Sheepdog with fine matted hair
65 Wrong for the situation
68 Yacht's dir.
71 Catch slyly
74 Reply from Boris
75 Dins
76 This and that
78 "Step ___!"
80 Headdress, maybe
81 1974 hit by Chicago
82 Unaware
84 Bric-a-___
87 ___ Reader's Encyclopedia (classic literary reference)
88 Their home was the Astrodome
89 Rock guitarist ___ Ray Vaughan
90 Shoot
91 "Voila!"

by Robert H. Wolfe

92 "I Love a Parade" composer
93 "Touched by an Angel" co-star
94 Where to see "The Last Supper"
95 Lit
97 Decrease
98 Bishops' group
100 Beat it
101 Broiler
102 Guadalquivir and others

38 PAPER CHASE

ACROSS

1 Cutaneous
7 Rock group that sang "Let's Go"
14 Splendid
19 Conductor Toscanini
20 Like some shoes
21 Grammy-winning single of 1958
22 Groundskeeper's bagful at an Atlantic City newspaper?
24 Armpit
25 Companion
26 Oregon __
27 Playboy Khan
28 Library ref.
29 Where "Falstaff" premiered,1893
32 Start of a string of 13 Popes
34 Dish alternative, maybe
36 Loudness measure
37 Musician who co-starred in "Trespass"
38 Descartes conclusion
39 Horse owned by a Boston newspaper?
42 Hired hands at Microsoft
44 Sponsorship
46 Camera since 1924
47 Bank sitters
49 Some picture frames
52 Used rubber
56 Garden, in a way
57 Correspondence to the editor of an Allentown newspaper?
60 Allan-__
61 Obviously sleep-deprived
63 End of a Burns title
64 Prepare to get juice
65 Madonna's "La __ Bonita"
67 Kind of law
69 Yeshiva product
71 Off, so to speak
72 Drink with 87-Across
74 Concert memento
76 Like a clover leaf
78 Take over, in a way
79 Columbia, S.C., newspaper's security department?
81 Vane dir.
84 Like a mule
86 Mars, to Aries, in astrology
87 Ingredient in a 72-Across
89 Thunderstruck
91 __ facto
93 Like Chippendale furniture
94 Way into the bathroom at a Macon newspaper?
99 Start to function?
101 Snake oil, purportedly
102 Hungary was a member of it
103 Suffix with sect
104 Named before
106 Do some roadwork
107 Automobile sticker fig.
108 Jack-in-the-box part
109 I.Q. recordholder Marilyn __ Savant
111 Prize
113 Associated
115 Shell shot at a Harrisburg newspaper?
120 Come
121 Nobel physicist Becquerel
122 Frank
123 Rather awkward
124 Mouthing off more
125 Crackers

DOWN

1 Skip, as a stone on water
2 Muff
3 Hwy.
4 Sweet wine
5 Some insurance fraud
6 __ Tay, Scotland
7 Part of an old Greek fleet
8 In the know about
9 Subject of a psych. experiment
10 Do
11 Permanent-magnet alloy
12 Seize again
13 60's campus grp.
14 Popular theater name
15 Bulldog
16 Big goon
17 50's–60's "What's My Line?" panelist
18 Beginning of a tape
21 Harper, for one
23 "Come Back, Little Sheba" wife
27 Edits
29 Book before Nahum
30 Likeness: Prefix
31 Come-on at a Lakeland newspaper?
33 "Enough!"
35 Handsome, as Henri
36 Carmichael classic
38 Sharon, for one
40 Attorney-to-be's exams
41 In base 8
43 Shipping dept. stamp
45 Pupil's reward
48 Roy Rogers's real surname
50 A great dist.
51 ". . . and last in the American League" team
53 Recruiter at a Wichita newspaper?
54 Inter __
55 Say it ain't so
58 __ squares (statistical method)
59 Malcontent
62 They're full of beans
64 A clip may hold it in place
65 "Look at me, __ . . ."
66 Start of some Italian church names
68 Tutsi foe
70 __-a-brac
73 Cutting down
75 Misrepresent
77 Eddie Rickenbacker's 94th __ Squadron
79 City on Resurrection Bay
80 Great Fire of London diarist
82 Pelvic bones
83 Tempter
85 Acting Day
88 Gets via computer

by Fred Piscop

90 Prefix with 1-Across
92 Name dropper?
94 Gong in an orchestra set
95 Run out
96 Hybrid cats
97 Humidor item
98 Fife player
100 "As You Like It" servant
105 In unison
106 "Jurassic Park" mosquito preserver
108 Roman historian
110 Some B'way shows
112 Bird whose male hatches the eggs
114 Bad-mouth
115 Stage setups, for short
116 "Superman ___"
117 ___ bind
118 Baseball's Dykstra
119 Before, once

39

ROCK TOUR DOUBLE BILLS

ACROSS

1 Favorite Degas subject
8 Behave
11 ___-Ball
15 It often has its arms out front
18 Gorged oneself
19 Classified
21 "Windsor Forest" poet
22 Dinner offerings
24 Services, in a way
25 "Mr. Basketball" Holman et al.
26 Gray remover, maybe
27 "Suzanne" songwriter
28 Orbital point
29 "The Simpsons" tavern
31 Show of affection
33 Backgammon piece
34 Oater affirmative
36 Engine conduits
37 Hits errantly, in golf
38 Impassioned
41 State to be in
42 Word with ready or shy
44 Reef
45 Hair-raising site?
47 Undercover operation
52 #2 at the 1994 U.S. Open
54 Swing voter: Abbr.
55 Lodge
56 CD-___
57 Ice cream parlor order
59 "La vita nuova" poet

60 Captures, in a way
63 Rachmaninoff's "___-tableaux"
64 Indian stringed instruments
65 Make up
66 Like some muscles
67 Poop
68 Impetuous
69 Listen: Sp.
70 British noble, briefly
72 "___ in my memory lock'd": Ophelia
73 Certain berth
76 Kind of pie
79 Community spirit
81 Majors in acting
82 Ruling groups
83 Farm resident
84 Part of a split personality
86 Orchestral works
88 Considerable irritant
91 Word in many business names
92 "Star Trek" role
93 Soup kitchen offering
97 Taradiddles
100 Puffball relative
101 Release upon
102 Hotfooted it
104 Clock sound
106 Make money
107 Health care group
110 Sews up
111 Reserved
112 Totals
113 Christie contemporary
114 Musical syllables
115 Never, in Nuremberg
116 Least irrigated

DOWN

1 Butler's expletive
2 Col. Hannibal Smith's group
3 Cool
4 Relative of an agate
5 Plumbing piece
6 Chancel entrance display
7 Collar inserts
8 Collar
9 Animator's unit
10 Parcels
11 "___ is Love" (1962 hit)
12 They provide prayer support
13 Brings in
14 1997 U.S. Open champ
15 Long-term pollution concern
16 Data transmission path
17 Actress Armstrong and others
20 Tend the hearth
21 Toaster treat
23 Couple or so
28 Word before and after "to"
30 Parasol
32 Quite a while
35 Fund-raising grp.
37 Seemed funny
38 Sit-up benefactors
39 Squeal
40 Travels of Shane, e.g.
41 Locale
42 Mention
43 Breeze through
46 Items in sync?
47 Imaginary

48 Chaplin and others
49 Mil. transports
50 "Are you nervous?" response, a la Don Knotts
51 Diamond execs
53 Gist
58 Hairsplitters
59 Pronouncements
61 Charge with
62 Bribe money, in slang
63 Chacon of the 1962 Mets
64 Still-life subject
65 Hasty
66 Pocket item
67 Holiday purchases
68 Diamond target
71 Company that made Photophones
72 Ford sobriquet
74 Sniggler's quest
75 Fam. reunion attendee
77 Castle features
78 "Paper Moon" actor or actress
80 Breakfast orders, briefly
83 J.F.K. posting
85 Emulated Mme. Defarge
86 Kind of meeting
87 Prize
88 Aquarium acquisitions
89 Track and field events
90 Secure
93 Topps rival
94 Gaucho gear
95 Mil. address
96 Longtime Guy Lombardo record label

by Rich Norris

THEY WHAT?

ACROSS

1 Steady
6 Sauteed dish
10 Edison's middle name
14 Dessert item
19 Silver Ghost, informally
20 Lohengrin's love
21 Activist
22 Up
23 Title for a cleric's book?
25 Teen fantasy?
27 Do type
28 Gone
29 1995 Pitt flick
30 Product of the press?
32 Quickly apply
37 Goodfellow ___, Tex.
40 It may be black or green
41 Deep bell sound
42 Mr. Hyde, e.g.
44 Cybernetics pioneer ___ Wiener
46 Firm
48 Pinochle combo
49 "Dirty dog," for one
50 City discussed at the 1954 Geneva Conference
52 Senate support
54 Cows, maybe
55 Opposite of baja
56 Black spot
58 Kind of expression
60 They cross the line
62 ___ one
64 Bank deposit
65 Sewing tool
66 Masseuse's target
67 "Was ___ blame?"
68 Program
70 Ring org.
73 70-Across weapon
75 Miss America attire
77 Dweller across the strait from Singapore
79 Stadium sight
81 Horrible
84 Prefix with mechanics
85 Thick fog, in slang
86 "___-Man" (1974 spy/sci-fi film)
88 Center of activity
89 Wit
90 Part of a W.W. II exclamation
91 Search for x
93 Bit of business attire
96 Kind of apparel
99 Foreign refusal
100 Shower with flowers
101 Certain model railroads
102 Ardent and then some
103 Cavern, in poetry
105 "Backdraft" concern
107 Old piece
109 Wedding locale in a Crosby film
112 Anorexic?
116 Simple beachwear?
119 Provide, as with some quality
120 For fear that
121 Split, so to speak
122 Pen patter
123 Not thinking straight
124 Douay prophet
125 Heart of the matter
126 Desert drainage basin

DOWN

1 Support ___
2 Virginia Senator
3 Lily relative
4 Hints
5 Artsy one
6 Engage in a food fight at KFC?
7 Out of this world
8 Sight at Dulles
9 "That'll show you!"
10 Deem
11 Screw (up)
12 Hero-worship
13 Like Australia's western plateau
14 Famous Tuesday Club member
15 ___ bark beetle
16 Actress Myrna
17 Repeatedly
18 Ultimate
24 Fin
26 Bounce
30 Do a salon job
31 Hitchhiker from Calcutta?
33 Hammer in manufacturing
34 Tiny Christmas decoration?
35 Was coquettish with
36 Auction actions
37 Cochise player Michael in 50's TV
38 Succeed
39 Unbearably hot holiday?
41 Quite a thrill
43 Capriole
45 Small fastener
47 Foreign refusal
51 Jerks
53 1953 title role for Rita Hayworth
56 Treat
57 Talk fondly
59 "Field of Dreams" setting
61 What a padlock may fasten
63 Org.
67 Where Mt. Carmel is: Abbr.
69 Kindly spirit?
71 Inner-city area
72 Current terminals
74 Disable
76 With bated breath
78 Small fastener
79 City ESE of Bombay
80 Water ring
82 Chilling
83 Go up and down the dial
85 Budge
87 Whitens
92 It might come out of a summit
94 Rose-red dye
95 Stove workspace
97 Fictional ghost
98 It passes between decks
104 Clangor
105 Be ready for
106 It meant nothing to Caesar
108 Capital of Manche
110 North or South district in Hawaii
111 Black
112 Drops outside
113 Musician Brian
114 Hubbub
115 Procter & Gamble soap
116 Oomph
117 Year in Nero's reign
118 Fed. property overseer

by June Boggs

ACROSS

1 Like putty in one's hands, maybe
7 Teen's woe
14 Rum cocktail
20 Rockville __, L.I.
21 Musical instrument with finger holes
22 Tigers' school
23 Soup ingredient
24 Start of a quip by 67-Across
26 Backgammon impossibility
27 Tab topic
29 Ring thing
30 It has a red coat
31 Quipu maker
33 It might be sung on one's birthday
37 Skins
39 Part 2 of the quip
44 Exploits
45 Hot
46 Say further
47 Place, as a bet
48 Traveller's check
49 Lucky draw
50 Drudge
52 Sharp taste
53 With 56-Down, city near Knoxville
56 See 72-Across
59 Withdraws
61 Part 3 of the quip
65 Trouble
66 Show stoppers
67 Author of the quip
69 Bumbling beast
72 With 56-Across, like some shares
73 Part 4 of the quip
75 Zones
79 Ball girls
80 Downing and others: Abbr.
81 Some W.B.C. outcomes
82 Briny

83 Suffers from
85 Examines, with "over"
86 Prado treasure
87 Charles, e.g.
88 Norwegian king
92 Beet variety
94 Part 5 of the quip
101 50's TV comedian
102 Concurred
103 Pig
104 __-humanité (crime against humanity): Fr.
105 Historic grp.
107 Airport line
109 Alert, for short
110 End of the quip
115 Elusive subject, familiarly
117 Deep-frying need
118 Ex-con, maybe
119 Rubber ring
120 Ticket order
121 Jacks or better, in poker
122 Blurs

DOWN

1 Nova follower
2 Spelling
3 What pronouns refer to
4 Local org.
5 Skater Heiden
6 Struck out
7 Shalikashvili's predecessor
8 90's brew
9 Warp, say
10 It comes before adolescence
11 "__ Darlin' " (1957 hit)
12 Sphinx
13 Copy to a floppy
14 Enthusiastic exclamation
15 They're boring
16 In the same place

17 Deli option
18 Composer Khachaturian
19 A keeper may keep it
25 Ties up
28 Contact, perhaps
32 Hanging clear of the bottom
34 A.M. TV offering
35 Mythical bird
36 "__ questions?"
38 Relief
40 Female octopus
41 "Pillow Talk" actress
42 1993 Kevin Kline comedy
43 Choice beef cuts
48 Bust, so to speak
49 Bleated
50 Fugitive's trail
51 "Jurassic Park" girl
52 Its slogan was once "The things we do to make you happy"
53 Wrinkle-resistant fabric
54 Govt. agent's employer
55 Opera's __ Te Kanawa
56 See 53-Across
57 Biting
58 Pea stabbers
60 Olympics great Janet
62 He doubted God's ability to bring water out of a rock
63 Wards (off)
64 Film director Bunuel
68 New York __
69 Popular dessert
70 "The Dukes of Hazzard" spinoff
71 Jour. staff

72 Airline to Karachi
74 Attacks
75 It might have the shakes
76 Tannish
77 TV pal of Mary and Rhoda
78 Ought to have, informally
84 Certain look
85 Accelerator
87 Map abbr.
88 Saturn's wife
89 __ Fresnos, Tex.
90 Black and tan ingredient
91 Bordeaux business owner
92 Popular cereal
93 Stashes
95 Absentee
96 Where the Tagus flows
97 Cap attachment
98 Conditions of equilibrium
99 More silly
100 __ Field
104 British emblem
106 __ Snaps (dog treats)
108 Petticoat junction
110 "Name him!"
111 England's Isle of __
112 Before, in poetry
113 Sun follower?
114 Big cheer
116 Compass dir.

by Peter Gordon

ACROSS

1 Buzzing
6 Billiard stroke
11 Name in computer software
16 Hinder
21 Oscar Madison's secretary
22 Hero of the first opera written for TV
23 Ain't right?
24 Leaf
25 GREEN
27 GREEN
29 Bank deposit
30 Keep for oneself
31 Concert finale
32 ___ League
33 Kansas city
35 Raiders' chief
38 Subjects of modern mapping
39 Bitty's partner
40 V-chips block it
42 Column couple
44 Trojan War figure
46 GREEN
52 Corsair and Citation, for two
56 ___-a-porter
57 Feature of Roy Lichtenstein's art
58 Genealogist's abbr.
59 Eastern attire
61 Dit's partner
62 Come to
65 Kind of testing
67 Novarro of silents
69 City on the Mohawk
71 Jimmy Dorsey's "___ Mine"
72 Watering holes
74 GREEN
77 GREEN
79 George ___
80 Stretch
81 Colleen
82 Detergent
83 French toast portion?
85 Easily handled, as a ship
87 Lhasa ___
90 Beethoven's "Choral" Symphony
93 Service station offering
94 GREEN
98 GREEN
101 Commencement
102 Voyage preceder
103 1993 N.B.A. Rookie of the Year
104 "Forget It!"
105 Where firings take place on a daily basis
107 Spicy stew
109 Mineral suffix
110 Gospels follower
112 Commuters' ways
114 Financial aid criterion
116 Dexterity
117 What some fans do
119 GREEN
123 Smoking container
126 Foam at the mouth
127 Petitions
128 Pulitzer dramatist Connelly
131 Ancient city in 2-Down
133 Food item usually picked wild
136 Abases
140 Jerusalem's Mosque of ___
141 Aristocracies
143 Arm
145 Granada greeting
146 GREEN
148 GREEN
150 Reason for 55-Down's rebellion
151 Underground worker
152 Petitions
153 Math measurements
154 Blackthorn fruits
155 Colonel's insignia
156 Digression
157 To wit: Lat.

DOWN

1 Out of place
2 Aleppo's land
3 Coloratura's specialty
4 Provoke
5 Bowl sound
6 County in NW Ireland
7 City once called Philadelphia
8 One born on a kibbutz
9 Most likely to collapse
10 Annex
11 Victoria, e.g.
12 Rubber gasket
13 With 15-Down, some chains
14 Outfoxed
15 See 13-Down
16 Newt
17 Costly sweaters
18 Say suddenly
19 Target
20 1955 film robot
26 Lewis of children's TV
28 Rankle
34 Go-ahead
36 Takeoff, approx.
37 The Lone Ranger's real identity
41 It may be living or dead
43 She's still with Stiller
45 Ignominy
46 Squarely
47 ___-Detoo
48 Some Balts
49 Lonesome George of early TV
50 Address nos.
51 Shades
53 Woman on TV's "Ab Fab"
54 They're fit to be tied
55 1786 Springfield insurrectionist
59 Lounge
60 Assumed names
63 Off
64 Vietnamese port
66 Populous place
68 Team V.I.P.: Abbr.
70 Flat sign
73 Discerning
75 Shoptalk
76 Hole enlarger
78 Sicilia, for one
79 Shipmate of Starbuck
84 Panzer
86 ___-tat
87 French 101 verb
88 It's spotted in westerns
89 Driving hazard
91 Sgts., e.g.
92 Service station offering
94 Private
95 Sub
96 Rally
97 Record
99 Winged
100 Film used for recording tapes
101 Dairy aisle buy
106 Bush leaguers
108 Advances
111 Tall player
113 Sting
115 Pat
118 Grow together
119 Babbling

by Nancy Nicholson Joline

43 DISPOSSESSED

ACROSS

1 Mailing supply
7 Leaves of metal
12 Coped
19 A Musketeer
20 Cliched movie ending
21 Better
22 Most ghastly
23 Hose-wielding serf, perhaps?
25 Slangy acumen
26 1977 film killer
27 "The Clan of the Cave Bear" author
28 Charlotte's web site
29 Developmental period
30 Trumpeter Ziggy
31 Rabin's successor
33 Fact about unladylike habits?
37 Chow
41 Cries akin to "Shucks!"
42 Clingmans Dome locale: Abbr.
43 T or F, e.g.: Abbr.
44 Overhauled
46 Charleston dancer
49 "This means ___!"
51 Expert witness at a trial
52 Samplers
53 Ones peeking at rams and ewes?
56 Winter Palace dweller, once
57 Loser to Braddock, 1935
58 Emollient source
59 Rent
60 Famed Chicago boat?
65 Invitation word
69 "Mine!" in France
70 Pilgrim's pronoun
71 Blood: Prefix
75 Long-winded oration of Andrew, e.g.?
78 Heavenly host
81 Bureaucratic stuff
82 John Dos Passos trilogy
83 Pass in some bowls
84 Yak in the pulpit
85 Qt. couple
87 More than chuckle
89 The Nittany Lions: Abbr.
90 Early pulpit
91 Stifling of a happy bird?
96 Hotfoot it
98 Refreshing spot
99 Get nosy
100 Vacation sites
104 Ancient Roman wheel
105 Lt. Kojak
106 Prefix with graph
109 Seedy place?
112 Live, as a game ball
113 Pen
114 Habituates
115 The Green Wave
116 Popular Christmas gift
117 Like Batman
118 Volcano, e.g.

DOWN

1 Napkin holders
2 Composer Khachaturian
3 Back talk, to one prophet?
4 Crop up
5 Conversation starter
6 J.F.K. jet set
7 1995 cop on the spot
8 Like some garages
9 Montreal, for one
10 Guitar designer Fender
11 Buckle up
12 Stephen King title
13 Capacious
14 Member-supported org.
15 Abu Dhabi denizen
16 "Naked Maja" painter
17 By any chance
18 Laura or Bruce of film
20 Hot
24 Political debates, often
30 Washstand toppers
32 Palmists, e.g.
33 Go with the wind
34 Certain fledgling
35 Suffix with hoop
36 Modern Maturity grp.
38 Emulate Mia
39 Thomas Mann's "___ Kroger"
40 Mean grin
44 Event for those who know the ropes
45 Irish offshoot
47 Span. coin: Abbr.
48 Short wave?
49 Coaster rider's cry
50 Makes bubbly
51 Swamp critter
53 ___ law (ancient code)
54 Worked with alfalfa
55 Additionally
57 Hecklers' chorus
61 Nobel-winning Bunche
62 Captain Hook's sidekick
63 Ostrich cousin
64 Sharpen
65 Kvetch
66 Kind of hat or house
67 Web user's need
68 Cornerstone abbr.
72 Afore
73 Irish side dish?
74 Humble
76 Guadalajara lunch
77 "Tom Thumb" star Tamblyn, 1958
78 Kind
79 Ruin
80 Cast aspersions on
85 It's a snap
86 Huge
87 Mended
88 ___ Hound (Canis Major)
91 Low-frequency speaker
92 Tallies
93 Pakistani city
94 Unfold
95 Big hit
97 Hag
100 Bursae
101 Fore-and-after's fore
102 Tops
103 Remote location
106 Rests
107 Silver hair
108 ___ and terminer
110 Weimar "with"
111 Spanish queen until 1931

by Cathy Millhauser

ACROSS

1 Kindergarten stuff
5 Deduce
11 Like some socks
14 Outdoes
19 Loser in an upset
20 Part of the iris bordering the pupil
21 Implant
22 Grammar subject
23 Dancer's apparel?
26 Money substitute
27 Preacher's apparel?
28 Factory worker's apparel?
30 Florida's ___ National Forest
31 "Cheers" setting
33 Start of many criminal case names
34 The universe on day one
37 Unexpected blows
39 Actor Peter et al.
43 Home, to Hans
44 Psychiatrist's apparel?
49 Brutally dismiss
50 Suffix with disk
51 Kansas town
52 Amount to be raised, maybe
53 A regular type
54 Cable network, briefly
55 Miner's apparel?
59 Burns's partner
60 "Ditto"
62 Send
63 Earthy deposits
64 Conners
65 Saki, really
66 Author Marsh
68 Separates, in a way
70 Now
71 Election times
74 ___ as a pig
75 Projectionist's apparel?
77 One of the 13 orig. colonies
78 Rhineland town heavily bombed in W.W. II
79 Apt family name in "The Wizard of Oz"
80 Constellation animal
81 "___ cost to you!"
82 Suffix with special
83 Entomologist's apparel?
87 Silent actress Naldi
88 Highly seasoned stew
90 TV Mr.
91 Joyous hymn
92 Country
95 Govt. intelligence org.
96 Meeting room staple
99 Referee's apparel?
103 Pro athlete's apparel?
107 ___ friends
108 Lawyer's apparel?
111 Compact matter
112 Elevs.
113 Flower part
114 Mountain known locally as Mongibello
115 Kind of skill or home
116 Luggage marking
117 Restful
118 Barrier breakers

DOWN

1 1956 Peck role
2 Island south of Borneo
3 Plagiarize
4 Free
5 Nero's successor
6 Dizzy
7 Edison contemporary
8 Holler's partner
9 Polar worker
10 Snitch
11 Fed. watchdog
12 Opportunities, so to speak
13 Resided
14 1956 Marilyn Monroe film
15 Collectible Dutch print
16 Hindu garment
17 Letters of rejoicing
18 Library Card Sign-Up Mo.
24 Gumshoes
25 Sealy competitor
29 Ivy Leaguer
31 Fella
32 "___ Lay Dying"
34 Castle locale
35 Kind of yoga
36 Mechanic's apparel?
37 One of the Marianas
38 Become suddenly aware
40 Engineer's apparel?
41 Shine
42 Penn and others
44 Certain office worker
45 Surf sounds
46 Composer Siegmeister
47 Old dagger
48 Paper size: Abbr.
53 Highlander's pride
55 Treasure site
56 Day after mercredi
57 Skeletal parts
58 Saint ___ College of California
59 Stock up
61 Form of Spanish "to be"
65 Continue
66 Sip
67 Intimate
68 Master
69 4 × 4 name
70 E-Z Pass payment
71 One of the Monkees
72 Nosy one
73 Longtime G.M. chief Alfred
75 Evil, to Yves
76 1884 literary hero, informally
79 Physicist Ohm
81 Lab reports
83 Son's designation, with "the"
84 Hollywood's B. D. and Anna May
85 Certain H.S. teams
86 Good bond rating
89 Yankee
91 Anne McCaffrey's dragon land
93 Don Marquis character
94 Airs
96 Wonderland message
97 "Men in Black" menace
98 River at Lyon

by Michael S. Maurer

MAGAZINE MERGER MANIA

ACROSS

1 Routine responses?
6 Least amiable
12 One who sets up shots
18 Make ___ for
20 Radiators and such
22 Camden Yards player
23 One of the Beverly Hillbillies
24 The World ___
25 Lab vessel
26 View surreptitiously
28 Concubine's room
29 Tart
30 How the celebrity's mom and dad survived?
37 Contemptible one
38 Theme park transport
39 Hit man, so to speak
40 Novelist Nin
42 Name of three English rivers
43 Be against change
47 How the case of commercial espionage is halted?
52 ___ du Diable
53 Cry of delight
54 Bitter, to a Brit
55 Chatter
56 Nonplussed
58 Birchbark
60 Bowling game
63 Commute overseas regularly?
68 Quit
69 Top
70 More monumental
71 Short test for brains?

72 Base figure: Abbr.
73 Annual hoops event, familiarly
74 Taste
77 Evening hours, to Larry King?
87 Ready for a vacation
88 Sundance's girl
89 Pour ___ troubled waters
90 Where the Via del Corso runs
91 Elath resident
94 Small toymakers: Var.
95 President Bush writes part of his autobiography?
101 Andretti, for one
102 1920's White House nickname
103 Greenish-yellow hue
104 Sit in on
106 "King Rat" novelist
110 Birdie of Broadway's "Bye Bye Birdie"
113 Diving Instructions, maybe
114 Barely perceptible
115 Heavy hammer
116 Lay hold of
117 ___ verité
118 Krupp family city

DOWN

1 Muslim pilgrimage: Var.
2 Cousin of a lemur
3 Weekly radio program
4 Heatless
5 It can go in brackets
6 Angry words
7 Animator's sheet

8 Words before and after "what" for Popeye
9 LAX abbr.
10 Counterpart for madame
11 Wall Street figure
12 Stole
13 Hardware
14 Chutists' needs
15 Keen
16 80's TV divorcee
17 Strapped
19 Arizona native
21 Mayo Clinic test
27 S.A. country
30 Master
31 Not dissonant, musically
32 Beat it!
33 Emulate Tyra Banks
34 Agassi, at times
35 Challenger of Stalin
36 Sign of damage
41 Mollify
43 When repeated, cry at a celebratory party
44 Intimidate, with "out"
45 "To fetch ___ . . ."
46 Combining the ideal characteristics of its variety
48 Nipped, with "out"
49 1973 World Series stadium
50 Reached in amount
51 "The Time Machine" people
56 Letters on a telephone bill
57 Redressed, with "for"
58 Williams title start
59 "So then what?"

60 Specter
61 Left and right, maybe
62 Midpoint: Abbr.
63 Camp vehicles
64 Strain
65 Big name in golf
66 Light: Prefix
67 Tax-free bond, briefly
74 Banking game
75 "See ya!"
76 English 101 subject
78 Most gamesome
79 Having equal angles
80 Salinger dedicatee
81 Interpret
82 She had a "Tootsie" role
83 List ender
84 Tpkes.
85 "Das Rheingold" locale
86 Telephone connections
91 Leaning to the right
92 Corned beef alternative
93 Important sports org.
95 Exams for advanced study, briefly
96 Noted stationer
97 "Coffee ___?"
98 Churchly: Abbr.
99 Some office equipment
100 Eleve's place
105 Letters after Gov. Jeanne Shaheen's name
107 Sportscaster Scully
108 Compass heading
109 Thrash
111 Sensitive subject, often
112 Stereo site

by David J. Kahn

ACROSS

1 Cry or relief
7 Actress Campbell of "Martin"
12 Greenery
19 Stainless
20 Bony
21 Mammals like camels
22 Minnie's mama
24 Amount of fun
25 James Whitcomb Riley's "___ I Went Mad"
26 Make waves, for short?
27 Request for permission
29 A small one is white
30 Jodie's mom or dad
34 Unmannered
38 Changing places
41 Tops
42 Lawn mower maker
44 Where area code 813 is: Abbr.
45 Pad, so to speak
46 Zip
47 Partridge locales?
49 Side-channel, in Canada
50 Mel's daughters
54 Farm females
55 Tentativeness
57 Synthetic fiber
58 Mawkish
59 Life's strange turns
60 Throws off
61 Not esto or eso
62 Univ. grant source
63 Member of Glenn's family
67 Elemental ending
70 Competitor of Bloomies

72 Part of a candlelight ceremony, maybe
73 Where zebras and giraffes graze
75 They travel on foot
77 Subatomic particle
78 Unruffled
80 Soprano in "Louise"
81 Michael J.'s kids
83 Understand
84 Gym equipment
86 One for Juan
87 Kind of alphabet
88 Hurricane heading: Abbr.
89 50's–60's teen idol
90 French bench
92 Hoarder
94 Side in a Euro conflict
96 Jasmine's family member
99 Uranians, e.g.
101 Kind of exhaust
102 Provide, as with legal authority
103 Lizard, old-style
106 Hitched
110 Member of Joyce's family
114 Sautéed seafood dish
115 Lots of potatoes
116 Designer Pucci
117 Follows a sidewalk preacher
118 First name in cosmetics
119 Holds off

DOWN

1 Tip
2 God with iron gloves
3 Midnight or beyond
4 Hair color
5 Initial instruction
6 Cherished name in Calcutta
7 Kitchen meas.
8 Suffix with Manhattan
9 "Able" one
10 Capital once known as Salisbury
11 Masefield's "___ That Pass By"
12 Testing site
13 Ben-Gurion carrier
14 Liqueur flavor
15 Traveler
16 Close friend, in slang
17 Hoedown date
18 Squiggly shape
20 "What's to become ___?"
23 Dog bowl bits
28 Investor's concern
30 Film editing effect
31 Union demand
32 Charles's game
33 ". . . ___ a good-night!"
35 Anita, Bonnie, Ruth and June
36 Sore labour's bath, to Shakespeare
37 Flip, in a way
38 Return, as chips
39 Doubleday et al.
40 Donna's sons
43 Penn Sta. traffic

46 Big Apple's 30 Rock occupant
47 Ship commanded by Martin Pinzón
48 Caboose
50 Highlanders
51 ___ many words
52 "Give me an example, smarty"
53 Bar's partner
56 Sounds of time passing
58 Allen or Martin
60 He played Robin and Don Juan
61 Tracks
64 "Braveheart" setting
65 Bridge positions
66 Tropical spot
68 Nervousness
69 Climbing plant with a dye-yielding root
71 Burnoose wearer
74 Straddling
75 Deliveries to a butcher
76 Cut back
77 Silvers role
78 Shell
79 Tic-tac-toe failure
81 Football Hall-of-Famer Ford
82 Candid Allen
85 Fortification
87 Spring part
90 S.A.T.'s
91 Solvent
92 Stress, for one
93 Tousled
95 Old Texaco star
97 Broadway salute to Blake
98 Times to call, in classifieds

by Randolph Ross

100 Elated
103 Vogue rival
104 So-so
105 Terrible time
106 Vandalize
107 Honest name
108 Grammy category
109 Paris's
Parc ___ Princes

111 Not just any
112 Ground breaker
113 Tiny carp?

ACROSS

1 March event
7 ___ law (i = v/r)
11 They may appear in the long run
16 "The Phantom of the Opera" star, 1962
19 Appear
20 TV actress Spelling
21 Sound from the bleachers
22 She played Sarah in "The Bible"
23 Hardly Mensa material
25 Kind of session
26 Understanding
27 Hard rock, maybe
28 Suburb north of Seattle
29 Mole, for one
30 Directional suffix
31 Warhol icon Sedgwick
33 Medit. nation
34 Tricked
35 Stem joint
36 "The ___ Adventure" ("Star Wars" spinoff)
37 Group of planes
39 Bitsy beginning
40 Like
41 "Gilligan's Island" actress
43 1974 hit subtitled "Touch the Wind"
45 Composer Prokofiev
46 "Exodus" role
47 John of York
48 Pizzeria patron
49 Property of housepets?
50 Tackled
51 Hay morsel
52 Reassurer's words
54 Animation
55 Perfect
57 Ending with blind or broad
58 Kilowatt-hour fraction
59 Congratulations, of a sort
60 Decline
62 Bereavements
64 "It Happened One Night" producer
67 Violinist Jean-___ Ponty
68 Dosage amts.
71 Diamond of records
73 Nigerian language
74 Book stores?
76 Cozened
77 First lady of 1900
80 Magazine that debuted 2/17/33
82 Cheer
83 ___ Darya (Asian river)
84 When repeated twice, a 1964 pop hit
85 Botswanan problem
86 Go-getters
88 Portray
90 Grenoble's river
91 Battle of Coronel admiral, 1914
92 Drunk's woe, with "the"
94 "The Dark at the Top of the Stairs" playwright
95 Better than never?
96 Pancreas, e.g.
97 Time to look ahead
98 First name in spydom
99 "___ only knew"
100 Intersecting street
101 Sammy Davis Jr. had one
103 Drop the ball
105 Small songbird
106 Come about
107 Site of Chief Big Foot's last stand
109 Clockmaker Terry
110 ___ citato
111 Not well-done
112 They're not in the nuclear family
113 Matter for a judge
114 Thrills
115 "My Way" songwriter
116 Sensible to the nth degree

DOWN

1 ___ Fjord (inlet of the Skagerrak)
2 Preview programs for computers
3 Contract
4 Transfix
5 Possible change in Russia
6 Not lethargic
7 Idle
8 Center of a roast
9 Rocky Lane spoke for him
10 Tom Sawyer's half brother
11 One letting go
12 Couch potatoes, often
13 "The Furys" novelist James
14 Wrapped up
15 School reward
16 Lausanne lies on it
17 Is intemperate
18 Quirks, say
24 Lead singer of "Heart"
29 Maniacal
32 Guitar-picking pioneer Everly
35 Math calculation
36 North Holland seaport
37 Delicate
38 In a difficult position
40 Tackle
42 Open tract
44 Drip site
45 Ethel Merman and Jack Benny, e.g.
52 "Children of the Albatross" author
53 Conductor ___ Klas
56 Hold
57 Logging-on need
59 Sorority letter
61 Torpedo
62 A.M.A. members
63 Disgusted
64 .6102 cubic inch
65 Frederick Forsyth best seller, with "The"
66 1975 James Taylor hit
68 Euripidean work
69 Angler's hope
70 Chaldeans
72 The maximum, often
74 ___-majesté
75 Turns away
76 Put to use
78 Duds at work

by Frank Longo

79 Pot grower?
81 To be, in Bordeaux
87 Cave
89 Inlet
91 Oscar Madison, for one
93 Donald's daughter
96 Bellyache

98 Kind of hound
100 U.S.N. personnel
101 Enter
102 Itchings
104 Unwind
107 Depression-era inits.
108 Resource to be tapped?

ACROSS

1 In a fog
7 Fattening sites
12 School founded by a brewer
18 Comic Judy
19 Fusilli's shape
20 Delta, for one
21 John Knowles book about the tortoise's winning strategy?
23 Paper launched in 1944
24 Its setting is a setting
25 Color close to aqua
26 Makes sound
28 Slumber party guest
29 Public outcry
32 Frasier's brother
35 Debate position
36 Diamond corners
37 John Kennedy Toole book about a desert union?
41 Luke's sister
42 "Whip It" singers
43 Wrong
44 Parkers plug them
46 Peruvian coin
47 Musical based on "La Bohème"
48 "___ So Fine"
51 Discussion groups
52 Sine, cosine and tangent
55 Recess
57 Duke is part of it, for short
58 Henry James story about a mutiny?
62 Minimal swimwear
65 Tour-planning org.
66 Island ring
67 Islam's largest branch
68 Jane Austen book about Rosa Parks?
74 Moral misdeed
75 Ring combo
76 Patch sort
77 Strasberg subject
80 Was a pioneer
81 Door feature
84 Horror director Craven
85 Kite-flying need
86 Be cyclical
87 Writer Tarbell and others
89 Superwide shoe specification
90 Thomas Hardy book about a taxpayer's deductions for groceries?
96 Prophets
97 City on Guanabara Bay
98 Pianist Peter and family
99 Doughy snack
101 Robust
102 Start of many Latin American place names
104 Dubai native
106 Filing asst.
107 It's not wall-to-wall
109 John Grisham book about fashion show critics?
114 Ordinary
115 Sheathe
116 Frosh topper
117 Sudden contractions
118 TV event of January 1977
119 Baseball card number

DOWN

1 Harts
2 Coin of Córdoba
3 Lacking in substance
4 Trophy
5 Pilot's projection: Abbr.
6 Blowgun ammo
7 Relieved
8 Service award
9 401(k)'s kin
10 Singly
11 Happy colleague
12 Competes
13 Radius setting
14 Campaign poster inscriptions
15 Gary of "Forrest Gump"
16 Guitarist Segovia
17 Cassette parts
19 Sobersided
20 1984 Steve Martin/Lily Tomlin film
22 Dido's love
27 Like appreciative fans
30 "Jefferson in Paris" star
31 Use a prie-dieu
33 1974 foreign-language hit
34 Knowledge, in France
36 Stirs
38 Historic event
39 Upended umlaut
40 Alice's cat
44 Kind of shop or language
45 Prepared for transmission
48 Meddles
49 Vespers time
50 Ross's forte
51 Recon unit
52 Win
53 "Computers for people" company
54 Old five-centesimi coin
56 Heart ward, for short
59 Swindled
60 Sinn ___
61 Behavioral quirk
63 Clear
64 Rubbernecks
69 Time being
70 Field marshal Rommel
71 Actor Baker
72 Precarious
73 Corroded
78 Floorboard sound
79 Soundtrack album, e.g.
82 Scandal reaction
83 Bobby Orr, from 1966 to 1976
85 It has its ups and downs
86 Enjoys a favorite book
88 "Die Fledermaus" composer
90 Shred
91 "All's Well That Ends Well" heroine
92 Cad
93 "Deed I Do" singer
94 Andean beast
95 Morale
96 Pillow covers
100 He introduced the Easter egg roll on the White House lawn
102 Stars

by Mike Shenk

103 Cry of despair
105 Rum cake
108 Fishes-Bull go-between
110 "The Island of the Day Before" author
111 Snitch
112 In addition
113 Quick punch

ACROSS

1 Old Turkish aristocracy
6 ___ Gailey of "Miracle on 34th Street"
10 "He" and "she" follower
14 Hold off
19 Wasn't upright
20 Actress Anderson
21 Crown
22 Mideast's Gulf of ___
23 Heckles, say
25 Rare book dealer's abbr.
26 1989 Tom Hanks film, with "The"
27 UXS
29 Examines closely
30 Temper
31 Afr. nation
32 Obeyed a flasher
33 Timely girl's name
34 Deplorable
35 Bleat
36 In ___ (not yet moved)
37 Down
39 "To Evening," e.g.
40 0X
44 Early American orator Fisher ___
45 Jerusalem artichoke, e.g.
48 Tabloid, maybe
49 Pays what's expected
51 Western tribe
52 Problem for a dentist
54 "___ Baby" ("Hair" song)
56 They lack refinement
58 ___ Town
59 Razor-billed bird
60 Cutty ___
61 Some theater
64 Mil. drop site
65 TH000X
68 Grp. that conducts many tests
69 Runner's jersey
71 Pro side
72 One of 13 Popes
73 French count, maybe
74 Flurries
75 Not solid
76 Old-fashioned lady
77 "___ Agnus Dei" (Christian phrase)
78 Former
81 Roll
82 Inevitable
83 Spell
85 IX
90 Copy
91 Bluejacket
92 Before long
93 Player's grp.
94 Barbecue sound
97 Tangs
99 Tie again
102 Stable nibble
103 Shooter
104 Temple architectural features
105 bXw
109 Jousting
110 Morales of "La Bamba"
111 Free of criticism
112 King protectors
113 Regnum
114 Ring foe
115 Noted Civil War biography
116 Pick up
117 Spawning fish
118 Ending with hoop
119 Chicago's ___ Expressway

DOWN

1 Common defenses
2 Equus and others
3 Covered, in a way
4 Over
5 Decoration for a newlywed's car
6 Threw toward
7 Fibrous
8 Inner beginner
9 Dropping, in a manner of speaking
10 Indy occurrence
11 Soft drink name
12 "Who's there?" reply
13 Figure in a murder mystery
14 Lightly touches
15 Accouter
16 10 X
17 It's on its way out
18 Struggles with, as a varmint
24 Let go
28 Kind of horn
36 Afternoon fare
38 Gray
40 Onetime Chicago V.I.P.
41 Early wheels
42 Eastern verse
43 Suffix with glass
44 A celebrity may have one
45 Big brass
46 More romance
47 ? X
50 Breaks down, in a way
52 Kind of society
53 "Star Wars" name
54 Showed wonderment
55 Warner ___
57 Win over
60 Eye-opening problem
61 Word in a billet-doux
62 Pion's place
63 Saddled
65 What's more
66 Film director Sam
67 S.C. Johnson spray
70 Joint deposit?
73 Kind of ears
75 Announcement makers, for short
76 Tony-winning producer Theodore
79 Some TNT sports coverage
80 Backside
81 Certain illustrations
82 Utensils
83 Church events
84 Shoe style
86 Major news media
87 Sicilian resort
88 Object of a charity search
89 More than "Gosh!"
91 Dangerous pest
94 "___ Nacht" (German Christmas carol)
95 Fine liner fabric
96 Nobel and others
98 Summits
100 Succeed
101 Hoops
106 Cat's-paw, e.g.
107 Rhine feeder
108 Sped

by Robert H. Wolfe

ACROSS

1 Freight
6 < Player with this retired number
12 Overly smooth
15 ". . . this sceptred ___": "Richard II"
19 Site of Joan of Arc's demise
20 Dutch royal house
21 Goof
22 Switchblade
23 Words before clear or way
24 < Player with this retired number, informally
25 Famed railsplitter
26 TV
27 Mideast capital
29 Center of Anytown, U.S.A.
31 Golfer Juli
33 Tennis's Nastase
35 Film director ___ Lee
36 Exceed
38 Hearty cheer
39 Without a date
42 "___ at 'em!"
44 Johnson of "Laugh-In"
45 Throat projection
47 Where the Paraná River is: Abbr.
48 First name in horror
49 Prank
50 Honored
51 Shadow companion
53 Dumps
56 "East of Eden" co-star
57 Garlic segment
58 State tree of Missouri
59 Transcript
60 < Season record for which 3-Down had this number

62 Caviar
63 Gypsy, traditionally
65 ___-European
69 Upper, in Saxony
70 Open tract
72 Champ of 10/30/74
73 New Mexico resort
74 Colleague of Farrar and Maleska
75 Travel aid
78 Hex, of a sort
80 Convention activity
82 Pathetic
84 Waxy bloomer
87 Cousin of a loon
88 Clippers
91 Roosevelt quartet
92 Parrot's word
93 It's missing in manana
94 Duck
95 Meat stamp
97 Romanian coin
98 Copier button
99 Slow-moving
100 Race official
102 Boxer Willard
103 Uris hero
104 Brand name at picnics
106 Know-how
107 London gallery
109 < Team that won this many games in 1961
111 Member of the first A.L. team to win more than 110 games in a season
114 Classic action figures
118 Boast
119 Free (of)
121 Wield
123 Supercharger

124 Height: Prefix
125 Debenture, basically
126 More cunning
127 Open
128 Bygone era
129 Charlotte-to-Raleigh dir.
130 < Season record for which Rickey Henderson had this number
131 Actress Young and others

DOWN

1 Lit — (college course)
2 Top-flight
3 < Player with this retired number
4 < Player with this retired number
5 "Peyton Place" actor
6 Decimate, with "down"
7 ___ and Thummin (Judaic objects)
8 Obeisance
9 Kind of skate
10 Curing, in a way
11 Noted Virginia family
12 Shade of green
13 Umpire
14 Movement
15 Practitioners' suffix
16 < Season record for which Grover Cleveland Alexander had this number
17 One smeared in England
18 Big name in batteries
28 Blue ___
30 Sink

32 < Player with this retired number
34 Sought lampreys
37 Western Athletic Conference team
39 Skating jump
40 Object with three round projections
41 Nickname
43 Like certain elections
44 < Player with this retired number
46 Clothing
48 Rabbit or Fox preceder
49 Murmur
52 Swampy tract
54 Hubris source
55 Nor. neighbor
56 First TV series to show a baby being born, 1955
59 60's chess champ
61 Impugns
64 Harshest sentence
66 Enclosed part of a blimp
67 < Season record for which Earl Webb had this number
68 Bony
71 Printemps follower
76 Region of 101-Down
77 Rundown
78 Vegetable container
79 Plastic ___ Band
81 Turkish title
83 "___ Good Times Really Over" (1982 country hit)
85 Golly
86 Good will, e.g.
88 Meower
89 V.I.P.

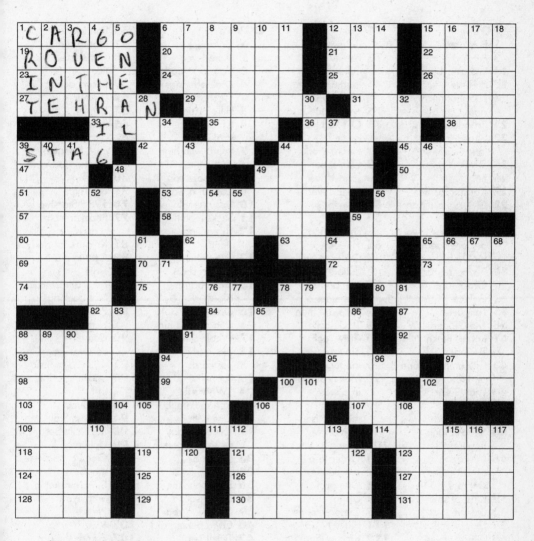

by Derrick Niederman

THAT'S AN ORDER

ACROSS

1 Puts down
8 Puts up
14 Passover breads
20 Surplus
21 Fish that hitches rides
22 Broadcast, e.g.
23 Order to a longshoreman?
25 Surgical probe
26 Busy
27 Caesar, for one
28 Civil rights leader Medgar
30 Antique car owner's need, for short
31 Perfect number
32 Order to a C.P.A.?
35 Fatigues
38 The Gipper
41 Robert Blake TV series
43 City on the Saône and Rhone
44 That Geller feller
45 Garden pests
46 Snaps of the fingers
48 Order to an art gallery worker?
52 Kind of sale
53 Spleen
54 Le __ Noël
55 Telecast over
56 Where to hear "O patria mia"
60 Give thumbs down
61 Some dances
63 Breathing fire
64 Polished
66 "Takin' It __ Streets" (1976 hit)
68 Order to a quarterback?

72 Over and done with
73 Family once called "the landlords of New York"
75 Hurray for José
76 Old "S.N.L." name
78 Pindar work
79 Gimlet or screwdriver
80 Soap seller
83 Dweeb
84 Anthem contraction
85 Wreck
87 Order to an editor?
91 Like Burns's "schemes o' mice an' men"
94 Thick locks
95 Crew tool
96 Siouan language
97 Makes potable, in a way
99 Grabs in monopolistic fashion
102 Strength: Var.
104 Order to a surgeon?
106 Gun grp.
108 Up to
109 Close to, once
111 Navy NCO
112 Kind of quarter
114 Making redundant
116 Order to a sloppy senator?
120 Park, for one
121 One who minds
122 One out?
123 Troubles
124 Rococo
125 Burr and Hamilton, e.g.

DOWN

1 Goldbrick
2 More level
3 Do piano work
4 Bank offerings, for short
5 Hill's partner
6 It may need stroking
7 Word with high or hunting
8 Like loose soil
9 Call, in a way
10 Hosp. employee
11 Sticks together
12 Three-legged stand
13 Letter encl.
14 Billiard shot
15 Small British island
16 Order to a D.A. with a hung jury?
17 Whole slew of
18 Like early postcards
19 Pepper, e.g.
24 "What's the __?"
29 Congo neighbor
32 One with a successful day on Wall Street
33 Indian ox
34 Push
36 Baja opposite
37 Snake sound
39 Calendar abbr.
40 Can-opening aid
42 Ticket info, maybe
45 Jewish pledge of faith
47 They're on a sched.
48 Imply
49 Musical composition
50 Adjoining
51 Medium pace
52 Use the spade again

55 Fan sound
57 Not alfresco
58 Transferred the title
59 Bean counters
62 "Cheers!"
63 Fannie __
65 Progress
67 Order to a cue card handler?
69 Tarzan portrayer
70 Quirks
71 Sch. type
74 1986 Starship hit
77 Recover from a drenching
81 Knight's fair lady
82 Off the mark
86 Flair
87 Fountain treat
88 Not backing
89 Prescription for burnout
90 Common correlatives
91 40's–50's music
92 Showing a lot of feeling
93 Sendups
94 Actress Stapleton
98 Rock climber
99 Uplifted
100 Open a package, maybe
101 Supermarket employee
103 Pens
105 Vs.
107 Primes the pot
110 Sonar signal
112 Time-honored name?
113 It's east of the Caspian
114 Dynamite
115 It fits under a head
117 Nabokov novel
118 End amount
119 Big Ten inits.

by Nancy Salomon

ACROSS

1 Red-faced
8 Metal found in meteors
14 Defiled
20 1963 Hepburn-Grant film
21 Social instability due to a breakdown in values
22 Mandarin, e.g.
23 Like some Greek odes
24 Standup comedian who wrote "Letters From an Adult Child"
26 Byrnes and Hall
27 Exaction
29 Long, in a way
30 Badminton call
32 "ER" doc
34 John Hancock: Abbr.
35 "___ Mio"
39 Before, once
41 Joins, as long-lost friends
45 Shoe with a puckered seam
47 Construction piece
48 Summarizes concisely
52 "___ y Plata" (Montana's motto)
53 Choose by divine election
54 Is suitable (for)
55 Plastics workers
57 Needle
58 Slow
61 Football positions: Abbr.
63 Stairmaster part
64 Give out
65 "Oh, ___!"
66 Fly-by-night
68 ___ vu
69 U.S. foreign aid, mostly
71 70's TV detective
74 Lump together
76 Heads up
77 Some retreats
78 Not miss ___
79 Superlative
80 Appreciates
81 Stares absentmindedly
82 One of the Bobbsey twins of fiction
84 Object of decoration
86 Redline
87 Org. for advocates
88 "Sleeping Gypsy," "The Snake Chamber," etc.
93 "At Random" autobiographer
95 Port with a natural harbor
96 Crabwise
97 50's political inits.
98 Land
100 School of whales
102 Sci. course
103 Arles water
105 Mine railway
109 Quartet for first graders
111 ". . . or ___ me?"
114 Tree surgeon, maybe
118 Odds and ends
120 Hardened
121 Theater area
122 Unusual house shape
123 Ticks off
124 Clerk
125 Kind of sandwich

DOWN

1 Ne plus ultra
2 Like plowhorses
3 Try to get mystical messages
4 Was mentioned
5 Magazine since 1952
6 Bowdlerize, with "out"
7 Politesse
8 Reports by phone
9 "Double Fantasy" artist
10 Spell
11 Flandre friend
12 Bank rights
13 Late afternoon, usually
14 Kind of list
15 "There ___ losers . . ."
16 Most collectible
17 Hospital V.I.P.'s
18 Something that can get in the way
19 Place for a VCR
25 Useless
28 She was Jennifer on "WKRP"
31 Fictional detective Philip
33 Room in the game Clue
36 Popular feature in poetry
37 Emulated a siren
38 College founded by a king
39 Pleased as punch
40 Switch tags
42 Incomparable ending
43 Montgomery's field: Abbr.
44 Code word for "S"
46 Seaplane inventor Glenn
49 Grape yields
50 Early influence on Baryshnikov
51 Car weight without fuel or load
56 Traveled unaccompanied
58 Asphalt
59 "Animal House" frat man
60 Urdu is spoken here
62 Muzzle
65 Old French headdress
66 Peg with a concave top
67 Stars
70 Directs
72 Three-time A.L. M.V.P.
73 Review, as damage
75 Cut
78 Harry's Veep
80 Edam relative
81 River at Liège
82 Veneer
83 Poser
85 Former French toastee?
86 "Midnight Lace" actress, 1960
89 Lions
90 Bill collector?
91 Med lab specimen
92 Admit a mistake, so to speak
94 Old Ford model
99 Intro
101 Daring
104 Set sights on
106 Boosts
107 "Be ___!"
108 Big name in computers

by David J. Kahn

110 Chief, in Italian
112 Sikorsky or Stravinsky
113 Where Dollywood is: Abbr.
114 Familial moniker
115 Tolkien creature
116 "__ hora es?"
117 Part of an itin.
119 A lot of Colo.

ACROSS

1 Split
7 Skiing type
13 Pressing machines
20 Closer to base?
21 See 60-Across
22 Impute
23 Start of a verse
26 Azerbaijani neighbor
27 Missouri feeder
28 Salt, perhaps
29 Faxed
30 Land in Genesis
32 European fruit tree
34 Leases
36 River inlet
39 Jack in oaters
41 Agt. such as Ness
43 B.C. Judean king
47 Part of A.D.
49 Sounding startled
52 Power problem
55 Old record label
56 Part 2 of the verse
60 With 21-Across, an 1861 literary hero
61 Kind of sax
62 Route
63 "___ It Romantic?"
64 Changes a Life sentence?
65 B. A. Baracus's group
66 Tag
68 Suddenly shrinks
70 Costa del Sol section
73 Launch of 7/10/62
77 Ferber's "Giant" ranch
79 Caravan maker
81 Basso Tajo
82 Yours, in Yonne
85 Mrs. David Copperfield
87 Month after Nisan
88 What optimists have
89 Part 3 of the verse
94 Afore
95 It's often underfoot
96 Stopped lying
97 Art Deco notable
98 Mythical queen of Thebes
100 Dickens girl
102 Medicare-eligible, maybe
104 Draft org.
105 Neighbor of 26-Across
108 Kissers
111 Burden of proof
113 Stand in ceremony?
116 Verdant
118 Head lock
120 Clearing
124 End of the verse
128 Kind of counter
129 Dogear mark
130 Custodians, colloquially
131 Custody
132 Impaired
133 Neverending, once

DOWN

1 ___-plié (ballet movement)
2 Actor-songwriter Novello
3 Start of a cheer
4 Kristen on "Ryan's Hope"
5 Mock
6 Goof
7 Lowell and Tan
8 Mahayana monks
9 Ragú rival
10 Book extra
11 Fresh
12 Lassie creator Knight
13 Slalom champ Phil
14 Cinereous
15 Cpl., e.g.
16 ___ Pointe, Mich.
17 In play
18 Bacheller's "___ Holden"
19 Spanish muralist
24 Expression of respect
25 Coward
31 King Harald's predecessor
33 Student body pres., e.g.
35 Lt. Kojak
36 Grower
37 Private
38 Like some of the early English
40 Peter Weiss drama "___/Sade"
42 "The Clan of the Cave Bear" author
44 Rotations, in garages
45 Awaited sign
46 Tabloid talk
48 Handel's "Messiah," e.g.
50 Drag
51 Attar source
53 Related on the father's side
54 Diving bird
57 Actor Davis
58 Wandering
59 Old-fashioned cooker
65 Famed furrier's family
67 Name meaning "My God is he"
69 Burdened
71 Shows wild instability
72 "Battlestar Galactica" commander
74 Some church lighting
75 Advisories
76 Media executive Steven and others
78 Incendiary sinner
80 Actress Scacchi
82 Yemeni capital
83 Geometric solids
84 Muffin topper
86 Equipped
90 One in a heat
91 Like elvers
92 1931 Dracula portrayer
93 Receptive
99 Miter wearer
101 Snit
103 Waiting place in a park
106 Sergeant York
107 "The Caine Mutiny" captain
109 Father of Paris
110 Brains
112 Incline
113 Gumshoe
114 Avis pair
115 Latin pronoun
117 High: Ger.
119 Variety listing
121 Say it's so
122 "After Dark, My Sweet" actor, 1990
123 Highland tongue
125 Christina's father
126 Singsong syllable
127 Literary inits.

by Cathy Millhauser

54 SUIT YOURSELF

ACROSS

1 Strikes out
6 Res ___ loquitur
10 Drink mixer
15 Actor ___ Phillips
19 Atlanta institution
20 Biblical kingdom
21 Shade of green
22 Some eagles
23 Burdened
24 Ranch menace
25 Nathan Hale was one
26 "So ___"
27 Ill omen
29 Echolocation device
31 ___ Sutcliffe, early Beatle
32 Kind of vaccine
33 Suffix with 20-Across
34 Kind of pigeon
37 Played
39 Got on
41 N.B.A. center Longley and others
42 Nags they're not
43 First golfer to win all four majors
46 Like a March wind
48 Schoolboy collars
49 Command at sea
50 Flourish
52 Astronaut Bean et al.
53 Oktoberfest sight
54 Leaf collectors?
55 Suffix with free
56 One of a watery quintet
60 Sign
61 Powwow
64 Gay Nineties bon vivant
66 "___ cannot wither her": Shak.

67 Cabins and such
68 Tickles
69 "Wow"
70 Comics girlfriend
72 Quiet craft
73 60's chess champ
74 This, to Cervantes
75 Space station supply
76 Affair
77 Welles's "The Third Man" role
78 Lets go of
80 Steamboat stops
82 Target
83 F.B.I. storage
84 Creepers
85 Weasels' cousins
87 Lights out
89 Hang
90 Pocahontas's husband
91 Undiminished
92 Yule decorations
94 Skater Midori
95 Wine choice
99 Poetic time of day
100 Dentist's instruction
102 Vegas bookings
105 Originator of cutout dresses
107 ___-um (gnat)
109 "Picnic" playwright
110 Sole supporter?
111 Padre's brothers
112 Preliminary drudgery
113 Live wire, so to speak
114 Like Pegasus
115 Cheers
116 Kind of organ
117 Goals
118 Cub Sandberg and others

DOWN

1 Wallops
2 Union Pacific terminus
3 Runway sight
4 It may be continental
5 In ___ (harmonious)
6 Ineffective
7 Not flat, as hair
8 "The Maltese Falcon" role
9 Ruffle
10 Intimate
11 Needing Dramamine, maybe
12 Some synthetics
13 Eager
14 "Jacta est ___" ("The die is cast")
15 Neighbor of Syr.
16 Electra's brother
17 "Welcome aboard" sloganeer
18 Ear ornaments
28 Where Slyne Head is
30 Sell down the river, in a way
35 Best Picture of 1968
36 Ruminates
38 Ceremonial burner
40 Much-discussed drug
42 Hem and haw
43 Gorge
44 Squares accounts
45 Most foul
46 Best Picture of 1995
47 Splits
48 Precocious 1955 fictional heroine
51 Plunges
52 Decree

57 E. L. Doctorow best seller
58 Think tank member
59 Grommets
61 Way of standing
62 Wears off
63 Sarges' superiors
64 Kimberley features
65 Chem. majors' degrees
68 Still going
71 Tea
72 A Jackson
76 General Motors' birthplace
77 Strictly speaking
79 Composer Bernstein
81 Overwhelms
82 Woof alternative
83 Jai alai locale
84 They're always thin
86 Loads
87 Kind of contract
88 Marilyn's "Bus Stop" role
89 Transfer
90 Fixed
92 Maine Senator
93 Nasty
96 Milieu for Queen Elizabeth 2
97 What a star may stand for
98 ___ Park, Colo.
101 Without restraint
103 A party to
104 Bar on wheels
106 Hook shape
108 Scrape (out)

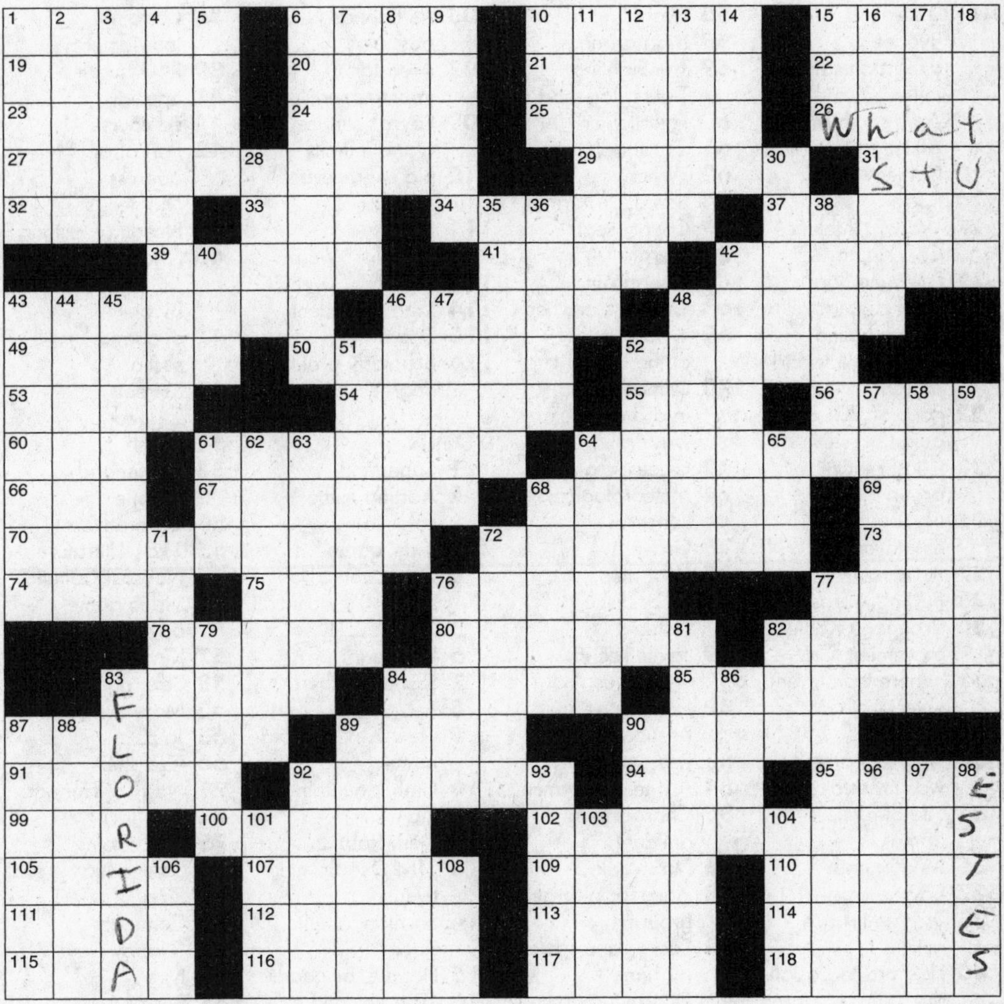
What
S+U
FLORIDA
ESTES

by Nancy Nicholson Joline

ACROSS

1 Bygone geographical inits.
4 Area south of the Atlas Mountains
10 Copier
14 Spots
17 Western Athletic Conf. team
19 Five-time Sugar Bowl champs
21 Opera based on two Wedekind plays
22 Popular 20's auto
23 Conservative group
25 Newspaper employee
27 Arouse
28 Parting words
30 Wolfgang Köhler's movement
31 Where the current enters
32 Ran
33 His real name was Ernesto
35 Site of ancient Samos
36 Kind of eng.
37 Boys
38 Tour de France activity
40 Hartford-to-Boston dir.
41 Parts of hoops
42 Hair-dyeing job
44 P.R., so to speak
45 "The Magus" setting
47 St. Lawrence Seaway terminus
48 Sultanate on the South China Sea
52 Apt. divisions
53 Canary relatives
54 ___ hawk (American bird)

55 Host
58 High ground
59 The Fighting Tigers, for short
60 Fa follower
61 ___-di-dah
62 Wreck
64 San ___ (Marin County seat)
67 Literary monogram
68 George's brother
69 Woosnam of the P.G.A.
70 Demonstrated, in a dramatic way
72 Ogees, e.g.
74 Meteorological concern
76 Grave
77 Heat meas.
78 Mogadishu resident
79 Jamie Lee in "Halloween"
80 Home runs, in baseball slang
83 Resentment
84 A one ___ chance
85 Character builder?
86 Nav. rank
88 Place for a target group?
92 Rocky Lane spoke for him
93 Slangy turndown
94 Some museum rooms
95 With 89-Down, a casino cry
96 Nuremberg negative
97 Andy Kaufman role on "Taxi"
99 Family reunion attender
101 In installments
104 More comely

105 As tight as possible?
107 Area for improvement?
109 Payroll service giant, initially
110 Big sports event sponsor
111 Excel
112 Nobelist Wiesel
113 Thou
114 Kind of student
115 Drove
116 Scholarly prof.'s degree

DOWN

1 Superficial
2 Adding some color to
3 Kids' game
4 Controversial 70's–80's sitcom
5 "That's ___!"
6 Ushers in
7 LSD and others
8 Set
9 New York stadium name
10 High mountain
11 Rid
12 Gen. Robt. ___
13 "The Deer Hunter" event
14 Fashion label since 1975
15 Handle, as goods
16 "The Volcano Lover" novelist
18 Motley
20 R–V connection
24 English source
26 Prepare for an emergency, in a way
29 Lawn-care products brand
32 Recognition
34 Talk (over)
37 Some contractions

38 Certain tournament
39 RNA sugar
41 Special ed course
42 Part of an address
43 "Romeo Is Bleeding" actress
46 "Maid of Athens, ___ we part": Byron
47 Supermarket section
49 Retreats
50 Jagged
51 British ___
53 Marienbad, for one
54 Covered
55 1981 Literature Nobelist Canetti
56 Video game adventurer
57 Kind of school
58 Beverage servers
63 More compliant
65 To ___
66 "___ sher!"
71 Nagy of Hungary
73 Ask (for)
75 Proxy votes
76 Serenaded
77 Ring
79 Come-on
80 "Happy Days" type
81 Building manager's schedule
82 Hooey
85 Caused distress
87 Was overrun
88 Not uniform
89 See 95-Across
90 Parlor treat
91 Panhandle site
92 Nixon's "In the Arena," e.g.
96 Suitable spot

by Rich Norris

97 Ballad
98 Suffix with
   concession
100 Rabin's
   predecessor
102 Marksmanship
   org. founded
   in 1871
103 Georgia ___

104 Mister Rogers,
   for one
106 Clarinetist Lewis
108 Early evictee

56 C PLUS

ACROSS

1 Dr. Seuss character
7 Puzzle solver's exclamation
14 Big name in the metal industry
19 Iago's wife
20 "Amadeus" antagonist
21 Clips
22 Keep in touch with the kids I raised?
24 Family life, figuratively
25 Transport for Tarzan
26 Cove
27 Dismissal
28 Big name in action films catches game?
31 Thwart the progress of United We Stand?
34 Boxcar rider, maybe
35 Run-D.M.C., e.g.
36 Seven: Prefix
37 Looks for
40 Auberge
41 TV's "Murder __"
42 Dome home
47 Constellation north of Taurus
49 Costal fracture?
52 Tidbit
55 Deborah's "The King and I" co-star
56 Uniform decoration
57 Businesses
61 Updates an atlas
63 Spud bud
64 Actress Sorvino
65 Teetotaler's choice

66 Something too tough for talons?
68 "Like __ not!"
69 Not name
70 Free
71 Beat
72 St. __ University
73 Investor's concern
75 "__ in apple"
76 Draw forth
78 Country legend tees off?
80 Thick vegetable soup
85 Hilton alternative
86 Ad __
87 Atlantis docked with it
90 Pressure, in a way
91 Garth Brooks's birthplace
93 Former Davis Cup coach
95 Tasty
96 Sculptor's creation?
101 Overfill airplane areas?
104 Loser
105 "Gotcha"
106 Vacuum tube filler
107 "I Will Survive" singer
108 Psycho with intense desires?
114 Touches up
115 Rival of Oprah
116 Pledge
117 "Bullitt" director Peter
118 Unfriendly quality
119 Book of the Apocrypha

DOWN

1 Like some wine
2 Grp. with a staff in its symbol
3 Pressure unit
4 Algonquian Indian confederation
5 Prepare to shoot
6 Old-fashioned contraction
7 Cousin of -esque
8 Kind of curve
9 Jazzman Mose
10 "Mi __ Loca" (Pam Tillis hit)
11 Poet's adverb
12 Burn up
13 Shanty material
14 Lots
15 Buzz off
16 Mother Teresa, notably
17 Right at the beginning?
18 "It's worth __!"
21 The Beatles' "__ Woman"
23 Links rental
27 Pres. initials
28 Crack in the cold, maybe
29 "Frank & Jesse" co-star
30 First name in shipping
31 Glee clubs
32 Kind of artery
33 The U.A.E. belongs to it
38 P.I.'s
39 South, to the south
42 "__ Man Answers" (1962 comedy)
43 "The Taming of the Shrew" servant
44 Bebe's "Cheers" role
45 King of the fairies

46 To astronomers, they're hot and blue
48 Comparatively cantankerous
49 Durable wood
50 Nervous
51 Dial letters
53 Beverage for Beowulf
54 528i or Z3, e.g.
57 Toast
58 Hardly handsome
59 "Twelfth Night" countess
60 It may be pending
62 Israel's first U.N. representative
63 Squeezed (out)
66 "Phooey!"
67 Tucked away
72 Ballet jump
74 Spiker's barrier
75 Dispatch boat
77 Old radio's __ Stoopnagle
79 Pandora's boxful
81 Poster material
82 Pastor, sometimes
83 Proceed
84 Loaf pair
87 Man alternative
88 Archipelago components
89 Christogram letter
91 Crying
92 Cinerary vessel
94 On a par, in Paris
96 Not forthright
97 Andes climber
98 To date
99 Department north of Nièvre
100 Elbows
102 Pouring pot

by Frank Longo

103 "___ Dei"
105 Calling company?
108 ___ de coeur (pained utterance)
109 Sinbad's transport
110 Loser to Norton, 1973
111 It may be natural
112 Sade's "Is ___ Crime"
113 Young and Coleman

FOR PEANUTS

ACROSS

1 Shakespearean prince
4 In stitches
8 Lacked, briefly
13 Footnoted
18 Moscow's locale: Abbr.
19 Swift Malay boat
20 Grammy-winning Carey
21 One of the 12 tribes of Israel
22 Strip's bête noire
24 Poppy plant derivative
25 Seasonal songs
26 Experienced one
27 Plug
29 She follows an order
30 Math branch: Abbr.
31 They may be just
33 More apt to bore
35 Early alias of 68-Across
38 Snow construction
39 "Finnegans Wake" wife
40 Prime
42 Évian, notably
43 Best Director of 1992
47 Fashion designer Pucci
49 Noble
50 Direction at sea
51 Bra specification
53 Promotes
54 "___ Davis Eyes" (1981 #1 song)
55 News broadcast closer
57 Maynard G. of 60's TV
59 Peeper pleaser
61 Revulsion
63 "Dallas" Miss
65 Counting aid
67 Old geographical inits.
68 Strip's creator, born 11/26/22
72 Door sign
74 Having a gap
76 Depth: Prefix
77 Clean-lined
79 Manhattan neighborhood
82 Loud, resonant sound
84 Great Western Forum player
85 "The Prince and the Pauper" star, 1937
87 ___ profit
89 Pound sound
91 Giving
92 Western wolf
93 Grease pencil, for one
94 Skaters do them
96 Wing
97 Stove or washer: Abbr.
98 Gremlins, Pacers, etc.
101 Fluid ___
102 Strip's cry of disgust
104 "Hooray!"
106 Monorail vehicle
110 Mariner's dir.
111 Checkup sounds
112 Fully anesthetized
114 ". . . two mints ___!"
115 Adam of "Chicago Hope"
117 Short shots
119 Predecessor of the strip
121 Clark's big role
122 French town opposite Brighton
123 First name in exploration
124 The Lion of God
125 Particles
126 Cloyingly charming
127 Young newts
128 Capitol Hill V.I.P.: Abbr.

DOWN

1 Brought on
2 Designer Simpson
3 Alan and Cheryl
4 Song ___
5 Slip up
6 Strip's smallest character
7 Baby caretaker
8 Popular proverb from the strip
9 Greek nickname
10 Steak ___ (flambéed dish)
11 With 80-Down, Frieda's do in the strip
12 Next
13 Treat on a toothpick
14 Sicilia or Capri
15 Strip's apparition
16 Sushi offering
17 E.R. figures
20 Wear black, perhaps
23 Old-fashioned cold remedies
28 Training overseer?: Abbr.
32 Stepped
34 Unracy
35 Start with Cone or Cat
36 Playmobile
37 When to sing 25-Across
41 Petit chanteur
43 Brings in
44 Restrained, after "on"
45 Strip's comforter
46 "Melancholia" engraver
48 Seine sight
49 Govt. antidiscrimination org.
52 ___-mell
54 1992 Earth Summit host
56 Jelly ingredient
58 Blister
60 R.B.I. producers, often
62 Whale of a captain?
64 Book before Job: Abbr.
66 Sister of Helios
69 Pub fixture
70 Tobacco mouthful
71 Kind of card
73 They're not cool
75 River known for disastrous floods
78 Japanese hand scroll
80 See 11-Down
81 Indy quest
83 Strip's trademark remark
85 Dog hounder
86 "Damn Yankees" vamp
88 Type of tide
90 Fierceness
93 Abbr. on a ticket
95 Schedule listings
97 Airline employees
99 Perfume, as at Mass
100 But, to Brutus
103 Pool
105 "The best ___ to come"
107 Rum mixers
108 Hopping joint?
109 Gum
111 Pierce player on TV
113 Stylish magazine
115 Humerus site
116 Density symbol
118 DHL alternative
120 Plastered

by Christopher Hurt and Derek Tague

ACROSS

1 Tater
5 Start of a palindrome
10 Figurehead site
14 Silent one
19 Mata __
20 Yankee Conference town
21 Piquant
22 "Yond Cassius has __ and hungry look": Julius Caesar
23 President's vision?
26 You can get a rise out of it
27 High spots
28 Dances for Desi
29 Mario Cuomo, e.g.
30 Fraternity letters
31 Lasting forever
32 Red __
33 President's bird?
38 Spoiled child, perhaps
41 Athletic type, supposedly
42 Bones, in anatomy
43 Architectural flute
46 __-mo
47 Innocent, e.g.
48 Stable locks
50 Place to buy a pie
52 Prankster
53 President's injuries?
58 __-Unis
59 Parts of a baseball schedule
61 Archenemies, maybe
63 Czar's reply to protesters
64 Broad sash
65 Flaubert's birthplace
66 __ Khan
68 Shot, e.g.
71 They do the thinking
74 Superiors
79 Bar at night, perhaps
81 President's testament?
83 Annex
84 Banker types
86 London gallery
87 Spring time in Lisbon
88 Boston's Bobby
89 __ Prayer
91 Leave a mark on
93 Big garden products brand
94 Look into again, as a case
96 President's takeover?
100 Misjudge
101 Fictional weaver
102 Mouths
103 Does high-tech surgery, in a way
105 One of the Brady bunch
106 Baby's pastime
111 Protected bird
112 President's weapon?
114 Rice-__
115 ". . . __ saw Elba"
116 "Let __ cake"
117 Bewilder
118 Part of a ship's bow
119 Reddish-brown gem
120 One-sided tilts
121 Victory, to Wagner

DOWN

1 Popular dog name
2 Easter egg hunt sight
3 Constellation animal
4 Plan to take off
5 Angora
6 Sound reveille
7 Gives, old-style
8 Chemical suffix
9 The mornings after
10 Early infant: Var.
11 Some shades
12 Kind of liner
13 "Swiss Family Robinson" author Johann
14 President's fog?
15 Nikita's successor
16 President's beam?
17 El __
18 Airing
24 Link
25 Noted jazz bandleader
31 Nordrhein-Westfalen city
33 Hardly stimulating
34 Bouquet
35 Surprisingly cold
36 Busy one
37 Etiquette subjects
38 Emerald City V.I.P., with "the"
39 Bluebloods
40 Get hot under the collar?
44 Some rtes.
45 Upswing
48 Ape
49 Pink-slip
51 Old-fashioned heating devices
53 Apprehend
54 Aloof ones
55 Prefix with modulator
56 Stammerer's phrase
57 The 21st, e.g.: Abbr.
60 Dinner for the Cratchits
62 Mercury model
65 Electrical unit
67 Goop
68 Hardwear?
69 Often-recited Christmas poet
70 President's line?
72 Pitcher
73 Unwanted coat?
74 Honor
75 Snippet
76 Alliance until 1977
77 Root of diplomacy
78 Single-master
80 President's article of apparel?
82 Flight path
85 Fed. holiday, often
87 "Happy Days" father, informally
90 Less available
91 Actress Braga
92 Maid
93 Expo '70 site
95 Shows pride in one's appearance
97 Corsage staple
98 Attacks
99 Founds
101 Spanish actress Carmen __
103 Mother of Judah
104 Where Shah Jahan is entombed
105 U.K. honors
106 French tire
107 Common conjunctions
108 Sons of, to a sabra
109 Seep
110 Standard force
113 "Yo te __"

by Charles Deber

ACROSS

1 Ending with way or sea
6 Commercial fuel
13 Questions closely
19 Placed on a pedestal
21 Nazareth native
22 Expire
23 MASH member
24 Songbird's lament?
26 Extract
27 Without ___ (daringly)
28 Rand Corporation employee
29 Trophy locale
30 Sot
33 Hun king, in myth
35 B.O. sign
36 Match
38 Story of trouble in the Oriole clubhouse?
42 More inclined
44 Pitch in
45 Prefix with verse
46 Emulate Webster
49 New York neighborhood
50 Slip
51 Not our
53 Approaches
54 You, abroad
55 Having parasites in the hair?
57 Kind of test
59 Farm creature
60 Is faithful
61 1954 Maxwell Anderson play, with "The"
64 Where on parle français, perhaps
65 Looked

66 ___ paper, used for postage stamps
69 Turk. borders it
70 Hangs back
72 Mad states
73 Big bird
74 "The Open Window" writer
75 Like Jack Haley in "The Wizard of Oz"?
78 Short snort
79 "Phooey!"
82 Like pear tree leaves
83 Pothook shape
84 Go without
85 Auerbach of "The Jack Benny Show"
86 Julio, for one
87 Record label abbr.
88 Shop talk
89 Risk a blowout?
93 Clause connector
94 KLM competitor
97 MacLaine movie "Guarding ___"
98 Summer discomfort
100 L.A.P.D. call
103 It has pull
106 ___ the Hyena ("Li'l Abner" character)
107 Front line
109 Acknowledgment from Gen. Montgomery?
113 Pax ___
114 What's left
115 Horton Foote's "Tender ___"
116 Wet floor
117 Farm device
118 Largest in scope
119 Without any pizazz

DOWN

1 Big, so to speak
2 Designer Simpson
3 Statue of a repairman?
4 Actor Stoltz
5 Elocutionist
6 Part of a footnote abbr.
7 Circular
8 Reply to "Am too!"
9 Not on time for
10 Goldfinger portrayer ___ Frobe
11 Subject of a 1996 Oscar-winning documentary
12 Part of R.S.V.P.
13 Bowl setting
14 Dodge
15 Swenson of "Benson"
16 Towers
17 Like some landings
18 Dictator's assistant
20 Affect
25 Caron role
31 Food group
32 Goldbrick
33 "Tomorrow" show
34 Classic sports car, informally
37 Want ad abbr.
39 Had second thoughts
40 Dr. of rap
41 Some Monte Carlo Rally winners
42 Goes after
43 Showy, scarlet flower
47 Story of adoptive jungle dwellers?
48 Looking up to
50 Duck down
51 Prepared to drive
52 Suffers from
55 Sticky stuff

56 Otto I's realm: Abbr.
58 Total
61 Loser at Fredericksburg
62 Sign of spring
63 Conked out
66 Lap dog
67 Connecticut collegian
68 Back blocker
71 Size
72 Aug. setting
75 The Pyramids, e.g.
76 Actresses Judith and Dana
77 Discovery grp.
80 Rio relative
81 Dispatched
84 Standings stat
87 Moves (oneself)
88 Practiced for a rodeo
90 "Primal Fear" star
91 Show for which Liza Minnelli won a 1978 Tony
92 Presidential nickname
94 Eye sores
95 Emerged
96 Prepare, as mushrooms
99 Letter opener
101 Control ___
102 Bunch name
104 Jeremy's singing partner
105 Site of some Millais works, with "the"
106 G.P.O. items
108 Barbra's 1968 co-star
110 100th anniversary of the Potemkin mutiny
111 Senate approval
112 Fast way to J.F.K.

by Randolph Ross

60

HEY, IT'S A LIVING

ACROSS

1 Calculating machine inventor, 1642
7 Reach
14 Protest
20 Delphi temple god
21 Invented word
22 Fingerprint features
23 Supper
24 Job for a restaurant server?
26 Pesticide
28 Had dinner at home
29 Three-way joint
30 Professional org.
33 Milne marsupial
34 Yugoslav novelist ___ Andric
35 Mildew cause
39 Job for a statistician?
43 Hurting the most
44 Alan and Adam
45 Blintzes, e.g.
49 Dustup
50 Player for coach Marv Levy
51 Embargoes
52 Job for a plastic surgeon?
57 Skid row look
60 Tomato-impact noises
61 ___ man
62 70's All-Star ___ Otis
63 Most like a wallflower
64 Worry
66 Job for a mathematician?
72 Plays the siren
73 Quark/antiquark particles
74 Rudolf's refusal
75 Man-mouse link
76 Food on a tray

77 What squeaky wheels get
82 Job for a relay racer?
85 Like Mongolia
86 Photography woe
87 Scull
88 Summoned
90 Jack
92 Styx ferryman
95 Job for a critic?
97 London institution
99 Rhine feeder
100 Second-century date
101 Thumbs up
102 Airport info: Abbr.
103 1978 disaster film, with "The"
105 Ripoffs
108 Job for a debutante?
113 Panama party
117 Screenfuls
118 Caught by surprise, with "on"
119 Athlete's assignment
120 Lohengrin and others
121 Toast opening
122 Tempt

DOWN

1 Course number
2 Goon
3 Bread, maybe
4 Sound of shutters in the wind
5 Minor-party candidate
6 Avon products
7 Parrot
8 Word ending in "o" in Esperanto
9 Compass pt.
10 Solve
11 Check words
12 Chill
13 Not strong

14 Have a title
15 Scholarly type
16 One to remember, for short
17 Spiels
18 Like the best ruse
19 "Women Who Run With the Wolves" author
25 Collections
27 Landscaper's need
30 Iraqis, e.g.
31 Singing Osmond
32 Shackle site
34 Woes of the world
36 Dew times
37 Push
38 Speaker's name
40 It's west of Dublin
41 Benedictines
42 They're not free of charge
46 Frees
47 Like carpet
48 Outburst
51 Ring holder
53 Synchronized
54 Lone Star State sch.
55 Christmas stocking item
56 Lady of a 1918 hit
58 Bit name in morning radio
59 "___ won't be afraid" (1961 pop lyric)
60 Classic Alan Ladd western
63 Dish out messily
64 Ruckus
65 Place for bouquets
66 Delete, with "out"
67 Money in the making
68 Mrs. Katzenjammer, e.g.
69 Wards (off)

70 Manner of speech
71 Stage of a race
76 Bank
77 1982 Disney film
78 Al from New Orleans
79 Cosmetics brand
80 Urbane
81 Marine fliers
83 Chesterfield or ulster
84 Mata ___
85 Way off
89 Violate, with "on"
90 Cold symptom
91 Bibliophile's concern
92 Some trim
93 Screenwriter Mankiewicz
94 Leaves home?
96 Hotshot
97 Kind of approval
98 Buckle opener
99 Passion
104 It's just for openers
105 Unbending
106 Shot shooter
107 Branch
109 Swellhead's excess
110 Anthem preposition
111 Letters before many state names
112 "___ Girls" (Kelly musical)
114 Tackle moguls
115 Shamus
116 "___ we having fun yet?"

by Nancy Salomon

61

FIRST THE SHEEP, THEN . . . ?

ACROSS

1 1962 Tommy Roe hit
7 "I'd rather not hear about it!"
14 Go with the flow
19 "Casablanca" producer
20 Meteorological effects
21 "Beggars can't be choosers" et al.
22 Start of a verse
25 Ring thing
26 Toothpaste-approving grp.
27 "I Know" singer Farris
28 Christian ___
29 "Olympia" painter
31 Every, in prescriptions
32 Tot's transport
36 They may have soft shells
37 Filippo Lippi's title
38 Finger, so to speak
42 Muezzin's call to prayer
43 Unnerve
44 Plum pudding ingredient
45 From Umbria: Abbr.
46 Verse, part 2
52 Dolly, for one
53 Lust after
54 Sailplanes
55 Stag
56 O.K.
58 Attribute
60 Mug
61 Designer in J.F.K.'s White House
63 Take under one's wing
65 Thin
68 Nice touch
70 "Caught" star Maria Conchita ___

73 ___-garde
74 Netanyahu's predecessor
75 Starbuck's captain
76 Its capital is Altdorf
78 Verse, part 3
83 Galley feature
84 "How now! ___?": Hamlet
85 Caesar's wings
86 Malodorous
87 Christian Science founder
88 RR stop
89 Jelly Roll Morton biographer Alan
91 Locale of Ptolemy's lighthouse
93 Good name for a chef?
94 Hardly a sissy
95 West of Hollywood
96 Patch up
99 Princess Yasmin ___ Khan
100 Obvious clue
105 End of the verse
109 Person in a booth
110 ___ Trail (Everglades highway)
111 Testify under oath
112 Nervous, with "up"
113 Clytemnestra's killer
114 Sprung up

DOWN

1 Draft
2 Harness part
3 K-6: Abbr.
4 St. Pierre and Miquelon
5 Refuse
6 Classify
7 All there
8 Plunk

9 One of Knute's successors
10 Cheese made of 52-Across's milk
11 Cuts into
12 French Revolution leader
13 Toledo-to-Akron dir.
14 Extra
15 Not-so-mild oath
16 Stravinsky ballet
17 A Dumas
18 Lao-___
21 Lively, to Liszt
23 Dona ___ (Las Cruces' county)
24 The Magi, notably
29 Hampton Court feature
30 They're nonreturnable
32 Kind of warden
33 Boston Symphony conductor
34 Christmas tree hangings
35 Even one
36 Napoleon relative
37 W.W. II tyrant
38 Certain rating
39 Friend of Aramis
40 See 72-Down
41 Bugs bugs him
43 Desktop publisher's supply
44 Social climber's concern
47 Affirm under oath
48 Ragwort variety
49 Strange "gift"
50 They may be modified
51 Richard Leakey's birthplace
57 Set back?
58 Making no progress
59 Sticks in the mud
60 Stalin's persecuted peasant

62 Bygone delivery person
64 Source of the Truckee River
65 It may be toxic
66 Work around
67 Broken
69 Shakespearean verb ending
71 Babydoll
72 With 40-Down, Down East university town
74 Discompose
75 Bon Ami alternative
77 Rubs the wrong way
79 More odious
80 Crimson Tide, for short
81 Panache
82 Blue Eagle inits.
89 Mesquite or mimosa, e.g.
90 Muscateers?
91 Shanxi shrine
92 Marilu of "Taxi"
93 Socked away
94 Helga's husband
95 Thou squared
96 First South Korean president
97 Hard to hold
98 Mayberry's Goober
100 Biol., geol., etc.
101 Name of two ancient Egyptian kings
102 Cries of surprise
103 Kind of wave
104 The Untouchables, e.g.
105 "Naughty!"
106 W.W. II arena
107 Make an antimacassar
108 Cockney residence

by Frances Hansen

62 BLANKETS

ACROSS

1 Heist gain
5 East German secret police
10 "Star Wars" princess
14 Attack moves
20 S
23 Alpo competition
24 P
25 Threatening finale
26 Clinton has two
27 Buys or leases
28 Miller hero
30 Downed
31 Shakespeare, e.g.
32 Here on the authority of
35 Ripken, Jr. and Sr.
36 "And I Love ___"
37 Had the know-how
39 Mo. parts
40 Hot
42 Knots
43 "Cabaret" director
45 Tract
46 1968 track and field gold medalist
48 Former Swedish P.M. Palme
49 J
55 Water around the Ijsselmeer
56 Wrap
58 Medium-range U.S. missiles
59 Some feasts
60 Dolphin leader
62 She's put out to pasture
63 Horror film staple
66 Vocal style
69 Sat at home
70 The first "M" of M&M's
73 Heroine of Tennessee Williams's "Summer and Smoke"
74 N
79 Basso Pinza
80 Existentialist concern
81 From Tabriz
82 Wayne genre
83 Whitish
84 Printed
86 Popular museum exhibits
88 Anatomical cavities
91 Irk
92 Big dictionary section
93 Break
96 L
101 Pinball paths
102 Hill and Bryant
103 Horseshoer's need
104 Hostilities
107 Greek architectural feature
108 Circus
110 Wheat part
112 Old-time actresses Markey and Bennett
113 Oscar-winning Gibson
114 Moravian, e.g.
116 Some clouds
118 Bit of fancy footwork
119 Live
120 Correo ___ (airmail)
122 Make eights, maybe
124 Kind of hotel
127 Unlearned
129 M
133 Made out
134 G
135 Positions
136 The best
137 Call it quits
138 Complete

DOWN

1 "Dog Day Afternoon" character
2 Blame
3 Switch settings
4 "The Crucifixion" painter
5 Tariff co-sponsor of 1930
6 Common powder
7 When the sun goes down
8 Near misses, maybe
9 "Wie geht es ___?" (German greeting)
10 Flight
11 Two or more periods
12 "___ be all right"
13 Partner-to-be
14 Toast
15 Alerts
16 "Bravo!"
17 Choctaw for "red people"
18 Attached, in a way
19 Derisive
20 Not just any
21 Remnants
22 Ski run
29 "Buddy"
31 Bit of a drag
33 Thin nails
34 Yesteryear
37 King ___ Trio (popular 40's combo)
38 ___ d'amore
39 Baby
41 Actress Harper
42 Bettors bet on them
43 Dickens alias
44 Traveled horizontally
46 Cold one
47 Heroine of 1847
50 Alley mewers
51 Lover of Pyramus
52 The duck in "Peter and the Wolf"
53 Armor-plated warship
54 Black Sea port, new-style
56 Kind of path or pay
57 ___ about (approximately)
60 Karate school
61 Blows away
63 Run for it
64 First name in bridge
65 Pinup features
66 Over
67 Shah ___ Pahlavi
68 Game-ending pronouncement
70 Have it in mind
71 When shadows almost disappear
72 Grand slam foursome
73 Lawyers: Abbr.
75 Touch, say
76 Largest Greek Island, to locals
77 Rawls and Reed
78 1968 Chemistry Nobelist Onsager
84 Santa ___
85 Egyptian menaces
87 Seemingly forever
88 Greek cheese
89 Reaches
90 On-line periodical, for short
91 Subject of a 1982 best seller
93 Mapmaker's aid
94 Crackerjacks

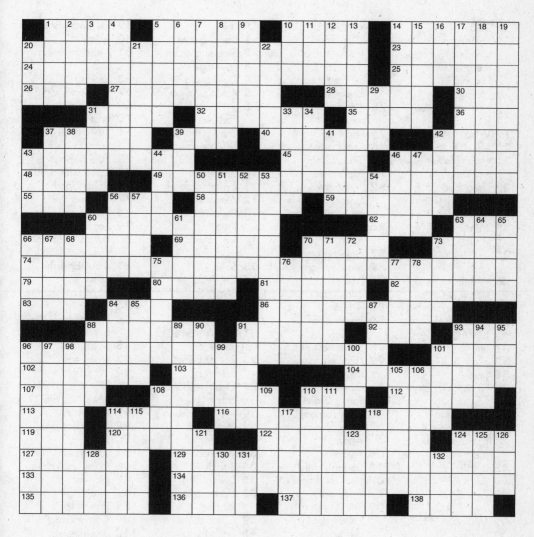

by Matt Gaffney

63   HEARD AT THE AIRPORT

ACROSS

1 River name meaning "where the goods are brought in"
8 "Shane" man
12 He's well-sooted for the job
19 Womb-related
20 Mine, in Amiens
21 Most volatile emotionally
22 "Hey, babe, wanna sit with me on the plane?"
24 Transport to ecstasy
25 Game for two of four
26 "While we're in the air, write an essay on aviation"
28 "Don't waste your breath!"
31 Still
32 Some M.I.T. grads
33 Spree
36 Nods, perhaps
37 "I'm an unattractive woman who'll gab the whole trip"
43 Revolt
45 Burden
48 Deanna of "Star Trek: T.N.G."
49 "Mulholland Falls" actor
50 One of the clan
51 Bad-mouth
53 "___ out!" (ump's cry)
55 Manor near Twelve Oaks
56 "Follow orders in this plane area or else!"
62 Court huddle
64 Twice 79-Down
65 Sen. Cochran
66 Roman called "The Elder"
68 Trackers, e.g.
69 "Prepare to do a spoof on airports"
73 Accused's retort
74 Middling
75 Cross letters
76 Sine ___ non
79 Pilot's wear
82 "Executives, today's lesson is on jet financing"
86 Years of Nero's reign
87 Found groovy
89 Bush, for one
90 Bits
91 Bank deals
93 A Bear
96 Prefix with biology
98 Housekeeping
99 "First I'll read, then watch the movie, then . . ."
101 Fen-___ (diet drug combo)
103 Through working: Abbr.
104 Astonish
105 Spanish article
107 Lions and tigers and bears, e.g.
109 "What's that knitter doing during air turbulence?"
114 Rhyme scheme
118 Conspicuousness
119 "My suitcase is better than yours"
122 Pollen, e.g.
123 Lake near Jacobs Field
124 Put into motion
125 North Pole family
126 Pick-me-up
127 Bums steers?

DOWN

1 Darts' places
2 Siouan speaker
3 Jets, e.g.
4 Gold braid
5 Among, in poetry
6 "Wheel of Fortune" buy
7 Used a thurible
8 Wash against
9 Part of a Latin trio
10 "Indeed!"
11 Examine closely
12 Assemblage
13 Psychoanalyst Karen
14 Joy of wild animals?
15 Split
16 Chow ___
17 Secy.
18 Last in line, usually
21 "Don't blame ___ voted for . . ."
23 Zeit or polter follower
27 One telephone button
29 They're missing from a roll
30 Contest
33 American finch
34 Beeish
35 Diving bird
38 Lichtenstein, for one
39 ___ condolence
40 Spills the beans
41 Gillette brand
42 Landing ___
44 It's "here" in Le Havre
46 Pitches
47 Greek letters
52 Basic sugar
54 Hardships
57 Discontinued, with "out"
58 "Wild!" to a dude
59 Ice cream brand
60 Teller
61 Airport monitor abbr.
63 Lacking
67 Tom Joad, e.g.
69 Harassing
70 Watch chain
71 1997 Rose Bowl winner: Abbr.
72 50% of Bonn
73 Porch with a view
76 Doha's land
77 Treatment
78 Plus
79 See 64-Across
80 Hydroxyl-carbon compound
81 Small English coins
83 ___ d'Orléans
84 Veto
85 First name in horror
88 Lass
92 Trees, e.g.
94 N.F.L. sacker Bryce ___
95 Poe's "___ Lee"
97 Aria area
98 Mayo, for one
100 Pang
102 Jet's home
106 Computer game pioneer
107 Sire
108 French toast
109 Convention site
110 Stewpot
111 Place
112 Not spec.
113 Pre-weekend cry
115 Canaanite deity
116 Fishing luck
117 Home of the Cyclones
118 Small pouch
120 Old French coin
121 Change for a dol.

by Mark Danna

64   SOUTHERN-SPEAK

ACROSS

1 Signals at sea
8 "War and Peace" heroine
15 Indian dwelling
20 Like Miss Congeniality
21 Christie and others
22 Madonna role
23 Tar?
25 Connoisseur
26 Reception site, maybe
27 Catty comments
28 Even
29 Red __
30 Tolkien creatures
31 Sprint competitor
32 Crazy, in Cannes
33 Distance between pillars
36 Yorkshire river
37 60's org.
38 Heyum?
41 Some are "great"
42 Common setting for a joke
43 Mme., in Madrid
44 Check out
46 Not separately
50 Last choice on some lists
53 Come-__
56 Destined
57 Commitment
59 Encouraging words
61 Sleuth Lupin
62 Kind of mail
63 Minnie?
66 Phone trio
67 A.A.A. recommendations
68 Eliot's Grizabella, e.g.
69 Popular White House souvenir
70 It precedes "com"
71 Part of a comparison
72 "Exodus" role
73 Furner?
76 They move in a charged atmosphere
77 Request of an equestrian
79 Corn __
80 Multipurpose truck, for short
81 "Home Alone" actor
82 Meg, among the "little women"
83 Stranger
85 Teach, with "up"
87 Strong
90 Prog. Cons. rival, in Canada
92 Med. drama sites
93 Guns
95 Purty?
99 L-1011 alternative
102 Athos, to Porthos
103 Salon offering
104 Cable inits.
105 Less than diddly
106 Bank posting
107 Broadcasting feed
109 "Aladdin" prince and namesakes
111 Whip
112 Two-dimensional extent
113 Mexican waters
114 Hail?
117 Critical
118 Becomes understood
119 "Your Show of Shows" name
120 Person with a net, perhaps
121 Begins to like
122 Waterloos

DOWN

1 Dissipates
2 Threaten
3 Fairy tale characters
4 All's partner
5 16th President, familiarly
6 Inklings
7 __ Lake, N.Y.
8 Nopes
9 __-old
10 It's only skin-deep
11 Museum room, maybe
12 "Leaving Las Vegas" actress
13 Participatory
14 "Don't __!"
15 Hercules
16 Elliptical
17 Dah?
18 Pied-__
19 Port on the Loire
24 Dweebs
32 Kind of house
34 Movie ratings
35 It paves the way
38 Spar
39 Show disapproval
40 Caterer's need
41 "Hamlet" has five
42 Deposits
45 Drogheda's locale
46 Welcoming or parting gesture
47 Like some corners
48 Mayun?
49 Poland Spring competitor
51 Hit a four-bagger
52 Nicholas Gage book
54 Intensify
55 Restrains
58 Available
60 Mubarak's predecessor
64 Turn topsy-turvy
65 Dog treats
68 Procession
71 La Scala features
73 It may be feathered
74 Was bossy?
75 Antique shop item
78 Perfect ones
81 Actor's goal
84 London greeting
86 Occasion calling for grace
88 Easter starter
89 Onetime U.N. effort site
91 Cause for hitting the forehead
93 Sack
94 Baryshnikov, e.g.
96 Actor Alan of "Hope & Gloria"
97 Haunt
98 Like some cousins
99 Allahabad attire
100 Tristram Shandy's creator
101 Rags
103 Toughie
106 Roam
108 Overhang
110 Limp, as hair
111 Pro __
114 Attention-getter
115 It may be thrown
116 Napoléon, for one

by Nancy Joline and Peg Conner

65 PROPHECY

ACROSS

1 Theater worker
8 Hank Aaron or Jesse Owens, e.g.
16 "Wild Thing" group, with "the"
22 Day in Hollywood
23 Breakdown
24 Capital of Zimbabwe
25 Part 1 of a prophecy by Martin Luther King Jr.
28 Marshal Dillon portrayer
29 Cone-shaped heaters
30 Grocery area
31 More than suggestive
32 Track pick, informally
33 Sharp
34 Jalopy
36 Fr. holy woman
37 Prophecy, part 2
48 Holmes girl
49 Soup holder
50 What Moses did
51 Prophecy, part 3
58 Bob Hope's "___ Russia $1,200"
59 1/6 fl. oz.
60 Extinct New Zealanders
61 Brown of renown
62 Sludge
64 Swindle
67 Seesaw quorum
69 Prepare to surf, perhaps
71 Category
72 Joint protection
73 Unpopular slice
75 Wreck
77 "___ here" (store sign)
78 Time to act
79 Prophecy, part 4

83 Big name in games
85 Mer makeup
87 Riveter of song
89 Some wait for this
90 Cooperative interaction
93 Hundred smackers
95 Halfhearted
98 Charisse of "Silk Stockings"
100 Laszlo player in "Casablanca"
101 Kin's partner
102 Child's play
103 Grape brandy
105 Kind of trip
107 Pretense
108 Prophecy, part 5
114 Salad topper
115 Where suits are pressed
116 Laundry woe
117 Prophecy, part 6
126 Split
127 Memorable 1995 hurricane
128 Buffoon
129 Half and half
130 Famous redhead
132 Make sense
135 Poker challenge
138 Shade
141 End of the prophecy
145 Whip
146 Bête noire
147 Correction, of sorts
148 "Grand" hotels
149 Well-worn
150 Biased

DOWN

1 Yielding
2 Enthusiastic
3 Moon shade
4 Make way?
5 Architect ___ vander Rohe
6 Literary olios

7 "___ Kelly" (Jagger film)
8 Vinegar radical
9 Item of interest
10 Mrs. Alfred Hitchcock
11 Short orders
12 "Wonderful!"
13 Film rating org.
14 Spot of wine?
15 Missouri town near the George Washington Carver National Monument
16 "Lyin' Eyes" singers
17 "Awesome!"
18 Like some votes
19 Most festive
20 Wall Street analysts' concern
21 Letter getter
26 Cameo carvings
27 Red or Card, for short
33 Geared down, perhaps
35 Crusty ones
38 Had a heart but used a club?
39 Some trains
40 Brit. award
41 8 1/2" × 11" size: Abbr.
42 It's often served at home
43 Two-toned treat
44 Savage
45 Plaster of paris
46 Fotomat abbr.
47 "Love thy neighbor" is one
51 Speedily
52 Admitted
53 Make up one's mind
54 Detached
55 Hole in the wall?
56 Unrivaled

57 The first Mrs. Copperfield
58 "E-w-w-w!"
63 Code breaker
65 Here and there?
66 11-Down extra
68 Very early
70 Old car with a 389 engine
71 Senator who made the rounds
74 "¡" lid
76 "For ___ sow . . ."
79 Model Cheryl
80 Cool, once
81 Violinist Paganini
82 Operative
84 Tennyson's "___ and Enid"
85 Theologian who opposed Martin Luther
86 "Oh, right!"
88 Wishing spot
90 Excluding
91 Tomorrow's woman
92 Giant gains: Abbr.
94 Mary Tyler Moore catch phrase on "The Dick Van Dyke Show"
96 Elaborate Japanese porcelain
97 Lifeboat support
99 Snuggery
102 Clairvoyants
104 Soothsay
106 Unified whole
109 Venus's home
110 Shavetails: Abbr.
111 Berlin-to-Cologne dir.
112 Problem of the middle ages?
113 "___ geht's?"
117 Something to catch or save
118 Unrefined

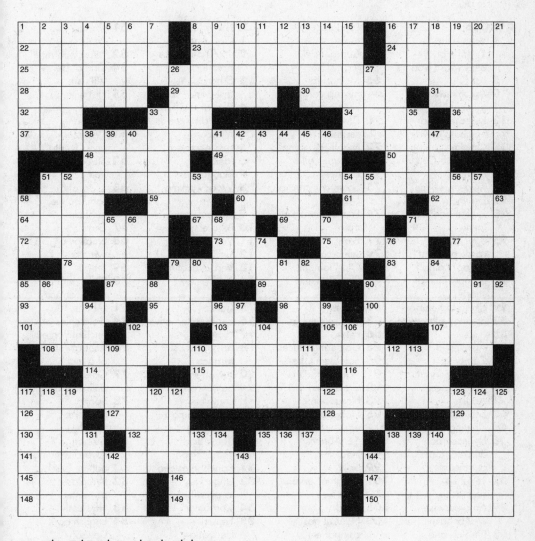

by Ed Early and Bob Klahn

119 "Peer Gynt" dancer
120 Fake fanfare
121 Dracula's mother-in-law?
122 Mutually fee-free
123 O.B.E., for one
124 Performance extension
125 Thatched
131 Powwow
133 Wrist attachment
134 Swamp thing
135 "___ hollers . . ."
136 Rubber Duck, for one
137 Baïonnette, e.g.
138 Prowling Wolfe
139 River to the Caspian
140 "Now I see!"
142 It goes to extremes
143 Polo Grounds legend
144 "___ Ramsey" (70's western)

SEEING DOUBLE

ACROSS

1 Where the 1986 World Series was won
5 Lot
9 Automotive pioneer
13 Prepare to go home, in a way
19 Onetime America's Cup champ
21 Kind of service
22 List ender
23 Coffee addict's meal?
25 Special correspondent
26 "Soap" spinoff
27 Humpty Dumpty short?
29 Like ghost stories
33 Saying nothing
35 Nets
36 Awakened
37 Computer program input
41 Ticket place: Abbr.
42 Sch. subject
45 Plowing woe
46 Hydrocarbon derived from petroleum
47 1962 NASA success
49 An otherwise well-behaved liar?
53 One-on-one sport
55 Chanel fragrance
56 "___ precaution . . ."
57 "Voices Carry" vocalist Mann
58 90's actor Epps
59 Luke's "90210" role
60 Panay seaport with a repetitive name
62 Landscaper's tool
64 Cupronickel, e.g.
65 Method for mixing cards, Illinois-style?
70 Divided into sections
72 Highflier's home?
73 Oceanus and brothers
75 Some construction beams
76 Part of a wagon train
77 Profit
79 Jump causer
81 Old "Tonight Show" theme writer
82 Grade
83 Tot's plaything?
86 Fumes
88 Gathering places
90 Sale item label
91 Wife, with "the"
92 Crew need
93 No-goodnik
95 Nobel or Celsius, e.g.
96 ___ Ababa
98 Had
99 Sells
101 What to serve stew in?
105 Hard
108 Natural gas component
109 Ice cream as still life?
115 Passes
116 Perfectly healthy, to the Army
117 Person who cracks a whip
118 Can't stand
119 Kind of home or room
120 Russian river
121 Tax

DOWN

1 Gal of song
2 1970's Chinese premier
3 Erhard's discipline
4 Part of a toll-free long-distance number
5 Less exposed
6 Identical
7 Haughtiness
8 Woodworking groove
9 Control
10 Blockers, e.g.
11 Vestige
12 Twilled fabric
13 Verbal dueling
14 God, with "the"
15 Cords
16 Purina alternative
17 "Later!"
18 Brickmaker's furnace
20 Jewish teacher
24 Sentence completer
28 Swiveling part
29 Family head
30 Some Bach compositions
31 Ranch infestation?
32 Underway to over there
34 Consumer
38 French clergyman
39 Bassoon, basically
40 Was overrun
42 Yeast, fruit and nuts?
43 Tree with pods
44 "The Gift of the Magi" feature
48 Monster in the Strait of Messina
50 Scottish landowners
51 Thread: Prefix
52 "___ cloud nine!"
54 One of Henry VIII's six
58 Flirt with, maybe
59 Less sane
61 "Wozzeck" and "Jenufa"
62 St. Patrick's home
63 ___ gratia
66 Land on the Rubicon
67 Guys
68 Smallpox symptom
69 Let go
70 Suffix with endo- or proto-
71 Li'l one
74 Gold coins of ancient Rome
76 Central vein of a leaf
77 One of a ballroom couple
78 Sport ___ (trucklike vehicles)
80 O. Henry Award-winning author Tillie ___
82 Whiplash preventer
83 Flawlessly
84 English poet Dowson
85 Cuss (out)
87 Marmots and such
89 Savers by profession
94 Had too much of
95 "What ___ thou?"
96 Swiftly
97 Deep, unnatural sleep

by Dave Tuller

100 Jean Renoir film heroine
101 Basis
102 ___ Reader (eclectic magazine)
103 Great, in slang
104 Dwindle
106 Rossini subject
107 Singer Adams
110 Basketball Hall-of-Famer Holman
111 Down
112 Somewhat exotic meat
113 Abbr. after a general's name, maybe
114 Aim

ACROSS

1 Rum-soaked cake
5 Tall, slender hound
11 Practical joke
15 Bleached
19 12th-century poet
20 Neckwear accessory
21 Uzbek sea
22 Fashion house ___-Picone
23 "At 9 A.M. breakfast will be supplied by ___"
25 Prohibit
27 Mastic, for one
28 "At 11 A.M. ___ will speak"
30 Comics sound
31 Unusually smart
34 First name in TV talk
35 Like R. L. Stine stories
36 "At 1 P.M. ___ will sing . . ."
39 Govt. property org.
40 River near Chantilly
41 O'Donnell and Perez
42 ". . . a tune from one of their ___"
48 Modern office staples
49 Jackson and Leigh
50 Handle a joystick
51 In post-career mode: Abbr.
52 Dance invitation response
53 Axis Powers, once
54 Jamaican sect member
56 "At 3 P.M. President Bush will ___ . . ."

61 First name among sopranos
62 The less-used end
63 Nonexistent
64 Key of Mendelssohn's Symphony No. 3
66 Kind of alcohol
67 ". . . on the subject of ___"
74 Initiated, legally
76 Europe/Asia dividers
77 Actress Suzanne
78 Ambient music pioneer
79 Mount Vernon, e.g.
81 Wristbone-related
82 Abbr. on a Mayberry envelope
85 "At 5 P.M. the Philatelic Society will discuss some ___"
87 Knot-tying place
88 Actress Ward
89 Hosts
90 "And at 7 P.M. there'll be a showing of the 60's film ___ . . ."
92 Snail trail
95 Slick, so to speak
98 Some pops: Abbr.
99 Wage news
100 ". . . starring ___ . . ."
103 Goes limp
104 Call to action
105 ". . . unless ___"
110 Grouper grabbers
111 Numerous
112 Dario Fo forte
113 Infamous Roman
114 Cobbler's need
115 Places for coats
116 Lively intelligence
117 Jersey Standard's other name

DOWN

1 Conk
2 Without form
3 Without foundation
4 Gallery event
5 British gun
6 It can be fresh or hot
7 Singer Peggy
8 Put ___ fight
9 Brick baker
10 Dr. Scholl products
11 I love: Fr.
12 Ball partner
13 City on the Ganges
14 Basic: Abbr.
15 Human-powered taxi
16 Province of Spain
17 Tongue-lasher?
18 Access
24 Ticket
26 Slangy tag-team member
29 TV dog
30 Boarding place
31 Sorry individual
32 Barcelona buck
33 Colorful spiral seashell
37 Mary of Peter, Paul and Mary
38 My, to Mimi
39 Lead pumper
42 [see other side]
43 Collins juice
44 Quite a while
45 Bearish
46 Underground systems
47 Fire escape route
49 Jupiter
50 "___, the heavens were opened": Matt. 3:16
52 Glove fabric
53 Film changes

55 Sheriff Lobo portrayer
56 Wound with sound
57 He's a weasel
58 Flatten
59 Talus area
60 Loss-prevention device
65 Blackbird
68 1984 Peace Nobelist
69 "Dies ___"
70 Familiars, often
71 Writer Singer and inventor Singer
72 Apathy
73 Drives forward
75 Prepare to land
80 Subj. of 60's protest
81 He helped topple Batista
82 Slaps a new head on
83 Dentists' kids, probably
84 Have the guts
86 Prodigious
87 Shift
88 Like some triangles
90 Dam agcy.
91 Hockey's Lindros
92 Hollywood dive?
93 Ostracized one
94 Ready to spit
95 Caterpillar hairs
96 Via
97 Case workers: Abbr.
101 Summer getaway, perhaps
102 School orgs.
103 Big letters in public broadcasting
106 Race car sponsor
107 Columbus, for one: Abbr.
108 Christina's dad
109 Prelude to a hickey

by Merl Reagle

ACROSS

1 Some calisthenics
7 Hardly stars
14 Promote
20 Avid
21 Japanese art of flower arranging
22 Take away
23 Gave in church
24 Indexed early man?
26 Ancient porch
27 "___ of troubles": Hamlet
29 Secret devices
30 It may lead to a strike
31 Twisted person
33 Some campers
34 Wall Street worker
36 Reply to "Is it Mr. or Professor Chomsky?"
40 Together
41 Hill climber
42 Like fabric by the yard
43 How some people seem to know
45 Old despot
48 Hugs
50 Staten Island Ferry litter?
55 Enterprise log signature
56 Toast for the holidays
58 Long time
59 Its cap. is Charleston
60 Showed, with "out"
63 Kind of test
64 They battle the Indians
66 Reply to "How many senators are there, child?"
70 Big name in computers
73 Friction easer
74 Wire
77 One of the Whitneys
78 From ___ Z
79 Oxford university since 1844
82 Part
84 Molly Pitcher, for example?
87 Sang
89 Indochine locale
90 East, in Essen
91 Electronic snoop
94 Words with word or way
95 Low voice
98 What the overheated passengers called the airline?
100 Nightclub charge
103 Line up well
105 Static
106 Brews
107 Site for Seurats
109 Chairs for prayers?
110 Answer, in brief
114 Question about a flashlight that lacks batteries?
117 Precisely
119 Sharp as a tack
120 "I like that!"
121 Family split?
122 Like the other evil
123 Some kids' bedtime reading
124 Nike rival

DOWN

1 NCO club members
2 Vacate
3 "For ___ us a child . . ."
4 Shocked
5 Common article
6 Some recyclables
7 "Great shot!"
8 Tex. neighbor
9 School org.
10 F.B.I. sting of the late 70's
11 Wall builder
12 Author Bagnold and others
13 Sometimes cracked container
14 City whose name is Spanish for "ash tree"
15 Library ref.
16 Least of all
17 TV debut of 1/14/52
18 "Luann" cartoonist Greg ___
19 Held another session
25 Portfolio contents, for short
28 "The ___ the limit!"
32 Goes to bat
33 Some pointers
35 Wave catchers
36 Moolah
37 In the dark
38 "Wheel of Fortune" songstress, 1952
39 Has
40 Abbr. in car ads
43 Sizing up
44 Like some deities
46 ". . . ___ forgive our debtors"
47 Go crazy
49 "Bottoms up!"
51 Walked awkwardly
52 Bloomsbury group member
53 "The Grapes of Wrath" family
54 More, in Monterrey
56 Continued
57 Sum (up)
61 80's TV adventure
62 Full chorus, in music
65 The first one opened in Detroit in 1962
67 Occupies quarters
68 Israeli city on the Gulf of Aqaba
69 Some radios
70 Bunny boss, briefly
71 Director Kazan
72 Pate toppers
75 Was admitted to
76 "Maria ___" (1933 song)
80 1984 skiing gold medalist
81 "If ___ be so bold . . ."
83 Cracker cheese
85 China rose, e.g.
86 Infantile remark
87 Make an impression
88 Dadaist collection
92 Modern mall features
93 Feel in one's bones
96 Fort ___ (where Billy the Kid was gunned down)
97 Dirty stuff
98 Mishandle
99 Bubble
100 Taj ___
101 Admission of defeat
102 Tiny amphibians
103 "___ coffee?"
104 Babe and Baby
108 Like workhorses
109 Jokes (around)
111 Pin, in a way
112 Clinton denial
113 Look-see
115 Got into a jam?
116 Seine contents
118 Full of: Suffix

by Manny Nosowsky

69 MIDTERMS

ACROSS

1 Heart monitor sound
4 Lizards, old-style
8 "Be that as __ . . ."
13 Befuddled
18 Genesis brother
20 Grandson of Methuselah
21 Horde
22 Does some exercises
23 Retaliatory tactics
26 PC fixers
27 One of a comical pair
28 Undercover types
29 Ground
31 Rap sheet letters
32 Engineer
34 Lunch order
35 Put away
37 Hot times abroad
38 Words of support
39 Clinton and Bush, e.g.
40 Jerk
42 D.C. toiler
43 __-Foy, city near Québec
44 Strains in the winter?
45 Having more leeway
46 Iran or Iraq vis-à-vis OPEC
52 Store stock: Abbr.
53 Myopic Mr.
56 Mail-order specification
57 Minneapolis suburb
59 Hue and cry
61 Columbian vessel
64 Certain pass
67 Took for oneself
69 Old airline name
71 Ball participant
73 Attached, in a way
75 Gulf of Aden country
77 It has a lot to offer
78 Cape town
79 Subject of Form 1040, line 15a
81 Quake
82 Novel ending
85 Shoot-'em-up
90 Draw up, as cloth
92 Reveals, poetically
93 First mistake
94 W.W. II agcy.
97 "On the Rebound" pianist Floyd
99 Ward of "My Fellow Americans"
100 Lug
102 Cut, old-style
103 Single-celled organism
104 Kind of phenomena
105 It's read regularly
107 "As Time Goes By" singer in "Casablanca"
108 Cartoonist Wilson
110 Elvis's middle name
111 City SSE of Gainesville
112 Pang
114 Inventor's goal
117 Outré
118 Ohio natives
119 Annina in "Der Rosenkavalier"
120 Ratio of AB to BC, say
121 All in __ work
122 Aquarium denizen
123 Boardroom bigwigs
124 Some E.R. cases

DOWN

1 Flatters
2 Cut off
3 "If elected I will not serve" candidate of 1968
4 Copenhagen-to-Riga dir.
5 Popular retirement destination
6 Glazed fabric
7 Polishes
8 Roadblock requests
9 More than loyal
10 Aesop's foible?
11 Heads off
12 Recently: Abbr.
13 Decree
14 Movie projection?
15 Revulsed
16 Elevates
17 Blockhead
19 Parts of a curriculum
24 Hole opener
25 Anticipatory question
30 Chop
33 Pro __
36 Pound sound
39 Common street name
41 Dominion ended by Francis II: Abbr.
43 Shutterbug
44 Delirium
46 Storage of a kind
47 Hint
48 Basso Pinza
49 __ canto
50 Ijsselmeer Dam site
51 Actress Tushingham and others
53 Year in the papacy of Innocent III
54 Like a bump on __
55 Plymouth poky
58 Calls home, as a tree
60 Made a new hole
62 Menlo park monogram
63 Hosts
65 A6 manufacturer
66 "Fantasy Island" props
68 Destructive 1964 Florida hurricane
70 "The Silent Clowns" author
72 Type of 46-Down
74 __ grata
76 "Coming Home" subject, briefly
80 Slowed musical passage
82 "Go back!" on a PC
83 Clobbered
84 Rum-based liqueur
86 Argues vehemently
87 Cause for a magnifying glass
88 Social
89 Contender
91 Graycoat
94 Where Algonquin Park is
95 Approach the end of an ocean trip
96 Brightly colored attire
98 Piano piece
99 Field
100 Takeoff locale
101 "Becket" actor, 1964

by Rich Norris

ACROSS

1 Instrument superseded by the viol
6 W.W. I Allied plane
10 Switch's partner
14 Unappetizing fare
18 Dangerous strain
19 "I understand!"
20 Put __ question
21 Bagpipe part
22 Primitive Indian?
24 Former White House nickname
25 Rebelled
26 Not happy with
27 Words before "about"
29 Indian comic strip character?
31 Take a powder
33 Country name
35 "Carousel" choreographer
36 Where the Knicks play: Abbr.
39 PC menu selection
40 Simmons rival
42 Ending with iron or tin
43 Stopover for young Indians?
46 Hydroplane part
48 Brewery fixture
51 Anderson of sitcoms
52 C in a C scale, e.g.
54 What the Indian said after taking out a car loan?
57 Some computer program sequences
59 Bound collection
61 "The Capeman" composer
62 Kind of bank

63 Tot's cry
64 It bollixes up the machinery
66 Neighed
68 Indian's interpretation of Robert Browning?
73 In condensed format
76 "Well done!" in Italy
77 Vintner's prefix
80 One of L.B.J.'s beagles
81 Make a new connection with
83 Rest stop lineup
86 Jordan dropped it in 1949
88 Sound effects in an Indian haunted house?
91 Metronome settings
93 Dietary, in ads
94 It's sometimes "junk"
95 __ one's heels
97 Indian weatherman's forecast?
99 Echo
102 Advantage
104 Current: Prefix
105 Trainer's workplace, perhaps
106 Paint remover component
109 Give off intense light
110 "__ Thief" (1950 movie)
112 Indian's "Well, sorr-r-rry!"?
114 Detriment
116 Citroën model name
120 He caught his adversary's ear

121 Often underreported income
123 What the Indian said after his son's road test?
125 Does a warm-up (for)
126 "Biscuit" introduced in 1912
127 Jazz singer Jones
128 "The Family Circus" cartoonist
129 "Tom Thumb" star Tamblyn
130 Downright blue
131 It may be common
132 Bridge seats

DOWN

1 RCA products: Abbr.
2 River through Aragón
3 Yahoo
4 Cary of "The Princess Bride"
5 Former W.B.C. lightweight champion
6 Flag
7 Mekong River capital
8 ". . . and shall bring forth __": Matt.
9 Drive participants
10 Action at Christie's
11 Lorelei Lee's creator
12 Restlessness
13 Puffed, as a reefer
14 Bronco's locale
15 Store come-on
16 Hoopster/actor
17 p., as in Plymouth
21 College major
23 Like a body in Newton's first law
28 Lagoon perimeter

30 Patch up
32 Some choristers
34 "Road" film destination
36 Weigh, with "over"
37 Urban playing site
38 Salami choice
41 Turning about the vertical
44 "Fantasia" dancers
45 Loyal subject
47 Language of India
49 Roy Rogers, né Leonard __
50 Initiated, with "off"
53 West Indies native
55 Florida city, informally
56 Disentangle
58 Husband of Ops, in myth
60 They often accompany ejections
65 Precept
67 Channel swimmer Gertrude
69 It's found in sticks
70 Kind of kitchen
71 South American stamp word
72 Temple of Zeus site
73 One who takes orders
74 Sleek, in car lingo
75 Some wimple wearers
78 Babes in the woods
79 Bunk position
82 Black and white cartoon character
84 Like a jam

by Fred Piscop

85 He notched 363 victories
87 Big name in games
89 Bibliophilic data
90 Long story
92 Martian feature
96 "Oh, go on!"
98 Cornmeal slab

100 High times?
101 Hartebeest kin
103 Female fowl
106 New York "Place" name
107 South American rodent
108 Hail
111 Lost

113 Goo
115 ___-tiller
117 "Stupid ___ stupid does"
118 Garment slit
119 Cool drinks
122 "Old" country
124 Author Fleming

71

POETIC INJUSTICE

ACROSS

1 Displaces
6 Atomic
12 Lowly ones
17 Portuguese city
19 Batting a thousand
21 Mercury: Sable:: Ford: ___
23 Poet's outlook on life?
25 Fighting force
26 Good earth
27 Grab
28 Poet's favorite 1972 hit?
30 Objective
32 Many people sit around it
34 With 68-Down, "Fame" actress
35 Shakespearean couplet description?
41 Did derbies
42 Derbies
43 Roar of the crowd
44 Ebon
47 What one gets reading poetry?
52 Pen
55 Iranian city
56 General assemblies
57 Meal starter
59 Don't waste
60 Sans nuts, e.g.
62 "Taras Bulba" author
65 Tamper-resistant
66 Result of poetic license?
70 Crows
71 Stand for Steen
72 "Eleni" director Peter
73 Too hot for tots
74 "Brain Trust" Prez
75 Bats
77 Hi-fi buys

80 Substance in soaps
82 What a disaffected Japanese poet might become?
87 Outdated poet suffix
88 Tel. listing abbr.
90 Kyrgyzstan's ___ Mountains
91 Certain vertebrae
92 Opinion of Keats poetry?
98 Some "Aïda" singers
101 Labor activist Chavez
102 Forum wear
103 Talk about Tennyson poems?
105 Hose hue
107 "Hard Lines" poet
111 Correction section
112 Conclusion of many a poet?
116 Emmy-winning Rob
117 Arabs, Hebrews, etc.
118 Hitches
119 She's married . . . with niños
120 Contend, colloquially
121 Designer Simpson

DOWN

1 More than simmer
2 Machinating
3 Provincial capital in the Dominican Republic
4 Vow taker
5 Jeff's "77 Sunset Strip" partner
6 Kinetic art form
7 "The Gondoliers" nurse
8 Pew locale

9 Suffix akin to -ity
10 Crag
11 Fictional Dinsmore and Venner
12 Lance
13 Pesky insect
14 Unconfirmed reports
15 Body build
16 Khartoum's country
18 Merlin of football and TV
20 Roof type
22 All there
24 Old-timer, of sorts
29 Xylophone striker
31 Senator of 1967 censure
32 High: Prefix
33 Flatten, in Britain
35 Babylon's land
36 Perfume billed as "The forbidden fragrance"
37 Swindle
38 Next
39 Wild things
40 Poetic contraction
44 10,000,000 ergs
45 Krupp works site
46 Ticked (off)
48 Reaches over
49 Friend of Coleridge
50 Hankered
51 It's got ewe covered
53 Crinkly cloth
54 Springs
58 "___ can eat!"
60 Sacred poem
61 It's played with matches
63 Need to reimburse
64 "The Fisher King" director
65 Bacchus attendant
66 Filmdom's Robert and Alan

67 People
68 See 34-Across
69 Horse height measure
70 Open wide
74 Chevy Chase title role
76 Sooner migrant
77 Bats
78 Manx "Thanks!"
79 Abide
81 Cabbage collector, for short
83 "Ford ___ better idea" (old slogan)
84 Winged
85 "Odyssey" peak
86 Protected, in a way
89 Tailor's tool
92 St. John, e.g.
93 Joust contestant
94 Job preceder
95 Pointless
96 Venetian official, once
97 Give off
98 Stand at wakes
99 Relevant, to lawyers
100 Neighbor of Turkey
104 Give a hoot
105 Derby doings
106 Noble, in Nuremberg
108 Church projection
109 King of a Handel oratorio
110 Promotional overkill
113 Peruvian Sumac
114 Lead head?
115 Actress Long

by Cathy Millhauser

72

WHAT A NICE PICNIC!

ACROSS

1 Backside
5 Chaff
10 Fluff up
15 Alum, for one
19 First name in daredeviltry
20 Fixed the pilot
21 Mix, in a way
22 Mixed bag
23 Part of a girl's magazine dealing with makeup?
25 Attempt to irritate?
27 Kind of sauce: Var.
28 Treasure State capital
30 Straight
31 Sing in a full, happy voice
33 Await judgment
34 Fowl place
35 Tops in quality
38 On the horizon
40 Goldbrick
44 Maker of the game Pong
45 Cinematographer Nykvist
46 Got up
48 1969 Peace Prize grp.
49 "___ Bell" (Stephen Foster song)
50 Go parasailing
51 Has a bug
52 E.T.S. offering
53 Connecticut Bulldog
54 Sleeves of a sports jacket?
58 Milk, in combinations
59 Dorm companion
61 Former West African capital
62 Infer
63 Epitome of hardness

64 Garfield's middle name
65 Grow past the hour
66 Shampooing aftermath
68 Utter impulsively
69 Kitchen cloths
72 Beautiful Berry
73 Little one bypasses the altar?
75 Script ending
76 Audio effect
77 Appealing
78 Sale caveat
79 Winter Palace resident
80 Afore
81 Kitchen gadgets
83 Slide in sleet
84 Swell top
85 Religious knights
87 Eucharistic plate
89 Help for a mountaineer
90 "Phooey!"
91 Jam session feature
92 Used stickum
94 Put forward
97 Emulate Isamu Noguchi
99 Side by side
103 Grange lacrosse team?
105 Philly champion?
107 Member of the Winnebago nation
108 Like "The X-Files"
109 Stowe character
110 Court defense
111 Bryn ___ College
112 52-Across and the like
113 Electrical setup
114 Cap'n Hawks of "Show Boat"

DOWN

1 Cause for Chapter 11
2 Eye layer
3 Bugaboo
4 In a flap?
5 Timber problem
6 Force back
7 Pay stretcher
8 Something to heave
9 Increase the slope of
10 Random bits
11 Veldt sight
12 ___ breve
13 Helios, to the Romans
14 Mask features
15 Tone down
16 Succulent plant
17 Penn Station initials
18 "Hold the Line" rock group
24 Ankles
26 Rank
29 Gamboling spot
32 Washing
34 Directs a hoedown
35 Phony
36 Author Calvino
37 Country's border?
39 At this point
40 Hurts badly
41 Army dog?
42 Overjoy
43 Chopper part
45 Out of ___ (grouchy)
47 Pool shot
50 Protection against tampering
52 Devonshire dad
54 "Get ready for the camera!"
55 Collector's book
56 Sojourn
57 Small type

58 Backing for plasterwork
60 One of the Thomases
62 Krypton and xenon
64 Tattered Tom's creator
65 Fat or wax
66 Night cover
67 Button material
68 Bunches of bits
69 Plying with pills
70 Understand
71 Mattress brand
73 Sounds of contentment
74 Winnebago, e.g.
77 Vestibule item
79 Sideboard
81 Bow on the screen
82 Married people
83 Cork
84 1920 Colette novel
86 Go for
88 The lot
89 Tube, over here
91 Theater backdrop
93 Caruso portrayer
94 Bit of physics
95 ___ precedent
96 Cold powder
97 Antitoxins
98 Prefix with -com
100 Before long
101 Fax
102 Yarborough component, perhaps
104 O.A.S. member: Abbr.
106 Nada

by Richard Silvestri

73

CENTRAL FIGURES

ACROSS

1 Overhaul
7 Inge dog
12 Oysters Rockefeller ingredient
19 Cry of success
21 Gretzky was one
22 Dragon's land, in song
23 Soprano Gluck kidnapped by a fundamentalist group?
25 Raging
26 River to the Ohio
27 Actor Baldwin trapped in a heavenly phenomenon?
29 Telescope-maker ___ Clark
32 Green around the gills
34 "Mickey" singer Basil
35 Flees to a J.P.
36 Supermodel Evangelista stuck in a dead end?
39 Party giver's abbr.
41 Overcurious
42 Poster material
43 VCR adjuncts
45 "___-Kid" (1995 comedy)
48 Sign, slangily
49 Where Jekyll became Hyde
52 Actress Garr discovered at a statue site?
58 Reporter under Perry White
61 Aspen asset
62 A abroad
63 Davy Jones's domain
64 Cowboy, at times
66 Remnant
68 Queequeg's captain
69 Actor Williams found in a 17th-century poem?
75 Near-miss exclamation
76 Casa chamber
77 "Mr. Clemens and Mark Twain" author Justin
78 Spitchcock
79 Like new recruits
82 A&W alternative
84 Like a flu sufferer, often
88 Singer Cochran unearthed in the food pyramid?
91 Gift for a haole
92 Aladdin's monkey
93 Consumer Reports employee
94 Years on end
96 Race with gates
99 "The Statue" actress Virna
102 Claim on an orange juice carton
105 Witticist Bombeck caught in a newspaper feature?
108 Strapped
111 Hebrides island
113 Bygone carrier
114 Peace
115 Artist Warhol accosted by the British police?
118 Hersey hamlet
120 Bach work
121 Statesman Doria seen in an idealistic vision?
126 Pricey homes
127 Bolshevism founder
128 Bradshaw was one
129 Calorie-crammed course
130 High-fives
131 Clinkers

DOWN

1 Periphery
2 First name in screwball comedy
3 Different sp.
4 Inflexible
5 Dillon of "A Christmas Story"
6 Arizona Indian
7 ___ Canals
8 "Java" trumpeter
9 "The Mill on the Floss" writer
10 Tip sheet buyer
11 Indo-Europeans
12 Part of a brake
13 Puerto Rican port
14 Totally
15 Avis alternative
16 City known in ancient times as Beroea
17 Discontinues
18 Reason for excommunication
20 Sri Lankan language
24 TV angel Munroe
28 "Les Misérables," e.g.
29 Simmering
30 Treeless tract
31 Singer Carr
33 Tennis do-over
37 Blazing
38 Actor Montand
40 Major fish exporter
44 "The Dunwich Horror" star
46 "Ladders to Fire" novelist
47 Philosopher Lao-___
50 Added stipulations
51 Contacts, modern-style
53 Holding a grudge
54 Fine-tune
55 "Hard Road to Glory" author
56 Uncluttered
57 Apply, as ointment
59 CNN anchor Bernard
60 100 qintars
65 Check the figures
67 Distort
68 Word on monuments
69 1966 Beatles concert site
70 Alternative to high water
71 ___ Mountains, part of the Tien Shan range
72 Ill-fated German admiral
73 Getting on in years
74 Actress Grey
75 It's catching
79 Retrovirus component
80 Masquerade
81 Display dolor
83 Lay up
85 Film actor Albert
86 Torpedo vessel
87 Short and stout
89 Brief operatic solos
90 Stonehenge worshiper
95 Lepidopterist's accessory
97 Hellespont victim
98 Gunsmith

by Frank Longo

ANAGRAMMATIC DISCLOSURES

ACROSS

1 Purloin a sirloin?
7 Not for sure
13 Hangers around the house
19 Necessitate
20 ___ de Balzac
21 Something too easily broken
22 Overdo the diet
23 Director Martin Scorsese's anagrammatic claim
25 Where a pupil sits
26 Recess for a joint
28 Emmy-winning Daly
29 Rotten egg
30 Jockey Eddie Arcaro's anagrammatic motto
32 Hors d'oeuvre cheese
33 Cartoon skunk Le Pew
34 Masthead figs.
35 Queen's servants
36 King of comedy
37 Hole-making bug
38 Fine subjects
39 Ulysses S. Grant's anagrammatic advice regarding hangovers
43 Protectors from splats
46 Cried "Yee-haw!"
47 Poetic preposition
48 A point in Mexico
49 Song-and-dance shows
50 Spree
51 Sternward
54 Artist Piet Mondrian's anagrammatic epigram
57 Capitalist?

59 Congress-thwarting move
60 Author ___ Mae Brown
61 Jackknife, e.g.
62 Farm prefix
63 Toothless
65 Kevin Costner's anagrammatic lament about his videos
69 What Leary tripped on
70 Wheel track
71 Sunshine in Québec
72 Babe Ruth, on the Yankees
73 Intent
74 Without rocks
75 Sneaker bottoms
76 Carmen Miranda's anagrammatic ballroom tip
80 What an ostiary guards
81 Oxlike antelope
82 Footless critter
83 Stuff in a muffin
84 Slugger's stat
87 Greet with old-fashioned etiquette
88 Bath's county
89 Len Deighton's anagrammatic avowal on writing
93 Beatles' "___ Loser"
94 MacGraw's namesakes
95 Any spider
96 Glaciated mountain peak
97 Poet Denise Levertov's anagrammatic urging
100 Tasselly hem
102 Blow up

103 Let
104 Melt down, as fat
105 "Sophie's Choice" author
106 Helmet plumes
107 Lots and lots

DOWN

1 Have a hearth
2 Virgin
3 Domestic flights
4 Ankles
5 Ullmann of moviedom
6 Classic work of Euclid
7 Trilled calls
8 Plantain lily
9 Bit of clowning
10 Whence the word "troll"
11 Canadian prairie tribe
12 Aye-aye
13 Many a lecturer
14 Setting for "Don Pasquale"
15 Org. with a much-quoted journal
16 Lobster part
17 Coop flier
18 Rustic sow-and-sows?
21 Like a Nosy Parker
24 Maroon
27 Mudder fodder
31 Shade
32 B. B.'s bag
33 Prepare to be shot
36 Quaker in the woods
37 Carrier in a canal
38 Auteur's order
39 Bara the "vamp"
40 Gad about
41 "It's ___ move"
42 Get a rise out of?
43 Whine pathetically

44 Urban transports
45 Emulated Demosthenes
46 Composed
50 Rock's Bon ___
51 Silky goat
52 Like fast marches
53 Tots' wheels, for short
55 Psychic shock
56 Oven ___
57 School door sign
58 Brit's accented reply
61 Rational faith in God
64 Put to the proof
65 Without letup
66 "Pure ___" (1994 jazz album)
67 Drive out of one's lane
68 Buff, so to speak
71 Grafting bud
73 Teen-y problem
74 Tariff
75 Alternately
76 Mocks
77 Foodstuff
78 How some country stars sing
79 Product of erosion
80 Trio abroad
83 Runs colorfully
84 Name in a Beach Boys title
85 In old show biz, he was no dummy
86 Forward line players, in soccer
88 Set straight
89 Singer Cara
90 Cupid's stock

by Emily Cox and Henry Rathvon

91 Start
92 Like whose eyes, in a Ben Jonson verse?
94 Of planes and flying
95 Say it's so
98 Alternate: Abbr.
99 Mythical monster
101 Abbr. on a boombox

ACROSS
1 Rikki-Tikki-___
5 1990's group Salt-N-___
9 Headpiece?
13 Off
18 February 1991 headline
20 Jordanian tongue
22 Like un ami to une amie
23 ___ Foundation (leading philanthropic organization)
24 Mrs. Yeltsin
25 Join for a ride
26 60's–70's German chancellor
27 Charleson of "Chariots of Fire"
29 Highway caution
31 Ushered (in)
32 Southern Mexican
36 Kind of plan
37 Suffix with room
38 Much-discussed 1991 film
40 Outlet type
43 Composer Bartók
44 Bar sounds
45 Rein
47 "Theogony" poet
51 Angle, in a way
55 Low tie
56 NASA seal
57 Happening
58 Cruise catcher
59 Settles
60 Hot shots
64 Govt. investigation grp.
65 Former TV host John
66 High riser
67 Milton's "Lycidas," for one
69 "Oh, sure!"
73 Dweller in Shiloh
75 Friendly questioning, in court
77 Religious leader ___ Muhammad
78 Treat
81 Clink
82 What that is, in a 1953 song
83 Skirts
84 Ancient land west of the Rhine
87 Author ___ Le Guin
88 Converted palace
89 Dance move
90 Axes
92 Communism battler, with "the"
93 Not a job for a claustrophobe
97 Inits. on a Soyuz rocket
101 1964 Streisand song
103 "She-Goat" artist
104 Home of Wheeler Air Force Base
105 Certain hammers
109 Ratio symbols
110 Decreaser?
112 Name after a name
113 Go's mate
115 Buzzers
118 Polo man?
119 Reagan adviser
120 Add up
121 Relevant
122 Fictional pirate
123 Squeezed (out)
124 Epitome of thinness

DOWN
1 Sound quality
2 Ham saver
3 Undeveloped
4 90–110, normally
5 Finish
6 Afr. nation
7 Little, in Lyon
8 Pope of 772
9 Role for Mia
10 Openings
11 1994 Peace Nobelist
12 "Spartacus" actress
13 It calls for a blessing
14 What some theaters won't do
15 Visored cap
16 A Walton
17 Flight
19 Like some numbers: Abbr.
21 Terrorist of renown
28 Do something
30 Line carrier
33 Netcom competitor
34 1797–98 to-do
35 Soft drink brand
39 Greetings
41 Information source
42 Site of Jesus' first miracle
43 Slows (down)
45 It's unpleasant to be in
46 Figurative powerhouse
47 Big name in book publishing
48 Jolliet's 1669 discovery
49 Expires
50 To begin with
52 "Casablanca" actor
53 As a team
54 N.B.A. stats
55 Endorse
57 Rock blaster
61 Kind of raise
62 1985 Nelligan title role
63 Some jewelry
66 Letter opener
68 Airfone corporation
70 Jewel
71 Nobleman
72 Certain Brooklyn-Manhattan train
74 Treasure-trove
76 "Make ___ good one"
77 They perform a balancing act
78 Bud
79 Acknowledge
80 "___ lost me"
84 Property receivers
85 Draw
86 Escape, in a way
87 Off-balance
89 Speaking block
91 His "E" was the same as J. R.'s
93 Deal (with)
94 Ardent cry
95 Fi lead
96 Message on a dirty car
97 Picnic staple
98 Harrier, for one
99 V.I.P.
100 Puckered
102 Downs spot
105 1993 Sugar Bowl winner, for short
106 "When I Was ___"
107 Way to get to N.Y.C.
108 Supporter of botany
111 Calls
114 Operation
116 Sturdy one
117 Small music-maker

by Robert H. Wolfe

ANSWERS

1

```
M A R C I A   L I L     W A C S   S P I N
A N O I N T   E D E R   O M A N   P O N E
D I D N T [BAT]A N E Y E   M I N A   A L T E
A L I C E   T O A D S   [BAT]T E R F R I E D
M E N O R A H   L E I F   Y A L E   C R I
    I C E   I N D U S     S E L E N E
[BAT]T L E M E N T S   E N A T E   U S S R
I R I D S   I O T A   M E R M A N
S I N S   D A N S E [BAT]O N R O U G E
T A N   C I N E   R A T A   S C R E A M
A L E M A N   S T I P E N D   H A S S A M
  S T I N G S   E A R N   E T A L   E R I
  S A B[BAT]I C A L   E S T H S   R O I L
    S Y S T E M   D O O R   S A U N A
S C A M   E L E N A   M O U N T[BAT]T E N
P A L A T E   D A C H E   S T R
A T E   V A S T   P R O P   T H I C K E T
T A K E A S T A[BAT]   O L L I E   C H O R E
I L S A   T I N A [BAT]M A N R E T U R N S
A P E S   O L G A   S E C O   D E T E S T
L A I T   N E O N   S E N   T R E A T S
```

2

```
S O F T G   R E S T E R   B R E T   A B A F T
O N E A L   E S K I M O   Y O Y O   N O B L Y
P U L L U P S T A K E S   A A R P   G R O A N
  S T E E L I E   I R I S H M E N   O Z O N E
    A G R   A T T A   O T R O
T R A D E I N S   P L A Y I T S T R A I G H T
R E L O A D   F E D   E R O I C A   R O I
A P L U S   C A R E S S   M P H   S C E N E
P L E B E   A T I P   P R I E S   P O U T E R
P E A L   Q U O D   P E E N S   B E T R A Y S
E T R E   U L N A   L E E K   B L E S T
D E S C   O K A Y B U D D Y D R A W   A F A R
  H O T E L   A M B I   A A R E   I R M A
S E C E D E D   A L E U T   M I N E   N E O N
P L A C E D   P R I S M   P A N E   I C E R S
R O C K S   S E M   P L E S S Y   T A B O O
I R A   F T R O O P   O A K   H E L I U M
G O O D B Y E M R C H I P S   S E A M L E S S
  V A I N   A I D E   U L T
S A Y O K   O P E N S E A S   F A C T O R Y
A D O R E   P A P A   A R T O F T H E D E A L
C I G A R   A C I D   T E E P E E   C E L L O
S N A K Y   D E C A   E D W A R D   H A Y E S
```

3

```
E L P A S O   █ T I E D U P █ S E T T E E
S O R B I C █ S E R P E N T █ A D O R E S
T W I C E T O L D T A L E S █ V I R I L E
E E N █ V A R Y █ █ C P A █ S A T A N █
█ █ T R A V E L E D T H R O U G H T I M E
█ A B E █ Y A R █ I T S M E █ O D O R
O B E S E █ █ R A T █ H U M █ C R A W L
R A S H A D █ A S T E P █ A R I A D N E
I L K █ N O D S █ S L A M █ O A T █
E D I T █ T A K E S T O T A S K █ O V E R
N E M O █ T I C T A C T O E █ R I D E
T R O N █ T E N T I M E S T E N █ A S A P
█ █ Y E W █ G O N E █ S P A R █ A M O
L A S T C A R █ G N O M E █ Y E A G E R
E L I H U █ O N S █ T A O █ █ A T E S T
F A M E █ P O O C H █ T V S █ S L O █
T I P T O E T H R U T H E T U L I P S █
█ L I M E S █ O S E █ A G E S █ P E R
G E E G A W █ T O T E L L T H E T R U T H
A R S E N E █ A G O N I E S █ P I E R C E
P E T R I E █ T E N S E D █ S C A T H E
```

4

```
A T T A R █ C R A V A T █ A L A C A R T E
M E R L E █ S A L A M I █ V A G A R I E S
B R O A D W A Y F L O P █ O C A R I N A S
O R I N D A █ S A L E █ N E S T █
Y E S S E S █ █ A B I E █ E A M E S
█ █ R A C K E T A N D B A L L G A M E
A R P S █ T H E R E █ G U I D E █ A R A M
R I O T S █ I S A █ M E C C A S █ V I I I
U S U A L S █ E T T E █ E S P █ P E A L S
B E L G I A N Y O U T H S █ T A O █
A N T E N N A █ B A A █ E L L E S S E
█ █ G A S █ T A X I D E R M Y N E E D
S C A M S █ C P A █ A L E X █ S P A R T A
L O N E █ R E A R M S █ C U T █ S C R I M
A R E A █ A N I M A █ C O R K Y █ T A N S
K I N D O F T R A I N O R B O A T █
E N T E R █ C L O P █ B U R I A L
█ I S L E █ R I A L █ B R E N D A
O L D J O K E S █ A M E R I C A N I C O N
V O C A L I S T █ M A R I N O █ E N U R E
A N I S E T T E █ I N S E T S █ D E R N S
```

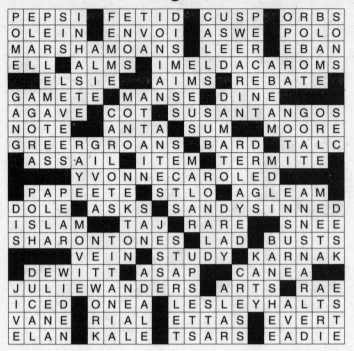

5

P	E	P	S	I		F	E	T	I	D		C	U	S	P		O	R	B	S
O	L	E	I	N		E	N	V	O	I		A	S	W	E		P	O	L	O
M	A	R	S	H	A	M	O	A	N	S		L	E	E	R		E	B	A	N
E	L	L		A	L	M	S		I	M	E	L	D	A	C	A	R	O	M	S
	E	L	S	I	E		A	I	M	S		R	E	B	A	T	E
G	A	M	E	T	E		M	A	N	S	E		D	I	N	E
A	G	A	V	E		C	O	T		S	U	S	A	N	T	A	N	G	O	S
N	O	T	E		A	N	T	A		S	U	M			M	O	O	R	E
G	R	E	E	R	G	R	O	A	N	S		B	A	R	D		T	A	L	C
	A	S	S	A	I	L		I	T	E	M		T	E	R	M	I	T	E
			Y	V	O	N	N	E	C	A	R	O	L	E	D
	P	A	P	E	E	T	E		S	T	L	O		A	G	L	E	A	M
D	O	L	E		A	S	K	S		S	A	N	D	Y	S	I	N	N	E	D
I	S	L	A	M		T	A	J		R	A	R	E		S	N	E	E
S	H	A	R	O	N	T	O	N	E	S		L	A	D		B	U	S	T	S
			V	E	I	N		S	T	U	D	Y		K	A	R	N	A	K
	D	E	W	I	T	T		A	S	A	P		C	A	N	E	A
J	U	L	I	E	W	A	N	D	E	R	S		A	R	T	S		R	A	E
I	C	E	D		O	N	E	A		L	E	S	L	E	Y	H	A	L	T	S
V	A	N	E		R	I	A	L		E	T	T	A	S		E	V	E	R	T
E	L	A	N		K	A	L	E		T	S	A	R	S		E	A	D	I	E

O	H	A	R	A		J	A	W	A	T		O	A	T	H		M	E	E	T
S	O	L	E	D		A	D	A	S	H		S	C	A	R		A	R	N	O
A	L	L	A	H		N	I	X	I	E		C	E	L	E	B	R	A	N	T
G	E	O	D	E		E	E	E		P	E	A	R	L		I	S	S	U	E
E	D	W	A	R	D	T	U	D	O	R	A	R	O	Y	A	L	H	E	I	R
		P	E	I			F	I	R		L	U	N	K
M	E	E	T	S	T	O	M	C	A	N	T	Y	A	P	O	O	R	L	A	D
O	D	S			T	A	O		C	H	E				K	I	L	O
B	Y	C	H	A	N	C	E	T	H	E	Y	S	W	A	P	R	O	L	E	S
	S	E	E	T	O		S	E	A			A	L	O	U		I	C	E
		S	T	E	N	T		E	N	G		G	L	I	N	T
D	I	S		A	N	N	A		D	O	E			L	U	I	G	I
E	D	W	A	R	D	W	I	T	H	T	O	M	S	S	U	P	P	O	R	T
E	L	A	N			H	A	H		M	E	L			B	O	A
R	E	G	A	I	N	S	R	U	L	E	B	Y	L	O	C	A	T	I	N	G
		N	A	T	E		O	P	E				O	N	A
T	H	E	G	R	E	A	T	S	E	A	L	O	F	E	N	G	L	A	N	D
E	A	G	R	E		M	A	T	S	U		X	I	V		O	L	L	I	E
S	T	E	A	M	P	I	P	E		P	A	I	N	E		R	I	A	T	A
L	I	S	P		O	N	E	A		E	L	D	E	R		A	S	T	E	R
A	N	T	E		M	A	S	K		R	E	E	D	S		S	H	E	R	E

```
  SARA   SAL   ODIST   CARBS
SHRUB   AGA   RESAW   OSHEA
TIESCORES   SPANISHHEEL
ARCH   FISHHOOKS   HECATE
GRAHAM     ONT   AURA
   OPERANTS   SENTENCED
LARUE   AGEE   CANDID   OLE
AMOR   SNARL   ALTON   ARTE
LES   ENGLISHHORN   TENOR
ASHTREE   ANNA   SHRINE
   HAIRDO   ERS   PATIOS
ELOPED   VETS   GUNSHIP
RIDES   HUSHHUSHING   HEE
AMER   DELTA   LEAST   SERA
TIS   CAREEN   CELT   OMNES
OTHERNESS   MENSSANA
   LOIS   BAR   MASHED
ETHICS   POLISHHAM   HERO
CRASHHELMET   OUTOFHAND
TOTHE   TUNER   ALT   LIVID
ONEAT   ASIDE   RAY   ATEE
```

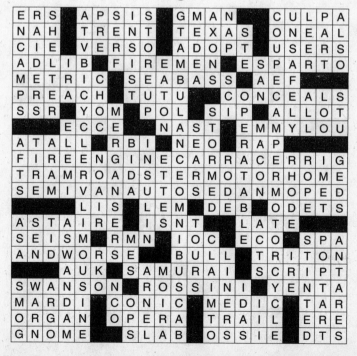

```
ERS   APSIS   GMAN   CULPA
NAH   TRENT   TEXAS   ONEAL
CIE   VERSO   ADOPT   USERS
ADLIB   FIREMEN   ESPARTO
METRIC   SEABASS   AEF
PREACH   TUTU   CONCEALS
SSR   YOM   POL   SIP   ALLOT
   ECCE   NAST   EMMYLOU
ATALL   RBI   NEO   RAP
FIREENGINECARRACERRIG
TRAMROADSTERMOTORHOME
SEMIVANAUTOSEDANMOPED
   LIS   LEM   DEB   ODETS
ASTAIRE   ISNT   LATE
SEISM   RMN   IOC   ECO   SPA
ANDWORSE   BULL   TRITON
   AUK   SAMURAI   SCRIPT
SWANSON   ROSSINI   YENTA
MARDI   CONIC   MEDIC   TAR
ORGAN   OPERA   TRAIL   ERE
GNOME   SLAB   OSSIE   DTS
```

```
  PRADO   BRAVADO   GRAHAM
TREMOR   RECITED   LATINO
SOFARIHAVENTMADEITFIT
UPSTAGED    NEO   RETAIL
     DIX   SWISS   ACT
SAILON   FLEET   AWL   DARK
PINE    SOAR    ALOU   AMON
IMPOSITIVEITCANBEDONE
RAU   OTOE   MACS   GARDE
OTTOMAN   SPACEK   GEISEL
    CELESTE   ONAGERS
SHEEHY   WISEST   UNITING
MARLO    ENTS    ASIA   NEA
AHNOWIVEGOTITTHISISIT
LAST   CATO   TROY   SEGO
LSTS   ENS   STEAM   SLATER
      API   SEAMY   ATO
  DEBRIS   CAT   OPERETTA
MERRYCHRISTMASEVERYON
REDOAK   COOLANT   INGRID
SPAWNS   ANNETTE   EASEL
```

```
SCATHE   MARSALA   SMEW
ARNHEM   CAROUSAL   APISH
WATERMOCCAPRIDE   MISSY
SWIT   ARCHIE   DEFENSES
OLGA   ILED   LBS   OBOLS
FEU   ASIT   MOO   BRAZO
FRANKCOVETOUSNESSATRA
   EARN   HUDSON    HUT
  MAPLE   THINMAN   GURGLE
MINT   CANTO   ETALIA
ENGULF   UNGLUES   LEVINS
KEENER   AUTRE    INGE
ORRERY   RIMSHOT   COOKS
NAG   DONATE   FALL
GLUTTONYDBADTHESAILOR
  LEONA   ROI   REEK   URE
  VALSE   DAB   GOLD   GRIN
FIRESALE   ARMIES   AKEE
ARISE   ENVYGAPORESLING
DETER   ATOMIZES   TRENTE
SOYS   HEXANES   HINGED
```

11

```
HOHUM  FANJETS  RUBITIN
AROSE  STEAMUP  INARAGE
WILMA  THERITEOFSPRING
HODAD  OED  SCALES  LIL
ALI  SPINES  ITER  STE
WENTAT  STREAMERS  EPIC
GULLET  INTERS  CLINT
SPANIEL  ACTON  DOINGS
PETEFOUNTAIN  ALONE
ORBS  SOW  NEWGATE  OTC
USA  MAITAI  SHAPES  CAR
TEY  LIVORNO  ENA  BENE
ELLEN  FLORALSPRAYS
METRES  CADRE  MARINAS
AXONS  CHACHI  FANONS
RPMS  POOLTABLE  TWEETS
LOW  RAUL  TIERRA  LAW
ONO  BASSOS  AMI  ADELA
WELLINTENTIONED  RAVEL
ENFORCE  MANNING  IRENE
STEALER  ENTENTE  DENTS
```

12

```
COULD  DACHA  OPERA  TBSP
OSTEO  ETHAN  PAPAL  HEIRS
ICIER  TBIRD  EROSE  AGGIE
LACKEDHANDSONEXPERIENCE
SRA  NERTS  BEVY  ESTEEM
COS  ISERE  BON  STDS
TRADEIN  STOL  FLOE
WASUNDERCAPITALIZED  PAM
APIECE  HALS  ALENE  ALAMO
STALE  CORY  SPEND  DROPIN
IAN  STEPS  COINAGE
RUBBEDPEOPLETHEWRONGWAY
ENRAGES  RIATA  HAM
SCOURS  FALLS  SAAB  TISCH
ELIDE  MATEO  AMIR  NICOLO
TEL  TALKEDMYSELFOUTOFIT
LIED  OILS  UNSNAPS
EMIL  LID  TRUST  ETC
SONATA  SEAT  ELSIE  BAH
QUITWHENPUSHCAMETOSHOVE
UNTIE  LOATH  ARECA  SINAI
EDINA  ALCOA  PARTY  ELGIN
SOAK  NOEND  ABYSS  STOLE
```

```
A G R A ■ S W A M I ■ G O N E R ■ S C A T
S L O B ■ S E W E R ■ A L A M O ■ T H R U
H O P E D R E A M S ■ L I V I A ■ R E I N
C R E T E ■ D I P ■ O V A L S ■ E L S E
A I R ■ B L Y T H E S P I R I T ■ A S T I
N A S S A U ■ S I L T ■ E R A ■ I M E A N
■ P R I G ■ S A R T R E ■ A S I A ■
T I D Y ■ G A P ■ N O R ■ T W A N G E R
R B I ■ D I S S E D H I L L A R Y ■ R C A
A E R I E ■ R Y N ■ S P O O K Y ■ D A L I
I R E N E ■ A C D C ■ S O L E ■ C U M I N
P I C K ■ O N H O L D ■ P I T ■ O O M P H
S A T ■ A L G O R E R H Y T H M S ■ A S A
E N L A R G E ■ F Y I ■ A A A ■ F R E T
■ Y W C A ■ O N S I T E ■ T U T U ■
E S T E S ■ T V A ■ N I P S ■ V E R B A L
T W O A ■ T H E B I G T I P P E R ■ I R A
H O Y T ■ E R R O L ■ S E E ■ S A S S Y
N O A H ■ S E I K O ■ S O C K S E S S E S
I S L E ■ T A C O S ■ A D I E U ■ K E N O
C H E R ■ S T E V E ■ G E E S E ■ S T E N
```

```
■ L O G E ■ M U S T S ■ S E W S ■ E L L A
T Y R O L ■ A B O I L ■ A L E C ■ F O I L
O C A L A ■ N O L T E ■ B A L I ■ F L E A
R E N D S ■ D A V I D G O L D F I E L D
N E G O T I A T E ■ F I T ■ S I N N ■
■ D I N T ■ D U R A N ■ U D A L L
D I R E C T E R ■ O L D G O L D S I D E S
I D E O ■ O D E U M ■ S E S A M E ■ I S T
K O L N ■ A T I P ■ S E R I ■ O N E S
E L I ■ B H U T A N I ■ E T C H
■ C A T O N A H O T G O L D R O O F
■ B U N S ■ O L E O O I L ■ A G A
N A G S ■ C E S T ■ N A N O ■ G R O G
E R A ■ O H A I R S ■ D O R I S ■ O G R E
H I Y O G O L D A W A Y ■ A N T E L O P E
I D E A L ■ E D E N S ■ D Y A D
■ K E Y S ■ E L O ■ P O W E R B O A T
■ G O L D A N D O L D L A C E ■ H E I N E
N O V A ■ L O A F ■ Y E N T L ■ A L L I N
A N E W ■ T O F F ■ N O D A L ■ R L E S S
P E N N ■ A P T S ■ E G A D S ■ T Y R E
```

15

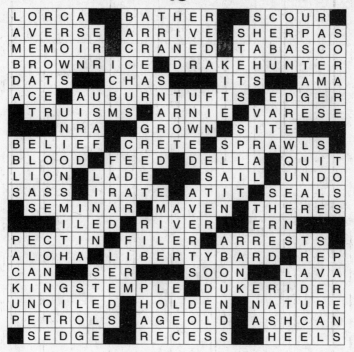

L	O	R	C	A			B	A	T	H	E	R			S	C	O	U	R	
A	V	E	R	S	E		A	R	R	I	V	E		S	H	E	R	P	A	S
M	E	M	O	I	R		C	R	A	N	E	D		T	A	B	A	S	C	O
B	R	O	W	N	R	I	C	E		D	R	A	K	E	H	U	N	T	E	R
D	A	T	S		C	H	A	S			I	T	S			A	M	A		
A	C	E		A	U	B	U	R	N	T	U	F	T	S		E	D	G	E	R
	T	R	U	I	S	M	S		A	R	N	I	E		V	A	R	E	S	E
		N	R	A		G	R	O	W	N		S	I	T	E					
B	E	L	I	E	F		C	R	E	T	E		S	P	R	A	W	L	S	
B	L	O	O	D		F	E	E	D		D	E	L	L	A		Q	U	I	T
L	I	O	N		L	A	D	E			S	A	I	L		U	N	D	O	
S	A	S	S		I	R	A	T	E		A	T	I	T		S	E	A	L	S
	S	E	M	I	N	A	R		M	A	V	E	N		T	H	E	R	E	S
			I	L	E	D		R	I	V	E	R		E	R	N				
P	E	C	T	I	N		F	I	L	E	R		A	R	R	E	S	T	S	
A	L	O	H	A		L	I	B	E	R	T	Y	B	A	R	D		R	E	P
C	A	N		S	E	R				S	O	O	N			L	A	V	A	
K	I	N	G	S	T	E	M	P	L	E		D	U	K	E	R	I	D	E	R
U	N	O	I	L	E	D		H	O	L	D	E	N		N	A	T	U	R	E
P	E	T	R	O	L	S		A	G	E	O	L	D		A	S	H	C	A	N
	S	E	D	G	E			R	E	C	E	S	S			H	E	E	L	S

16

P	L	A	C	I	D			S	C	U	S	I			U	L	U	L	A	T	E	
A	U	R	O	R	A		W	A	V	E	R		P	E	M	O	L	I	N	E
S	N	O	O	K	Y	O	O	K	U	M	S		B	A	B	Y	F	A	C	E
S	A	U	L		S	P	O	I	L		G	E	N	R	E		R	A	L	
A	T	S	I	X		I	N	N	A	M	O	R	A	T	A		S	A	S	E
D	I	E	O	F		N	E	G		E	R	A	T	O		C	H	E	E	R
O	C	S		I	B	I	D		A	N	D	Y	S		S	H	O	D	D	Y
			O	L	E	O		A	R	T	E		C	I	A	O				
S	O	T	H	E	R	N		D	E	A	R	H	E	A	R	T		V	O	W
P	H	R	A	S	E		O	V	A	L		A	R	F		S	T	I	L	E
U	B	E	R		T	U	B	E	S		G	R	I	E	F		A	N	D	A
N	O	N	E	T		T	O	N		C	A	P	E		R	I	N	G	E	R
K	Y	D		S	W	E	E	T	L	O	V	E		L	A	N	G	T	R	Y
		M	A	Y	S			A	M	E	R		U	N	D	O				
A	S	P	I	R	E		T	A	M	I	L		B	C	C	I		D	A	R
L	E	A	K	S		L	I	L	A	C		A	R	E		C	H	I	V	E
I	N	R	E		S	U	G	A	R	S	U	G	A	R		T	U	P	A	C
G	I	S		L	U	C	R	E			P	A	I	N	E		B	O	R	A
H	O	N	E	Y	P	I	E		L	I	T	T	L	E	D	A	R	L	I	N
T	R	I	P	L	E	T	S		E	T	H	E	L		A	P	I	E	C	E
	S	P	H	E	R	E	S		G	E	E	S	E		M	E	S	S	E	S

S	C	A	P	E		S	T	R	U	N	G	U	P		S	I	N	G	L	E
A	D	M	A	N		T	E	A	R	I	N	T	O		P	A	I	R	E	D
B	R	I	L	L	I	A	N	T	B	L	U	E	S	M	A	N	K	I	N	G
R	O	T	E		G	I	S	T		E	S	S	E	X			F	I	E
E	M	E	R	A	L	D		A	S	S			S	H	A	F	F	E	R
		M	I	O		B	I	T		K	A	I		A	L	L	E	N	S
A	U	T	O	M	O	B	I	L	E	J	O	C	K	E	Y	F	O	Y	T
B	S	A		I	S	L	A		L	U	R	K	E	R					
D	O	V	E	S		I	N	C	A	S	E		S	E	S	S	I	L	E
U	S	E	R		I	N	C	A		T	S	P		P	A	D	O	V	A
C	H	R	I	S	T	I	A	N	S	C	H	O	L	A	R	L	E	W	I	S
T	O	N	N	E	S		T	E	A		R	E	L	Y		A	B	C	S
	W	A	S	T	A	G	E		S	U	L	K	E	D		P	L	A	T	E
			A	T	E	A	S	E		R	E	E	L		L	E	T
	W	A	R	P	E	D	C	O	M	E	D	I	A	N	F	I	E	L	D	S
P	O	L	E	A	X		H	E	E		T	N	T		F	E	N		
R	O	T	A	T	E	S			G	O	T		R	O	S	T	E	R	S
A	D	E		T	R	A	S	H		O	V	E	R		I	S	E	E
Y	A	R	D	A	G	E	A	T	T	A	I	N	E	R	T	I	T	T	L	E
T	R	E	A	T	Y		M	A	I	N	M	E	N	U		B	L	E	E	D
O	D	D	M	E	N		S	T	R	A	P	S	I	N		N	E	S	T	S

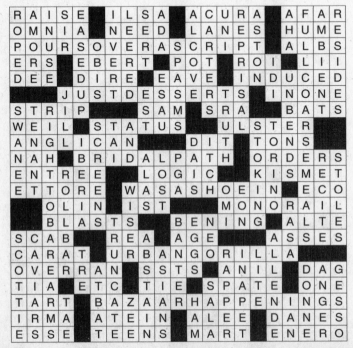

R	A	I	S	E		I	L	S	A		A	C	U	R	A		A	F	A	R
O	M	N	I	A		N	E	E	D		L	A	N	E	S		H	U	M	E
P	O	U	R	S	O	V	E	R	A	S	C	R	I	P	T		A	L	B	S
E	R	S		E	B	E	R	T		P	O	T		R	O	I		L	I	I
D	E	E		D	I	R	E		E	A	V	E		I	N	D	U	C	E	D
			J	U	S	T	D	E	S	S	E	R	T	S			I	N	O	N	E
S	T	R	I	P			S	A	M		S	R	A			B	A	T	S
W	E	I	L		S	T	A	T	U	S			U	L	S	T	E	R	
A	N	G	L	I	C	A	N			D	I	T		T	O	N	S	
N	A	H		B	R	I	D	A	L	P	A	T	H		O	R	D	E	R	S
E	N	T	R	E	E		L	O	G	I	C		K	I	S	M	E	T
E	T	T	O	R	E		W	A	S	A	S	H	O	E	I	N		E	C	O
	O	L	I	N		I	S	T			M	O	N	O	R	A	I	L
	B	L	A	S	T	S		B	E	N	I	N	G		A	L	T	E
S	C	A	B		R	E	A		A	G	E			A	S	S	E	S
C	A	R	A	T		U	R	B	A	N	G	O	R	I	L	L	A	
O	V	E	R	R	A	N		S	S	T	S		A	N	I	L		D	A	G
T	I	A		E	T	C		T	I	E		S	P	A	T	E		O	N	E
T	A	R	T		B	A	Z	A	A	R	H	A	P	P	E	N	I	N	G	S
I	R	M	A		A	T	E	I	N		A	L	E	E		D	A	N	E	S
E	S	S	E		T	E	E	N	S		M	A	R	T		E	N	E	R	O

19

20

21

S	A	D	I	S	M		E	C	L	A	T		S	H	I	P		C	A	B
A	G	A	T	H	A		A	R	E	S	O		E	A	S	E		A	N	A
L	I	F	T	O	P	E	R	A	T	O	R		A	N	A	P	E	S	T	S
A	L	F		P	L	A	N	T	M	A	N	A	G	E	R		A	T	I	E
D	E	Y		P	E	R		E	E	K		N	U	S		G	R	I	G	S
		W	E	S	T	E	R		G	A	L		W	A	L	N	U	T		
	M	F	A		H	A	S	A	B	A	L	L		A	M	I	G	A		
W	E	L	L	D	A	Y	S		I	A	G	O		K	N	E	E	D		
I	R	I	T	I	S		T	A	R	R	A	G	O	N		W	R	I	T	
F	I	G		S	Y	R		N	E	T		A	I	D	A		R	A	M	
E	D	H		C	O	U	R	T	R	E	P	O	R	T	E	R		E	R	A
Y	E	T		J	U	N	E		N	A	Y		S	A	D		C	P	I	
	N	A	T	O		G	L	A	N	D	U	L	A		T	E	U	T	O	N
	T	E	C	H	S		F	E	E	L		J	O	H	N	S	O	N	S	
	S	T	A	K	E		C	L	E	R	I	C	A	L		E	R	S		
S	H	E	R	E	E		H	A	D		O	X	I	D	E	S			
T	A	N	G	Y		P	O	M		O	N	E		V	I	S		C	A	N
E	D	D	A		M	A	K	E	U	P	A	R	T	I	S	T		R	I	O
R	E	A	S	S	U	R	E		S	T	O	C	K	A	N	A	L	Y	S	T
E	R	N		A	L	O	U		M	I	M	E	O		E	T	O	I	L	E
O	S	T		Y	E	L	P		A	C	I	D	S		Y	E	N	N	E	D

22

N	E	V	E	R		A	B	A	F	T		P	L	A	T		M	A	T
A	V	I	L	A		R	E	W	O	R	K		N	I	N	A	F	O	C	H
B	A	S	I	E		A	L	O	S	E	R		I	N	S	T	A	N	C	E
	N	A	H		B	A	L	D	M	O	U	N	T	A	I	N	D	E	W	
N	E	B	U	L	A			I	O	N	S				N	I	P	A	
O	S	I	R	I	S		C	Y	C	L	O	N	E		S	L	E	E	T	S
A	C	L	O	C	K	W	O	R	K	O	R	A	N	G	E	C	R	U	S	H
M	E	L	O		F	I	L	S			D	O	R	M			
			T	W	O	T	O		L	A	B	S		S	A	S	H	A	Y	S
G	I	L	B	E	R	T	G	R	A	P	E	N	E	H	I		A	L	E	A
A	D	M	E	N		N	O	M	I	N	A	L			P	I	L	L	S
R	E	N	E		F	R	E	D	A	N	D	G	I	N	G	E	R	A	L	E
P	O	O	R	B	O	Y		E	R	G	S		C	E	R	I	C		
			E	G	A	N			G	I	B	E		R	U	S	S
T	H	E	M	A	G	N	I	F	I	C	E	N	T	S	E	V	E	N	U	P
R	O	S	E	R	Y		L	O	C	U	L	U	S		T	E	A	Z	L	E
A	R	C	A			T	E	T	E			S	E	M	I	T	E
I	M	O	G	E	N	E	C	O	C	A	C	O	L	A		S	P	R
L	O	R	R	A	I	N	E		A	R	T	H	U	R		H	O	P	I	S
E	N	T	E	R	S	O	N		P	U	R	I	N	A		A	D	E	L	A
R	E	S		L	I	S	T		G	O	O	D	Y		L	A	D	Y	S

23

```
P A S T   N E O N     F O O L     H A G S
A G E E   E A T U P   O S L O   D A L A I
W H E N I P R O N O U N C E T H E W O R D
S A N D M A N     U S D A   S U C K E R S
    E E L S   S N E E R     B E E
    L A R A     P I C A S   D E R I D I N G
S I L E N C E I D E S T R O Y I T   C U L
E N I D   A X E L     O U R S   M I T A
E E N   L I T E R A T U R E   D I E T S
P R E T T I L Y   E C O N O   H E N R Y S
    R A C E   S C R O D   P O C O
I N D I G O   M O T E T   P U B O R D E R
S O A P S   P O L I S H B O R N     O V O
L I T E   R O L E     O L I O   C E O S
A S E   W I S L A W A S Z Y M B O R S K A
M E S S A G E S   E S T O P     R A T E
    A D S   D E L O S   F D I C
A G E N D U M   A P O P   R A N K L E S
N O B E L P R I Z E W I N N I N G P O E T
A T A L E   E D E R   N O N E T   O L G A
T O N Y   D A D S   B E D E   T A S S
```

24

```
F R A C A S   C H A R I S M A   F R A S
L O C A L E   D E C A M P E D   C O U N T
E N T R A N C E R A M P A G E   P U N T A
A N I   S N O   D E A N   W A L T E R
S Y N   K E N T S   S L O U G H   L O D E
    G N A T   E M C E E   N E E   I H A D
A M O U N T   N I A S   C H E T   N I T A
L A U D S   B D R M   N O O N   R E M E T
B Y T E   M E E K   P O O L A R E A
A H A   L I A R   R A S P Y   H I G H S
N E G R O S   F A U V I S M   O N E O U T
  M E O W S   O I L E R   E O N S   O R E
  C L A M O R E D   A S H E   O V E N
T A L K Y   I T E R   M U S S   C R E S T
A C A B   G L A D   V I D A   C H A R T S
K A B A   L E G   S E L I G   H E L D
E D E N   E R E C T S   S E R A C   A L A
F E L D O N   H A T S   I R K   M A X
I M E A N   C R I T I C A L M A S S A G E
V I R G O   R E L E G A T E   D I G G E R
E A S E   O P E R E T T A   E N T E R S
```

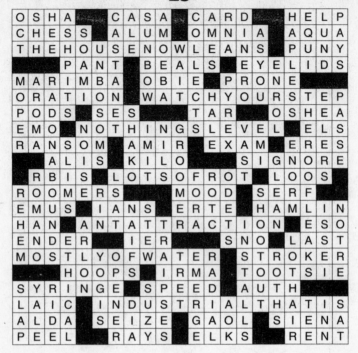

```
O S H A · C A S A · C A R D · H E L P
C H E S S · A L U M · O M N I A · A Q U A
T H E H O U S E N O W L E A N S · P U N Y
· · P A N T · B E A L S · E Y E L I D S
M A R I M B A · O B I E · P R O N E ·
O R A T I O N · W A T C H Y O U R S T E P
P O D S · S E S · T A R · O S H E A
E M O · N O T H I N G S L E V E L · E L S
R A N S O M · A M I R · E X A M · E R E S
· A L I S · K I L O · S I G N O R E
· R B I S · L O T S O F R O T · L O O S
R O O M E R S · M O O D · S E R F
E M U S · I A N S · E R T E · H A M L I N
H A N · A N T A T T R A C T I O N · E S O
E N D E R · I E R · S N O · L A S T
M O S T L Y O F W A T E R · S T R O K E R
· H O O P S · I R M A · T O O T S I E
S Y R I N G E · S P E E D · A U T H
L A I C · I N D U S T R I A L T H A T I S
A L D A · S E I Z E · G A O L · S I E N A
P E E L · R A Y S · E L K S · R E N T
```

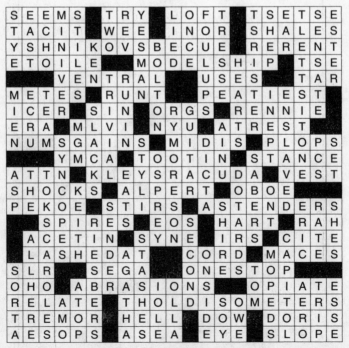

```
S E E M S · T R Y · L O F T · T S E T S E
T A C I T · W E E · I N O R · S H A L E S
Y S H N I K O V S B E C U E · R E R E N T
E T O I L E · M O D E L S H I P · T S E
· V E N T R A L · U S E S · T A R
M E T E S · R U N T · P E A T I E S T
I C E R · S I N · O R G S · R E N N I E
E R A · M L V I · N Y U · A T R E S T
N U M S G A I N S · M I D I S · P L O P S
· Y M C A · T O O T I N · S T A N C E
A T T N · K L E Y S R A C U D A · V E S T
S H O C K S · A L P E R T · O B O E
P E K O E · S T I R S · A S T E N D E R S
· S P I R E S · E O S · H A R T · R A H
A C E T I N · S Y N E · I R S · C I T E
· L A S H E D A T · C O R D · M A C E S
S L R · S E G A · O N E S T O P
O H O · A B R A S I O N S · O P I A T E
R E L A T E · T H O L D I S O M E T E R S
T R E M O R · H E L L · D O W · D O R I S
A E S O P S · A S E A · E Y E · S L O P E
```

27

Crossword 27 — completed grid:

```
M E A L P L A N   S H A S T A   S E E S T
A N N E R I C E   T E C T U M   E L M E R
R E A D O N E S F O R T U N E   R E E V E
I M H O M E   T I M   P A X   O G R E S
M I E N S   T O B A C C O   I T A I N T
B E I   P A R   C H A R S   F O N T A L
A S M A R A N   S H O W S U P I N T I M E
    R A W   L I S P S   D E M I
  S A M S N E A D   C A T   N O N C E
S E L F P E R C E P T I O N   M A L I
E X C U S E S   M E A R A   S P E E D E R
R E E L   L A R G E R T H A N L I F E
B R E S T   P I N   S H E L T E R S
    H T E N   A L L E Y   L E T
J E T P R O P U L S I O N   M A R S H E S
A G R E E D   S I T E S   C I S   E V A
M O A N E D   M I N E R A L   D A L E Y
A T B A Y   G T O   S U N   P E T E R S
I R E N E   R I G H T O N T H E M O N E Y
C I R C A   A R E Y O U   B A L I N E S E
A P T E R   D E S P O T   E Y E T E S T S
```

Crossword 28 — completed grid:

```
S N A P B E A N   S H A D   H A D A F I T
L E N A O L I N   L U X E   O P A L I N E
O B D U R A T E   A R I S T O P H A N E S
B R A L E S S   O N T O P O F   L I S Z T
    F O O T   O L D S M O K E Y
P A T   N I M B L E   T Y R E S   A B E
S H E D   C L A I R O L   O S L O   R E X
S O R E   S I D E S L I P   P O P E Y E
T Y P E A   A B O V E   T E A O R
    I M P A L A   A V E R A G E   I S N T
B B C   T R U E S T   L E S A G E   O D S
L E T A   C L O T H E S   E D G E I N
A F U S S   U N D E R   K N A V E
M O R A Y S   S N O W P E A S   T B A R
E R E   N E A R   S O I L A G E   O L I O
D E S   C A N I T   N A S A L S   E N S
    M Y D I G N I T Y   L E W D
O M I T S   B E N E A T H   O S T E O I D
D A N I E L O R T E G A   P R O T R U D E
E X A L T E D   E S E L   E N F E E B L E
A I N T H A Y   D E L L   D E F E A T E D
```

31

```
TOTEM  TONYAS   LOAND
ECOLES SWEEPEA MURRAY
THEYDOPENDANTS APIECE
ROSSINI    REAP NINERS
    CINCINNATIBANGLE
HEW CEASES   ROTE
OSHEA  LAI OBESE  SEAL
SAINTNECKLACE  SEEPAGE
PUTTIES   SLEEPY MORAN
  ESTATES CARA ASTRID
RAW THELOONYPIN   INS
ADAGIO  RUTH SANDMAN
DATED POIROT  SMUGGLE
INCLINE CALAMITYCHAIN
OOHS INGES SOO  HAITI
   ALTE  STANCE  DAD
 BIRDSANDTHEBEADS
MINEOS  TREE   RIPOSTE
ELTORO LOCKETORLUMPIT
OBRIEN ESTEVEZ ENRAGE
WOOLS  SALEMS  KITES
```

32

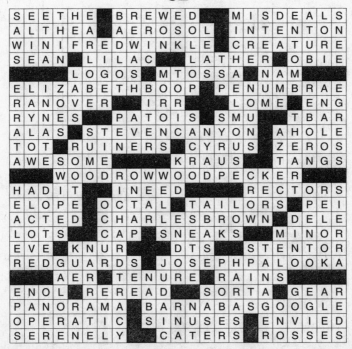

```
SEETHE BREWED  MISDEALS
ALTHEA AEROSOL INTENTON
WINIFREDWINKLE CREATURE
SEAN LILAC LATHER OBIE
   LOGOS MTOSSA NAM
ELIZABETHBOOP PENUMBRAE
RANOVER  IRR LOME  ENG
RYNES PATOIS SMU  TBAR
ALAS STEVENCANYON AHOLE
TOT RUINERS CYRUS ZEROS
AWESOME  KRAUS  TANGS
 WOODROWWOODPECKER
HADIT INEED  RECTORS
ELOPE OCTAL TAILORS PEI
ACTED CHARLESBROWN DELE
LOTS CAP SNEAKS MINOR
EVE KNUR  DTS STENTOR
REDGUARDS JOSEPHPALOOKA
 AER TENURE RAINS
ENOL REREAD SORTA GEAR
PANORAMA BARNABASGOOGLE
OPERATIC SINUSES ENVIED
SERENELY CATERS ROSSES
```

33

R	O	T	A	T	E		S	E	W	A	R	D		A	R	T		M	O	E
U	N	I	S	E	X		T	R	I	V	I	A		L	E	O	T	A	R	D
B	U	L	L	E	T	S	E	S	S	I	O	N		O	P	P	O	S	E	D
E	S	E		P	E	A	T		E	A	T	S		T	A	C	I	T	L	Y
		F	I	E	N	D		L	U	T	E			P	A	L	E			
W	A	I	T	E	D		S	U	P	E	R	M	A	N	E	T		R	B	I
E	R	S	E		S	M	U	G			I	B	A	R		S	P	A	N	
S	C	H	M	O		O	L	A	F		S	L	A	G		D	C	L	I	V
			P	U	N	K	R	O	C	K	E	T		B	E	R	A	T	E	
E	D	B		I	S	A	Y		S	H	I	R	E		R	E	I	N	E	R
L	E	A	R	N	E	D		S	T	U	D	S		P	E	P	P	E	R	S
E	C	L	A	I	R		S	P	E	N	D		S	O	A	S		T	S	E
V	O	L	V	O	S		M	A	R	K	E	T	T	I	M	E				
A	R	E	I	N		M	A	R	S		D	A	R	N		A	D	M	A	N
T	U	T	S		T	I	C	S				R	A	T	S		E	A	S	E
E	M	O		J	U	N	K	E	T	F	O	O	D		C	H	A	L	K	Y
	F	R	A	N			A	L	I	T		L	A	U	R	A				
O	F	F	I	C	E	S		A	M	I	N		S	E	N	D		M	T	A
T	R	I	P	O	D	S		R	A	C	K	E	T	A	N	D	R	U	I	N
R	A	R	E	B	I	T		A	L	K	E	N	E		E	L	A	T	E	D
A	Y	E		I	N	S		L	E	A	D	E	N		R	E	M	E	D	Y

34

H	A	S	T	O		S	P	A	R		G	A	Z	A		B	A	S	T	E
A	L	T	E	R		P	E	L	E		R	E	E	D		I	S	O	U	R
R	O	A	S	T		C	A	T	S		A	C	E	O	F	C	L	U	B	S
P	U	T	T	E	R	A	R	O	U	N	D			E	Y	E	L	E	T	
			E	G	O				R	E	E		M	E	E	C	E			
S	U	N	D	A	Y	D	R	I	V	E	R		B	A	L	L	P	A	R	K
U	N	O			S	E	A	B	E	D		G	A	R	N	I		V	I	E
M	I	N	C	E		P	R	E	Y	S	O	N		P	O	S	T	A	G	E
S	T	E	A	L		P	E	T			B	A	A	L		T	A	L	O	N
		V	I	A			C	R	I	S	P	U	S		L	O	R	E		
	W	E	A	R	I	N	G	O	F	T	H	E	G	R	E	E	N			
S	E	H	R		E	N	N	E	A	D	S			S	A	N				
A	R	E	N	A		S	E	E	S			T	I	A		S	T	A	T	E
D	O	E	S	N	O	T		S	T	U	D	E	N	T		E	S	S	E	X
A	D	Z		C	L	O	S	E		N	E	A	R	T	O		S	A	T	
T	E	E	S	H	I	R	T		M	I	S	S	I	N	G	L	I	N	K	S
		T	O	V	E	S		A	O	K			R	O	D					
S	A	F	A	R	I			I	N	T	O	T	H	E	W	O	O	D	S	
I	R	O	N	M	A	I	D	E	N		O	L	I	O		C	I	V	E	T
M	A	I	Z	E		D	E	L	L		P	E	N	N		A	D	E	L	A
I	M	E	A	N		I	F	F	Y		S	O	A	K		L	O	N	E	R

```
R O O S T S   ▪   F I N K S   ▪   C A C H E T
A N X I O U S   ▪ I N A N E ▪ A I R H O L E
M E E T M E I N S T P E R I O D L O U I S
S A Y ▪   M A K E ▪ S A N K ▪ O U S T S
▪ M E S A S ▪ H E R E S ▪ S I D ▪ T I E
▪   E X E S ▪   I D E S T ▪ E M B O S S
H E L P E X C L A M A T I O N P O I N T ▪
A V O I D ▪ Y E W S ▪   D R A P E R ▪
D I V A ▪ B L T S ▪ S K E E T ▪ D I A S
O L E ▪   O U L U ▪ T E A R ▪ B R O W N E
N O B O D Y A P O S T R O P H E S F O O L
E N U R E S ▪   D A H L ▪ L O T T ▪ J F K
S E G A ▪   A G E R S ▪ D E B S ▪ H I F I
▪   T A P I R S ' ▪ S A A B ▪ S U M E R
▪ Q U O V A D I S Q U E S T I O N M A R K
B U M R A P ▪ S A U N A ▪ T R I P ▪
R I P ▪   A A H ▪ A C H E D ▪ A P S E S
A X I O M ▪ M A A S ▪ O W E N ▪   L I P
S O R R Y C O M M A W R O N G N U M B E R
S T E E R E R ▪ B R I S K ▪ S O M E O N E
Y E S M A N ▪ I S L E S ▪ G A L W A Y
```

```
O F F H A N D ▪   D E F O G ▪ S E L E S
R E A I R I N G ▪ D E N O V O ▪ E X U L T
B R I T I S H R A I N C O A T ▪ D A M M E
▪ R A S E ▪ E D D O ▪ T L C ▪ U M B E R
S H A ▪ T I G E R S T E E S H O T ▪ E R N
T A M P A ▪ U N I T E D ▪ A C T E R ▪
A L O U ▪   R E P ▪ S A D ▪ T O N J O N
R O U T ▪ F U R ▪ F E L I C E ▪ C A G E
K E N ▪ K O S ▪ C A R L I G H T ▪ A C E R
▪ S T E E N ▪ G O B I ▪ E E E ▪ A S K E D
▪ M Y T H R E E S O N S R O L E ▪
R U M P S ▪ O E R ▪ B R E T ▪ G O D W E
O P A L ▪ B L A C K E Y E ▪ A R T ▪ U V A
E T N A ▪ R E V E R E ▪ U S E ▪ I N O R
G O I N T O ▪ E R A ▪ A N Y ▪ C D L I
▪ C E R T S ▪   F R E S C O ▪ R E E V E
T R U ▪ A H A U N T E D H O U S E ▪ R E S
H I R E D ▪ U N E ▪ V I E R ▪ I S A K
A G I L E ▪ C H A Y E F S K Y S A T I R E
N O S I R ▪ E A T E R Y ▪ S E A L A N T S
E R T E S ▪ S P O R T ▪ S L E D D E D
```

Puzzle 39 — Crossword grid:

```
DANCERS ACT SKEE   PUB
ATEALOT PERSONAL  POPE
MEATLOAFPLATTERS OILS
NATS DYER COHEN APSIS
 MOES SWEETKISS STONE
   YUP  HOSES  SHANKS
ARDENT ZEN   CAMERA
BAR SALON POLICESTING
STICH IND HOSTEL  ROM
  FRAPPE DANTE LASSOS
 ETUDES VINAS RECOUP
FLEXED FACTS MADCAP
OIR ARISTO TIS UPPER
BOSTONCREAM ETHOS LEE
 JUNTAS  ANT JEKYLL
SCORES THORN SON
UHURA FREEBREAD FIBS
MOREL LETAT SPED TOCK
MINT HEARTASSOCIATION
ICES SETASIDE COMESTO
TEY TRAS NIE ARIDEST
```

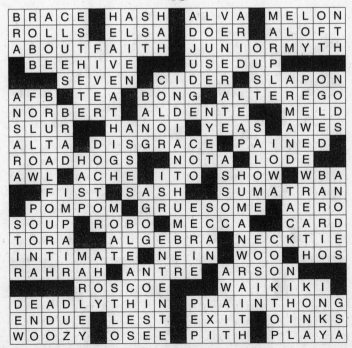

40

Puzzle 40 — Crossword grid:

```
BRACE HASH ALVA MELON
ROLLS ELSA DOER ALOFT
ABOUTFAITH JUNIORMYTH
 BEEHIVE  USEDUP
  SEVEN CIDER SLAPON
AFB TEA BONG ALTEREGO
NORBERT ALDENTE MELD
SLUR HANOI YEAS AWES
ALTA DISGRACE PAINED
ROADHOGS NOTA LODE
AWL ACHE ITO SHOW WBA
 FIST SASH SUMATRAN
 POMPOM GRUESOME AERO
SOUP ROBO MECCA CARD
TORA ALGEBRA NECKTIE
INTIMATE NEIN WOO HOS
RAHRAH ANTRE ARSON
 ROSCOE WAIKIKI
DEADLYTHIN PLAINTHONG
ENDUE LEST EXIT OINKS
WOOZY OSEE PITH PLAYA
```

41

```
S H A P E D   P I M P L E S   M A I T A I
C E N T R E   O C A R I N A   A U B U R N
O X T A I L   W E R E L I V I N G I N A N
T I E   C E L E B     G E M   E D A M
I N C A   T E L E G R A M   P A R E S
A G E W H E N L E M O N A D E I S M A D E
    D E E D S   R A C Y   A D D   L A Y
  R E I N         B Y E   S L A V E
T A N G   O A K   R A T A   S E C E D E S
W I T H A R T I F I C I A L   V E X
A D S   A L F R E D E N E U M A N   B E E
    P R O   I N G R E D I E N T S A N D
R E G I O N S   D E B S   S T S   T K O S
O C E A N   H A S           G O E S
O R O   R O I   O L A V   C H A R D
F U R N I T U R E P O L I S H I S M A D E
    G O B E L   A S S E N T E D   S L O B
  L E S E   D A R   T A X I S   A P B
W I T H R E A L L E M O N S   N E S S I E
H O T O I L   P A R O L E E   G A S K E T
O N E W A Y   O P E N E R S   S M E A R S
```

42

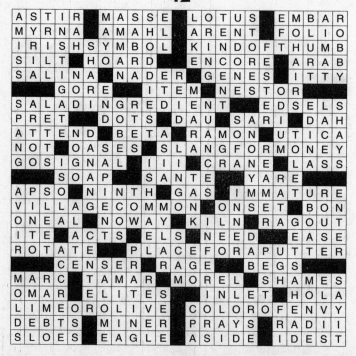

```
A S T I R   M A S S E   L O T U S   E M B A R
M Y R N A   A M A H L   A R E N T   F O L I O
I R I S H S Y M B O L   K I N D O F T H U M B
S I L T   H O A R D   E N C O R E   A R A B
S A L I N A   N A D E R   G E N E S   I T T Y
    G O R E   I T E M   N E S T O R
S A L A D I N G R E D I E N T   E D S E L S
P R E T   D O T S   D A U   S A R I   D A H
A T T E N D   B E T A   R A M O N   U T I C A
N O T   O A S E S   S L A N G F O R M O N E Y
G O S I G N A L   I I I   C R A N E   L A S S
    S O A P   S A N T E   Y A R E
A P S O   N I N T H   G A S   I M M A T U R E
V I L L A G E C O M M O N   O N S E T   B O N
O N E A L   N O W A Y   K I L N   R A G O U T
I T E   A C T S   E L S   N E E D   E A S E
R O T A T E   P L A C E F O R A P U T T E R
    C E N S E R   R A G E   B E G S
M A R C   T A M A R   M O R E L   S H A M E S
O M A R   E L I T E S   I N L E T   H O L A
L I M E O R O L I V E   C O L O R O F E N V Y
D E B T S   M I N E R   P R A Y S   R A D I I
S L O E S   E A G L E   A S I D E   I D E S T
```

43

Grid 43:

```
L A B E L S ■ F O I L S ■ M A N A G E D
A R A M I S ■ S U N S E T ■ I M P R O V E
P A L E S T ■ T H E L O R D S P R A Y E R
S M A R T S ■ O R C A ■ A U E L ■ B A R N
■ ■ A G E ■ E L M A N ■ P E R E S ■ ■
W O M E N S W E A R D A I L Y ■ E A T S
A W S ■ T E N N ■ A N S ■ R E D O N E
F L A P P E R ■ W A R ■ C O R O N E R
T E S T E R S ■ S H E P H E R D S P I E S
■ T S A R ■ B A E R ■ A L O E ■ T O R E
■ M R S O L E A R Y S C O W ■ ■
C O M E ■ A M O I ■ T H E E ■ H E M A
A P O S T L E S C R E E D ■ C H E R U B S
R E D T A P E ■ U S A ■ L A T E R A L
P R E A C H ■ P T S ■ R O A R ■ P S U
■ A M B O ■ W H I S T L E R S M O T H E R
■ ■ S C O O T ■ O A S I S ■ P R Y ■
S P A S ■ R O T A ■ T H E O ■ S E I S M O
A R O O M O F O N E S O W N ■ I N P L A Y
C O N F I N E ■ I N U R E S ■ T U L A N E
S W E A T E R ■ C A P E D ■ S P E W E R
```

Grid 44:

```
A B C S ■ G A T H E R ■ O D D ■ B E S T S
H A R E ■ A R E O L A ■ S O W ■ U S A G E
A L I T T L E S O F T S H O E ■ S C R I P
B I B L E B E L T ■ ■ E A R L Y S H I F T
■ ■ O C A L A ■ B A R ■ S T A T E ■
C H A O S ■ ■ G U S T S ■ L O R R E S
H A U S ■ F R E U D I A N S L I P ■ A X E
E T T E ■ I O L A ■ ■ A N T E ■ P I C A
S H O ■ C L A I M J U M P E R ■ A L L E N
S A M E H E R E ■ E L A T E ■ M A R L S
■ U S E R S ■ M U N R O ■ N G A I O ■
S I F T S ■ T O D A Y ■ T U E S D A Y S
A S F A T ■ M O V I E S H O R T S ■ D E L
H U L S ■ G A L E ■ U R S A ■ A T N O
I Z E ■ Y E L L O W J A C K E T ■ N I T A
B U R G O O ■ N O V A K ■ P A E A N
■ R U R A L ■ N S A ■ E A S E L ■
B O X I N G R I N G ■ ■ S A L A R Y C A P
A M O N G ■ C L A S S A C T I O N S U I T
R O U G E ■ H T S ■ S T A M E N ■ E T N A
M O T O R ■ Y S L ■ S E R E N E ■ S S T S
```

47

O	S	C	A	R	S		O	H	M	S		A	C	H	E	S		L	O	M
S	H	O	W	U	P		T	O	R	I		C	H	A	N	T		A	V	A
L	A	M	E	B	R	A	I	N	E	D		Q	A	N	D	A		K	E	N
O	R	E		L	Y	ᴺᴺᵂ	O	O	D		T	U	ᴺᴺᴱ	L	E	R		E	R	N

ROW 5: EDIE ISR WILED NODE
ROW 6: EWOK FLEET ITSY GOFOR
ROW 7: DA ᵂᴺᵂ ELLS ERESTU SERGEI
ROW 8: ARI LOO EATER TAM ᴱᴺᴱ SS
ROW 9: MET AWN NEVERFEAR VIM
ROW 10: HONE SIDED ERG PATS
ROW 11: WORSEN GRIEFS
ROW 12: COHN LUC TBSPS NEIL
ROW 13: EDO LIBRARIES HAD IDA
ROW 14: NE ᵂˢᵂ EEK ELATE AMU FUN
ROW 15: TSETSE TIGERS REPR ᴱˢᴱ NT
ROW 16: ISERE SPEE SPINS INGE
ROW 17: LATE GLAND EVE MATA
ROW 18: IFI CRO ˢˢᵂ AY GLA ˢˢᴱ YE ERR
ROW 19: TIT PIVOT WOUNDEDKNEE
ROW 20: ELI OPERE PINK NIECES
ROW 21: RES SENDS ANKA SAGEST

48

ROW 1: SPACED STIES VASSAR
ROW 2: TENUTA SPIRAL AIRLINE
ROW 3: ASEPARATEPACE LEMONDE
ROW 4: GEM TEAL HEALS GIRL
ROW 5: STINK NILES PRO BASES
ROW 6: ACONFEDERACYOFDUNES
ROW 7: LEIA DEVO AMISS
ROW 8: METERS SOL RENT HES
ROW 9: PANELS RATIOS ALCOVE
ROW 10: ACC THETURNOFTHECREW
ROW 11: THONG AAA LEI SUNNI
ROW 12: RIDEANDPREJUDICE SIN
ROW 13: ONETWO IRONON ACTING
ROW 14: LED KNOB WES STRING
ROW 15: RECUR IDAS EEEE
ROW 16: THERETURNOFTHENAIVE
ROW 17: SEERS RIO NEROS KNISH
ROW 18: HALE SANTO ARAB CPA
ROW 19: AREARUG THERUNWAYJURY
ROW 20: MUNDANE ENCASE BEANIE
ROW 21: SPASMS ROOTS ATBATS

49

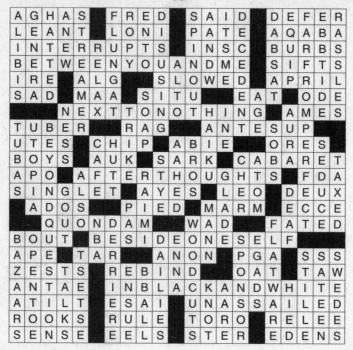

50

```
D E R I D E S █ E R E C T S █ M A T Z O S
O V E R A G E █ R E M O R A █ A I R I N G
G E T A L O A D O F T H I S █ S T Y L E T
I N U S E █ S I D █ E V E R S █ T L C █
T E N █ G O F I G U R E █ W E A R I E S
█ R E A G A N █ B A R E T T A █ L Y O N S
█ █ U R I █ S L U G S █ I N S T A N T S
H A N G I N T H E R E █ R E D T A G █ █
I R E █ P E R E █ █ R E R A N █ A I D A
N I X █ P R O M S █ M A D █ S H I N E D
T O T H E █ T A K E A H I K E █ E N D E D
A S T O R S █ O L E █ G I L D A █ O D E
T O O L █ A M W A Y █ █ N E R D █ O E R
█ █ D E R A I L █ M A R K M Y W O R D S
B E S T L A I D █ M A N E S █ O A R █ █
O M A H A █ D E S A L T S █ B U Y S U P █
P O T E N C E █ C U T I T O U T █ N R A
█ T I L █ A N E A R █ C P O █ L A T I N
F I R I N G █ C L E A N U P Y O U R A C T
A V E N U E █ H E E D E R █ E S C A P E E
B E S E T S █ O R N A T E █ D U E L E R S
```

```
A S H A M E D █ C O B A L T █ T A R R E D
C H A R A D E █ A N O M I E █ O R A N G E
M O N O D I C █ L O U I E A N D E R S O N
E D D S █ T O L L █ T E N T O O N E █ █
█ █ L E T █ R O S S █ S I G █ O S O L E
E R E █ R E U N I T E S █ M O C █ T N U T
L E A V E S M I N U T I A E O U T █ O R O
A N O I N T █ █ D O E S █ D R A W M E N
T A U N T █ P O K Y █ R T S █ T R E A D
E M I T █ M A M A █ T R A N S I E N T █
D E J A █ O V E R S E A I O U S █ T O M A
█ █ A G G R E G A T E █ R U N S █ S P A S
█ A B E A T █ A C E █ G E T S █ M O O N S
F L O S S I E █ H E R O █ █ D E L E T E
A B A █ H E N R I R O U S S E A U O I L S
C E R F █ R I O █ S I D E W A Y S █ A E S
E N D U P █ G A M █ A N A T █ E A U █
█ █ T R A M R O A D █ A B C D █ I S I T
S E Q U O I A E X P E R T █ R U M M A G E
I N U R E D █ R I A L T O █ O C T A G O N
S T E A M S █ S E L L E R █ W E S T E R N
```

53

```
D I V I D E ■ A L P I N E ■ M A N G L E S
E V I L E R ■ M A R N E R ■ A S C R I B E
M O V E R R H Y M E S W I T H H O O V E R
I R A N I ■ O S A G E ■ C U R E ■ S E N T
■ ■ ■ E D O M ■ S O R B ■ R E N T S ■ ■
R I A ■ E L A M ■ T M A N ■ H E R O D
A N N O ■ A G A S P ■ O U T A G E ■ E M I
I S G R O V E R H E N C E A G R O O V E R
S I L A S ■ A L T O ■ L I N E ■ I S N T
E D I T S ■ A T E A M ■ L A B E L ■ ■
R E C O I L S ■ P L A Y A ■ T E L S T A R
■ ■ R E A T A ■ D O D G E ■ I T A L O
A T O I ■ D O R A ■ I Y A R ■ H O P E S
D O L O V E R S B E C O M E L O U V E R S
E R E ■ I N S O L E ■ S A T U P ■ E R T E
N I O B E ■ N E L L ■ A G E D ■ S S S
■ ■ I R A Q I ■ Y A P S ■ O N U S ■ ■
D A I S ■ L U S H ■ T R E S S ■ G L A D E
I L L H A V E T O T H I N K I T O O V E R
C A L O R I E ■ C R E A S E ■ S U P E R S
K E E P I N G ■ H A R M E D ■ E T E R N E
```

54

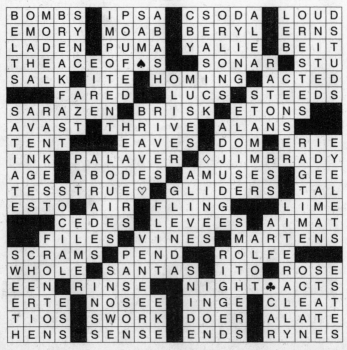

```
B O M B S ■ I P S A ■ C S O D A ■ L O U D
E M O R Y ■ M O A B ■ B E R Y L ■ E R N S
L A D E N ■ P U M A ■ Y A L I E ■ B E I T
T H E A C E O F ♠ S ■ S O N A R ■ S T U
S A L K ■ I T E ■ H O M I N G ■ A C T E D
■ ■ F A R E D ■ L U C S ■ S T E E D S
S A R A Z E N ■ B R I S K ■ E T O N S ■
A V A S T ■ T H R I V E ■ A L A N S ■
T E N T ■ E A V E S ■ D O M ■ E R I E
I N K ■ P A L A V E R ■ ◊ J I M B R A D Y
A G E ■ A B O D E S ■ A M U S E S ■ G E E
T E S S T R U E ♡ ■ G L I D E R S ■ T A L
E S T O ■ A I R ■ F L I N G ■ L I M E
■ ■ C E D E S ■ L E V E E S ■ A I M A T
■ F I L E S ■ V I N E S ■ M A R T E N S
S C R A M S ■ P E N D ■ R O L F E ■ ■
W H O L E ■ S A N T A S ■ I T O ■ R O S E
E E N ■ R I N S E ■ N I G H T ♣ A C T S
E R T E ■ N O S E E ■ I N G E ■ C L E A T
T I O S ■ S W O R K ■ D O E R ■ A L A T E
H E N S ■ S E N S E ■ E N D S ■ R Y N E S
```

59

60

61

S	H	E	I	L	A	■	S	P	A	R	E	M	E	■	■	A	D	A	P	T
W	A	L	L	I	S	■	A	U	R	O	R	A	S	■	A	D	A	G	E	S
I	M	E	E	T	S	A	N	T	A	M	O	R	E	A	N	D	M	O	R	E
G	E	M	S	T	O	N	E	■	■	A	D	A	■	D	I	O	N	N	E	■
■	■	■	■	E	R	A	■	M	A	N	E	T	■	O	M	N	■	■	■	■
G	O	C	A	R	T	■	T	A	C	O	S	■	F	R	A	■	N	A	M	E
A	Z	A	N	■	■	F	A	Z	E	■	■	S	U	E	T	■	I	T	A	L
M	A	N	Y	S	T	O	R	E	S	E	N	T	H	R	O	N	E	H	I	M
E	W	E	■	W	A	N	T	■	■	S	O	A	R	S	■	A	L	O	N	E
■	A	S	S	E	N	T	■	■	I	M	P	U	T	E	■	K	I	S	S	E	R
■	■	C	A	S	S	I	N	I	■	N	U	R	T	U	R	E	■	■	■	■
W	A	T	E	R	Y	■	C	A	R	E	S	S	■	■	A	L	O	N	S	O
A	V	A	N	T	■	P	E	R	E	S	■	■	A	H	A	B	■	U	R	I
S	O	M	E	O	N	E	M	U	S	T	B	E	J	O	K	I	N	G	O	R
T	I	E	R	■	A	R	A	T	■	■	A	L	A	E	■	■	R	A	N	K
E	D	D	Y	■	S	T	N	■	L	O	M	A	X	■	P	H	A	R	O	S
■	■	■	S	T	U	■	H	E	M	A	N	■	M	A	E	■	■	■	■	■
■	R	E	P	A	I	R	■	A	G	A	■	■	S	I	G	N	P	O	S	T
T	H	E	Y	V	E	B	E	G	U	N	T	O	C	L	O	N	E	H	I	M
S	E	L	L	E	R	■	T	A	M	I	A	M	I	■	D	E	P	O	N	E
K	E	Y	E	D	■	O	R	E	S	T	E	S	■	A	R	I	S	E	N	■

62

■	L	O	O	T	■	S	T	A	S	I	■	L	E	I	A	■	S	W	O	O	P	S
T	E	N	N	I	S	M	A	T	C	H	P	A	R	T	S	■	K	A	L	K	A	N
H	O	U	S	E	H	O	L	D	A	N	I	M	A	L	S	■	O	R	E	L	S	E
E	N	S	■	P	R	O	C	U	R	E	S	■	L	O	M	A	N	■	A	T	E	■
■	■	P	O	E	T	■	S	E	N	T	B	Y	■	C	A	L	S	■	H	E	R	■
C	O	U	L	D	■	W	K	S	■	E	R	O	T	I	C	■	■	N	O	D	I	■
B	O	B	F	O	S	S	E	■	■	A	R	E	A	■	B	E	A	M	O	N	■
O	L	O	F	■	■	W	E	S	T	S	I	D	E	S	T	O	R	Y	G	A	N	G
Z	E	E	■	B	O	A	■	T	H	O	R	S	■	S	E	D	E	R	S	■	■
■	■	■	D	A	N	M	A	R	I	N	O	■	■	E	W	E	■	F	O	G	■
A	R	I	O	S	O	■	W	A	S	I	N	■	M	A	R	S	■	A	L	M	A
N	E	W	J	E	R	S	E	Y	B	A	S	K	E	T	B	A	L	L	T	E	A	M
E	Z	I	O	■	E	S	S	E	■	I	R	A	N	I	■	O	A	T	E	R	S
W	A	N	■	R	A	N	■	■	D	I	N	O	S	A	U	R	S	■	■	■	■
■	■	F	O	S	S	A	E	■	G	E	T	T	O	■	E	S	S	■	G	A	P
G	I	V	E	S	P	E	R	M	I	S	S	I	O	N	T	O	■	A	R	C	S
A	N	I	T	A	S	■	R	A	S	P	■	■	E	N	M	I	T	I	E	S	■
S	T	O	A	■	B	I	G	T	O	P	■	A	W	N	■	E	N	I	D	S	■
M	E	L	■	S	L	A	V	■	S	T	R	A	T	I	■	J	E	T	E	■	■
A	R	E	■	A	E	R	E	O	■	I	C	E	S	K	A	T	E	■	S	R	O
I	N	N	A	T	E	■	S	H	E	A	S	T	A	D	I	U	M	G	R	O	U	P
N	E	C	K	E	D	■	A	S	S	U	M	E	S	O	W	N	E	R	S	H	I	P
S	T	E	A	D	S	■	T	O	P	S	■	D	E	M	I	T	■	A	T	O	Z

63

```
P O T O M A C ▓ L A D D ▓ ▓ C H A R M A N
U T E R I N E ▓ A M O I ▓ M O O D I E S T
B O A R D I N G P A S S ▓ E N R A V I S H
S E M I ▓ ▓ S E A T A S S I G N M E N T ▓
▓ ▓ S A V E I T ▓ Y E T ▓ E E S ▓ ▓
J A G ▓ B I D S ▓ ▓ C A R R Y O N B A G
U P R I S E ▓ T A X ▓ T R O I ▓ N O L T E
N I E C E ▓ ▓ D I S ▓ ▓ Y E R ▓ T A R A
C A B I N P R E S S U R E ▓ S I D E B A R
O N E ▓ T H A D ▓ C A T O ▓ G E O S ▓
▓ ▓ R E A D Y F O R T A K E O F F ▓
▓ L I E S ▓ S O S O ▓ I N R I ▓ Q U A
H E A D S E T ▓ B U S I N E S S C L A S S
A N N I ▓ D U G ▓ E L I ▓ ▓ I O T A S
L O A N S ▓ P A P A ▓ E X O ▓ M E N A G E
F L I G H T P L A N ▓ ▓ P H E N ▓ R E T
▓ ▓ A W E ▓ U N A ▓ B E A S T S ▓
▓ H O L D I N G P A T T E R N ▓ A B B A
S A L I E N C E ▓ B A G G A G E C L A I M
A L L E R G E N ▓ E R I E ▓ A C T U A T E
C L A U S E S ▓ L I F T ▓ R U S T L E S
```

64

```
W I G W A G S ▓ N A T A S H A ▓ H O G A N
A M I A B L E ▓ A G A T H A S ▓ E V I T A
S P A R E I N T H E T R U N K ▓ M A V E N
T E N T ▓ M E W S ▓ T I E D ▓ A L E R T
E N T S ▓ M C I ▓ F O U ▓ S P A N ▓ U R E
S D S ▓ M E A T F R O M H O G S ▓ A P E S
▓ ▓ B A R ▓ S R A ▓ I N S P E C T ▓
E N M A S S E ▓ O T H E R ▓ H I T H E R
M E A N T ▓ V O W ▓ O L E S ▓ A R S E N E
B U L K ▓ I N N U M E R A B L E ▓ G H I
R T E S ▓ C A T ▓ P E N ▓ D O T ▓ T H A N
A R I ▓ N O N A M E R I C A N ▓ I O N S
C A N T E R ▓ P O N E ▓ U T E ▓ P E S C I
E L D E S T ▓ O D D E R ▓ S M A R T E N
▓ I N T E N S E ▓ L I B ▓ E R S ▓
R E V S ▓ G O O D T O L O O K A T ▓ S S T
A M I ▓ P E R M ▓ H B O ▓ N I L ▓ R A T E
V I D E O ▓ A L I S ▓ B E S T ▓ A R E A
A G U A S ▓ P L A C E F O R S I N N E R S
G R A V E ▓ S I N K S I N ▓ I M O G E N E
E E L E R ▓ T A K E S T O ▓ N E M E S E S
```

67

Puzzle 67 solution grid:

```
BABA  SALUKI   JAPE  PALE
OMAR  TIEPIN   ARAL  EVAN
POSTCEREALS    INTERDICT
 RESIN    NORMANMAILER
SPLAT APT  LEEZA  SCARY
THELETTERMEN     GSA
OISE ROSIES  OLDALBUMS
PCS JANETS  AVIATE  RET
   LOVETO ENEMY  RASTA
DELIVERANADDRESS  KIRI
ERASER    NIL   AMINOR
AMYL  STICKTOITIVENESS
FILED URALS  SOMERS
ENO ESTATE  CARPAL  RFD
NEWISSUES  CHAPEL  SELA
    MCS    THECOLLECTOR
SLIME SUAVE  SRS  RAISE
TERENCESTAMP    WILTS
UPANDATIT   ITSCANCELED
NETS  MANY  SATIRE  NERO
TREE  PEGS  ESPRIT  ESSO
```

68

Puzzle 68 solution grid:

```
SQUATS  NONAMES   FOSTER
GUNGHO  IKEBANA   REMOVE
TITHED  CLASSIFIEDADAM
STOA ASEA  CODERS  LANE
   SICKO  VANS  ANALYST
JUSTSAYNOAM    ASONE
ANT UNSEWN  ESP  TSAR
CLASPS   NEWYORKJETSAM
KIRK  WASSAIL  EON  WVA
 TROTTED  DNA  YANKEES
  AHUNDREDGRANDAM
HEWLETT  OIL  MESSAGE
ELI ATO  OLEMISS  ROLE
FIGHTINGMADAM   RATTED
 ASIE  OST  HACKER  INA
  BASSO   FRYINGPANAM
MINIMUM  TRUE  NOISE
ALES  MUSEUM  PEWS  RSVP
HOWCANTHATBEAM  TOATEE
ASTUTE  OOHLALA  ESTATE
LESSER  DRSEUSS  REEBOK
```

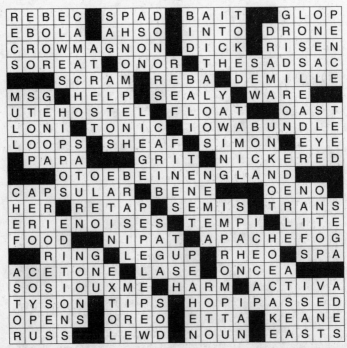

Grid 71:

```
B U M P S ■ ■ M I N U T E ■ ■ S E R F S ■
O P O R T O ■ O N A R O L L ■ T A U R U S
I T C O U L D B E V E R S E ■ A R M A D A
L O A M ■ S E I Z E ■ ■ I A M B W O M A N
■ ■ ■ I D E A L ■ A R E N A ■ I R E N E
I T S S O N N E T S L A S T L E G S ■ ■
R A C E D ■ ■ H A T S ■ O L E ■ ■ J E T
A B A R D S E Y E V I E W ■ E N C L O S E
Q U M ■ ■ P L E N A ■ O A T ■ R E U S E
■ ■ P L A I N ■ G O G O L ■ S E A L E D
■ A S S O N A N C E W I L L H A P P E N
G L O A T S ■ E A S E L ■ Y A T E S ■
A D U L T ■ F D R ■ L O O N Y ■ ■ L P S
P A L M O I L ■ A H A I K U D R O P O U T
E S S ■ ■ R E S ■ A L A I ■ ■ S A C R A
■ ■ I T S T H E S A M E O D E S T O R Y
B A S S I ■ C E S A R ■ ■ T O G A E ■
I D Y L L C H A T ■ B E I G E ■ N A S H
E R R A T A ■ R H Y M E D O E S N T P A Y
R E I N E R ■ S E M I T E S ■ T I E S U P
■ M A D R E ■ R A S S L E ■ A D E L E
```

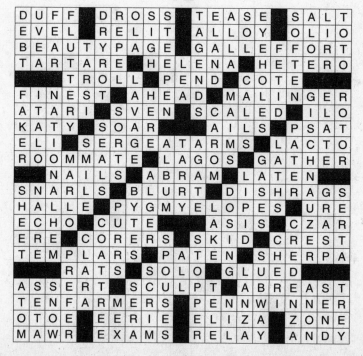

72

Grid 72:

```
D U F F ■ D R O S S ■ T E A S E ■ S A L T
E V E L ■ R E L I T ■ A L L O Y ■ O L I O
B E A U T Y P A G E ■ G A L L E F F O R T
T A R T A R E ■ H E L E N A ■ H E T E R O
■ ■ T R O L L ■ P E N D ■ C O T E ■
F I N E S T ■ A H E A D ■ M A L I N G E R
A T A R I ■ S V E N ■ S C A L E D ■ I L O
K A T Y ■ S O A R ■ ■ A I L S ■ P S A T
E L I ■ S E R G E A T A R M S ■ L A C T O
R O O M M A T E ■ L A G O S ■ G A T H E R
■ N A I L S ■ A B R A M ■ L A T E N ■
S N A R L S ■ B L U R T ■ D I S H R A G S
H A L L E ■ P Y G M Y E L O P E S ■ U R E
E C H O ■ C U T E ■ ■ A S I S ■ C Z A R
E R E ■ C O R E R S ■ S K I D ■ C R E S T
T E M P L A R S ■ P A T E N ■ S H E R P A
■ ■ R A T S ■ S O L O ■ G L U E D ■
A S S E R T ■ S C U L P T ■ A B R E A S T
T E N F A R M E R S ■ P E N N W I N N E R
O T O E ■ E E R I E ■ E L I Z A ■ Z O N E
M A W R ■ E X A M S ■ R E L A Y ■ A N D Y
```

```
R E V A M P   S H E B A   S P I N A C H
I M A D E I T   O I L E R   H O N A L E E
M O R A L M A J O R I T Y   O N A T E A R
    M I A M I   T O T A L E C L I P S E
A L V A N   I L L   T O N I   E L O P E S
B L I N D A L L E Y   R S V P   N O S Y
O A K T A G   T V S   R E N T A
I N K   L A B   E A S T E R I S L A N D
L O I S L A N E   S N O W   U N E   S E A
    H E R D E R   D R E G   A H A B
  S H A K E S P E A R E A N S O N N E T
W H E W   S A L A   K A P L A N
E E L   R A W   D A D S   R E D N O S E D
B A L A N C E D D I E T   L E I   A B U
    R A T E R   E O N   S L A L O M
L I S I   P U R E   W E A T H E R M A P
I N N E E D   I O N A   T W A   A M I T Y
S C O T L A N D Y A R D   A D A N O
P A R T I T A   A M E R I C A N D R E A M
E S T A T E S   L E N I N   S T E E L E R
D E S S E R T   S L A P S   E R R O R S
```

```
R U S T L E   C H A N C Y   D R A P E S
E N T A I L   H O N O R E   P R O M I S E
S T A R V E   I S T R E S S R O M A N C E
I R I S   M O R T I S E   T Y N E   C A D
D O R I D E A R A C E   B R I E   P E P E
E D S   A N T S   A L A N   B O R E R
    A R T S   T R Y S U N G L A S S E S
S M O C K S   W H O O P E D   E R E
N O R T E   R E V U E S   J A G   A F T
I P A I N T M O D E R N   G O V E R N O R
V E T O   R I T A   D I V E   A G R I
E D E N T A T E   N E V E R I N S T O C K
L S D   R U T   S O L E I L   T H R E E
    A I M   I C E L E S S   T R E A D S
D A N C E A R M I N A R M   D O O R
E L A N D   A P O D   B R A N   R B I
R I S E   A V O N   I D O L E N G T H E N
I M A   A L I S   A R A N E I D   H O R N
D E L V E I N T O V E R S E   F R I N G E
E N L A R G E   R E N T E D   R E N D E R
S T Y R O N   C R E S T S   O C E A N S
```

```
T A V I ▢ P E P A ▢ H O R N ▢ ▢ A S K E W
I R A Q O U T E D ▢ A R A I C ▢ C H E R I
M A C A R T H U R ▢ N A I N A ▢ H O P I N
B R A N D T ▢ ▢ I A N ▢ N A R R O W I N G
R A N G ▢ O A X A C A N ▢ F L O O R ▢
E T T E ▢ B O Y N T H E H O O D ▢ A C C
▢ ▢ B E L A ▢ H I C S ▢ S T R A P
H E S I O D ▢ F L Y F I S H ▢ O N E O N E
O R I N G ▢ A F O O T ▢ K I D M A N
L I G T S ▢ M A R K S M E N ▢ A T F
T E S H ▢ S P I R E ▢ E L E G Y ▢ I B E T
▢ E L I ▢ R E D I R E C T ▢ E L I A H
P A Y F O R ▢ T I N K E ▢ A M O R E
A V O I D S ▢ A L S A T I A ▢ U R S U L A
L O U R E ▢ P L I E ▢ C A N S ▢
▢ W E S ▢ C H I M E Y S W E E P ▢ C C C P
▢ P E O L E ▢ P I C A S S O ▢ O A H U
B A L L P E E N S ▢ P I S ▢ I R O N E R
A L I A S ▢ G E T U P ▢ H O U S E L I E S
M A R C O ▢ M E E S E ▢ M A K E S E N S E
A D R E M ▢ S M E E ▢ E K E D ▢ R E E D
```

The New York Times

Crossword Puzzles

The #1 name in crosswords

Available at your local bookstore or online at nytimes.com/nytstore

St. Martin's Griffin